D1072433

THE SEVENTH DAY

The Story of the Seventh-day Adventists

by BOOTON HERNDON

McGRAW-HILL BOOK COMPANY, INC.
New York Toronto London

Reprinted 1963
Review and Herald Publishing Association

THE SEVENTH DAY

Printed in the United States of America.

Library of Congress Catalog Card Number: 60-14998

Eighth Printing

Contents

1 In All the World

By almost any criterion of the Western world for human happiness, the more than one million and a quarter adult members of the Seventh-day Adventist church (three hundred thousand in the United States and Canada) must be rated as one of the most fortunate groups on earth. According to basic principles of general psychology as taught to college freshmen the country over, that an individual is happiest when striving for a worthwhile goal, these earnest and dedicated people are felicitously blessed indeed, for the prime mission of their lives is to strive for the eternal salvation of themselves and their fellow man.

If, as industrial surveys would indicate, the primary desire of the mid-century employee is security for his future years, then the Seventh-day Adventist must surely be content, for their security is assured. They are as positive in their own minds as mortal man can be that, if they meet the conditions of personal righteousness, made possible through Christ, their lives extend not only to the grave, but beyond it, forever and ever, in a steady and constant state of unimaginable joy. Considering the fundamental and primitive urge of creatures both low and high to fend for their young and to carry on the species, the fortunate million must again be given a ranking at or near the top, for they pass on a fine birthright to their offspring. Their children will enjoy better health, and enjoy it longer, than the children of their non-Adventist neighbors, they will be singularly free of such killing diseases as lung cancer, and they will have less than half the amount of tooth decay of their playmates (and their parents will have commensurately lower dental bills to pay!). Nor will many Seventh-day Adventist parents ever lie awake long past midnight, waiting for the overdue teen-ager to come home or the telephone to ring; precious few Adventist youths come even close to delinquency.

If the accumulation of worldly goods means happiness, then the Adventists pass this test as well. Though they are seldom the richest members of their communities, they nevertheless must manage to do all right, for, in America at least, they contribute four times as much money to their church on a per capita basis as the national average of the other denominations.

Finally, although the current generation of Adventists live in a period in which recreation and adventure are accented, they are second to none in enjoyment of both. It is true that, as people whose diet positively excludes pork and shellfish, and in most individual families other meats and fish as well, they will never dip a steaming piece of lobster tail into drawn butter, and most will probably live their lives out without ever savoring the succulence of rare roast beef. A few Adventists, as a matter of fact, even eschew milk, butter and eggs. They forego the stimulation not only of alcohol and tobacco, but the great majority even shun coffee and tea. They do not dance, or play cards, rarely go to the movies, limit, in the majority of cases, their television time to a minimum if they bother with it at all, and the women wear little or no cosmetics. But they're full of health and energy and most Adventists, though hardly ribald, have a humor that's bubbly and sharp. And everyone, from the Sabbath-school child contributing his nickel to the doctor, nurse or missionary using it for good in far-off places—one out of every nineteen members is an employee of the church—earns therefrom a close personal connection with Adventure.

And that, Adventure, is the subject of this book. Later on we will review the fascinating history of this seemingly paradoxical religion which speeds its emissaries over the world by jet to teach the most basic fundamentalism, and tell something about the life and motives of these little-understood people who live among us. But first you might be interested in the story of the missionary's pretty blond wife who lived alone for eight weeks in a haunted house on a South Sea Island inhabited only by primitive natives; of the pious young doctor who fought off a pack of river bandits deep in the interior of China, killing nobody knows how many; of the medical missionary—he'd have been a great old-time medicine show spieler—who brought medicine to the people of the Burmese jungles in bottles marked with the picture of a rabbit and the word of God with the aid of a sixteen-piece brass band; or even of the pioneer in Africa who was not above passing a bad check when the situation seemed to call for it.

Or an episode from the early career of Dr. Theodore R. Flaiz, the crisp but smiling administrator of the church's great medical program at home and overseas. Today Dr. Flaiz is respected the world over as both a man of God and a man of science, but few of his fellow Adventists, let alone the world leaders and eminent doctors with whom he rubs elbows, know the full story of how Ted Flaiz, armed to the teeth with a small arsenal of weapons strapped to the side of his chugging motorcycle, earned the respect and friendship of a village of thieves....

Like many another farm boy, Ted Flaiz practically grew up with a rifle in his hands, and many a time knocked over a varmint bent on making a meal of the Flaiz livestock or grain. As he grew into a tall, wiry young man, graduated from a Seventh-day Adventist college, and was assigned as a missionary to a primitive area deep in the southern peninsula of India, so too, did his guns grow from a .22 single-shot to a bruising .432 Mauser, and a 12-gauge double-barreled shotgun. As he made the rounds of his area, riding a battered old motorcycle over roads rutted by water buffalo–drawn carts, he carried his guns with him, for this missionary still loved to hunt.

Unfortunately, he was more successful at his avocation than at his vocation, for although he found plenty of game in the Indian jungles, he found few natives willing to listen to his message. White men were hardly popular in India at that time, particularly white men who spoke of a different religion and who advocated great changes in the centuries-old customs of the people. Even when a Christian doctor walked into an Indian hovel to bring surcease from suffering to the pathetically diseased, the occupants would run before him, pulling their pots aside so that his unclean shadow could not fall over them and violate them. Of all the people in India, it seemed that headway could be made with only one class, the shoemakers. And there was a reason. The cow is a sacred animal in India, and only the lowest of the untouchables, a person so base he had nothing to lose, would dare to remove the skin from the departed animal, then cure it, tan it, and make it into shoes.

Also because the shoemakers had nothing to lose, they had no compunctions about listening to the foreign devils, even embracing the strange religion they brought. In one sense those missionaries who successfully converted shoemakers were worse off than they had been before, for now they were definitely allied, in the minds of the higher castes, with the lowest of the low.

This was the situation when young Ted Flaiz first went to India. Though he cruised his region assiduously on his motorcycle, he seemed to be getting nowhere. In village after village he spoke only to deaf ears—except, of course, the ears of the local shoemaker. In his search for someone, *anyone* who would listen to him, Flaiz even paid regular visits to the local village which served as the official hangout for a band of thieves. Sometimes he would find no one in the village but women, children and old men; the men of the village were out on an organized foray into the surrounding countryside. After disposing of their loot, they would return to the village to live a life of ease until the next raid.

In the center of Flaiz's area was a small mountain range, about fifteen miles long, half again as wide. As he made his tour around the range, week after week, month after month, he learned that he was not the only living creature making his rounds in that area. An old tiger was also patrolling the beat, though for somewhat different purposes. Where Flaiz sought unsuccessfully to bring peace and contentment, the old tiger was highly successful in bringing terror and economic loss.

Over a period of two years, the tiger had destroyed three hundred cattle. The people were desperate; they would accept aid even from the white man with the strange religion. Flaiz began studying the tiger's movements, and he soon determined that the beast was set in his ways. Traveling in the fringes of the bamboo and thornbush thickets of the mountain range, the tiger always proceeded in a clockwise direction, and took about ten days to make the complete tour. Every day or so, when darkness fell, he would emerge from the thicket, kill a fat calf or even a large cow, eat his fill, take a nap, then be on his way again.

One day Ted Flaiz clattered into a village near the mountain range on his motorcycle to find the people milling around in a great state of excitement. The night before, the tiger had struck, killing a calf on the very fringe of the village. Though Flaiz had left his Mauser at his headquarters, his shotgun was with him, and he immediately volunteered to go out after the tiger. The people of the village became almost friendly at the suggestion. With a few of the braver men from the village, Flaiz set out for the forest, and began looking for tiger tracks. Sticking close together, they worked their way down the jungle trails. Suddenly Flaiz, leading the way, stopped short and pointed to the ground before him. There, in a fresh pile of dirt by a gopher hole, was the footprint of a tiger. And what a tiger! The footprint was as big as a bucket.

They proceeded cautiously, but saw no more sign of the tiger. The old killer had obviously left the trail to take a nap back in a thicket. Flaiz and the party went on until they came to a spot where five jungle trails came together. There Flaiz stopped and nodded to himself. From all he knew of the tiger's habits, the marauder would have to pass this point, and he would almost certainly pass it this night.

Back they went to the village, where Flaiz ate supper and borrowed a *machan,* or small cot. A couple of men helped him bring it back to the trail crossing, where they secured it in the branches of a large tree. A tired old water buffalo was led to the spot and tied by a strong rope to a thick, strong root for bait. Now night was coming on and the villagers hurried back home, leaving Flaiz alone in the forest.

Actually, he didn't mind the loneliness at all, for he had learned to find peace observing and listening to the wildlife in India. He made himself comfortable on his *machan* high over the trail, and listened for the cry of the wild peacock. He was not disappointed; soon the forest was filled with the piercing call, so loud that it could be heard for miles. Now the jackals and hyenas began yapping. He heard the graceful deer traveling the trails beneath him, giving a short, sharp bark when they unexpectedly came up to the old water buffalo. Elk, too, gave a barklike sound, only deeper, throatier. Far back in the hills came a cry like that of a baby; a leopard had seized a monkey. Then came the loud, nasal snort of a wild boar. Frequently, all during the long night, came the caterwauling of fighting wildcats.

Though noisy, the night was an unproductive one as far as tigers were concerned. The stage was set and the meal was ready, but the guest of honor did not appear. The old tiger must have been choosy, and had passed by the buffalo during the night, as Flaiz had been dozing. When the sun came up, Flaiz sighed, stretched, gave up and went on back to the village to give the people the disappointing news. But perhaps, the villagers suggested brightly, the tiger had been in no hurry, and had spent the night in the vicinity. Perhaps he would resume his patrol this night. Would Flaiz go back and try it again? He protested that it would hardly be worthwhile, but the people were politely insistent. On toward sundown he reluctantly gave in and went back to the *machan*.

He lay for a while listening to the jungle noises, watching the trail faintly illuminated by the moonlight beneath. But he was sleepy after the vigil of the night before and dozed off. Suddenly he came awake, as he heard something moving down the trail. He cocked his shotgun—one barrel was loaded with ball, the other with buckshot—and waited. Then he chuckled, and lowered the gun. Two black bears were gamboling down the trail, having a great time. A little later, here came a porcupine, padding along, looking to neither left nor right, pursuing his independent way. Flaiz yawned, made sure the gun safety was on, and dropped off to a sound sleep.

Sometime after midnight he came awake with a start. A low, deep growl had come from down the trail. The water buffalo heard it too, and let out a bellow of terror. Again the growl, this time closer, and then, with a snarl and a rush, here came the tiger, bounding through the splotches of moonlight. He was, Flaiz noted with a shiver, immense. *Tiger, Tiger, burning bright, In the jungles of the night....* Again the buffalo bellowed, but this time its cry was choked off in a gurgle, and Flaiz heard the sickening sound of mighty teeth crushing through bone. The lifeless body of the buffalo dropped heavily to the ground.

From his position on the *machan,* shotgun at the ready, Flaiz watched the scene beneath. The huge cat sat down and looked at his prey for a moment, then stood up and looked around him. He was sleek and beautiful in the moonlight. Then he got up, went to the carcass of the buffalo, got a grip on it with his powerful jaws, and tried to pull it back into the thicket. But the body was fastened tight to the heavy root, and the tiger couldn't budge it. Again and again he tugged. He snarled, shook his mighty head, roared with anger, then got a new grip and began tugging again. Flaiz, watching in awe, marveled at the tiger's strength and ferocity. If he kept this up, he might well pull the buffalo's body in two. Almost reluctantly, Flaiz sighted over the twin barrels of the shotgun, and waited. Again the tiger raised his head and roared in fury. Flaiz let go with both barrels, full into the animal's mighty chest.

This time the jungle shook with the fury of the tiger's roar. The wounded beast leaped, fell, writhed, snarled and yowled, just like a big tomcat hit with a shoe, and then crashed off through the jungle.

After a few seconds Flaiz heard the crashing stop, heard another roar, and knew that the tiger had sat down and roared again with pain and fury. Then he charged off again and the crashing grew faint in the distance. Then it stopped again, but this time there was no roar. The whole jungle was silent, as a kind of tribute to its cruel and ferocious but departed king.

Back in the *machan,* Flaiz quivered with excitement for a moment, his heart beating like a jungle drum. Gradually, he calmed down, lay back and soon he was sound asleep again.

Next morning Flaiz and a party of villagers set out, warily, to track down the tiger. They followed the trail of blood for several hundred yards, until it came to a patch of thornbush, several acres in size and completely impenetrable to humans. Only by following the trail on hands and knees could a man hope to track the tiger to his final resting place. Although Flaiz not only wanted to dispatch the beast, in case he were still alive, but to have that monstrous hide as a trophy, crawling into the thicket would be a foolhardy act. He and the villagers carefully circled the thornbush patch, making certain that the tiger was still in there. The next day they hacked their way in and found the body of the big cat; he had killed his last calf. Already the tropical heat had spoiled the hide.

But almost immediately the young missionary found that his reward was far greater than a tiger skin. The attitude of the villagers toward him changed that very day. No longer was he a foreign devil, seeking to uproot age-old customs; now he was the man who had delivered them from the beast of prey which had cost them their most precious material possessions. Word of the white hunter's feat spread throughout the entire area; from then on he was welcome in every village. Strangely, in the village of thieves he was probably most welcome of all, for they, more than any other natives, knew the law of the jungle; they needed it in their business, so to speak. When, at the insistence of the head man of the thieves' village, Flaiz recounted the story of the hunt and it became obvious that he, too, knew the jungle trails and the strange habits of the beasts which traversed them, the brigands looked upon him with a new and wholesome respect. Why, he might have been one of them!

Later, after seeing the great need of the Indian people for medical aid, young Flaiz returned to America and earned his medical degree at the College of Medical Evangelists in Loma Linda, California. Armed with the ability to heal, he returned to India, but even this new knowledge was secondary in the minds and hearts of the people he sought to help. He was, first and foremost, the man who had killed the tiger and he was welcome.

Some missionaries have earned the respect of the native people merely by being among them. In the case of Mrs. Zita Miller, a pretty young newlywed, "just being there" was hardly voluntary. She and her missionary husband, D. R. Miller, went out by mission launch to the new mission just set up on the atoll of Abemama, in the Gilbert Islands in the South Seas. The natives, big, brown, fuzzy-haired people, still wild and primitive, looked upon the newcomers with suspicion, even hostility.

The mission launch which had brought the Millers to Abemama had been picking up other missionaries in the islands to take them back to Suva. It would be a long run, of several days, and the little launch was terribly crowded. Someone had to stay behind. It could not be Miller himself; the launch had to be brought back, through the strange, shifting currents and coral reefs, and this type of navigation is something that girls just don't seem to take up. There was no way out of it; Miller would run the missionaries back to Suva—Zita would stay on the island.

"But I'll be here *alone,*" she wailed.

Her husband was sympathetic, of course, but what could he do? "The Lord will be with you," he said.

The condition of the tide gave them only two hours on Abemama, and then the launch would have to sail. Miller found the newly built mission house; its windows and doors were merely openings, and small things scurried in the thatched roof. They barely had time to unload a supply of canned goods for her before it was time to leave. The few natives they saw, though big, brawny fellows, made no effort to help.

Zita put on a brave front as she and her husband said goodbye, but as the little launch grew smaller over the wide Pacific, she began to get just a little bit scared. For one thing, although Miller knew more navigation than she did, that wasn't very much. Would he ever come back? And she dreaded the coming of night. Would the natives come with it? She scurried about in the few remaining hours of daylight preparing the house as best she could against intruders. She found a piece of plywood, nailed it up over the open aperture which served as a door. She fastened coconut blinds over the apertures which served for windows; they wouldn't stop anyone who wanted to come in, but at least she'd hear them fall and be ready.

A passageway ran from the front of the hut to a windowless little room in the rear. She found pieces of string and tied them across it as trip wires. There were some empty bottles lying around, and she stood them up in strategic places down the hall. As she worked she kept an eye out for natives, but no one came close to the little hut. They were waiting, she thought with a doomed feeling, for nightfall.

As the sun lowered in the west, she set about preparing her evening meal. Preparations for the bounteous repast consisted entirely of opening a can of beans and plugging a hole in a coconut for milk to wash them down with. And then the sun sank into the broad Pacific, and night came on with tropical suddenness. There was nothing else to do but retire. She had made her bed on a small platform, with some clothes rolled up for a pillow. Under that pillow she placed a native stone axe and a pair of manicure scissors for protection against any intruder. Thus armed, she lay down and tried to go to sleep.

During the night she heard many sounds, rustlings and murmurs and whispers, and the thumping of her heart as she lay rigid, one hand clutching the axe. But the sounds must have come only from the creatures of the night, and the rustles and whisperings from the wind in the eaves, for when dawn broke she found no sign that anyone had tampered with any of her makeshift barricades.

Night followed night, and still she was not molested in any way. Indeed as time went by, the natives seemed to become, if not friendly, at least respectful. For two whole months she stayed alone on that island, living on canned food and coconut milk, spending each night guarded by trip wires and bottles, with her stone axe and manicure scissors under her pillow. And finally the wonderful day came when the launch hove in sight, and her husband returned. Rarely has any husband received a more joyous welcome. Together, now, they set about working with the people of the island, treating their tropical sores and diseases, seeking to reach their souls. There was no question but that the respect all the natives seemed to have for Mrs. Miller made the work of the young couple easier. But what had caused it?

Finally, as they gained the confidence of the islanders, they learned the reason why. The little mission house had been built on a mound which was supposed to be haunted by evil spirits. No native would dare go near the place between sunset and sunrise. All that time Zita had been completely safe, protected by the devils she and her husband had come to fight. And the very fact that she had stayed there, alone, obviously with no harm befalling her, gave the natives strong indication that her God must indeed be stronger than the devils. Today the natives of Abemama are among the most devout members of the church.

Sometimes an enterprising Adventist missionary has been able to deliberately use native superstitions in his work, or, as it has been put in another line of endeavor, if you can't lick 'em, join 'em. Eric B. Hare, a twinkling-eyed Australian blessed with the gift of gab—he is currently assigned to General Conference headquarters in Washington, D.C.—started his missionary work among the Karen people deep in the interior of Burma. Hare had received medical training, and went to help the jungle people physically as well as spiritually. Not only did he want to cure and prevent such tropical ailments as malaria and tuberculosis, eye disease, malnutrition and ringworm for the sheer pleasure of serving mankind, but also as a practical means to performing his life work. For, he thought, as do many Adventists, if he could restore a wasted and pain-wracked heathen to health and happiness, then surely that heathen would be willing to listen to his message of the eternal health and happiness that comes only from salvation.

Hare and his wife set up their dispensary in a beautiful spot called Ohn Daw on the Salween River, and prepared to administer to the wants of the shy, gentle Karens. But days, weeks and months went by, and they had precious few customers. The people were suspicious and afraid. On one occasion, entering a new village, Hare saw the people look up, heard them shout, *"Daw Taka! Daw Taka!"*, and then saw nothing but the backs of fleeing men, women and children. He later learned that a *Daw Taka* was a half-breed between the devil and a ghost. A *Daw Taka* steals babies, fattens them up—and then eats them. No wonder the natives were afraid of jovial little Eric Hare; they thought he was a *Daw Taka.*

One of the more enlightened Karens, a man who had been down the river to Rangoon and knew some English, overcame his fears and permitted Hare to pay him for tutoring sessions in the Karen language and customs. One day the teacher told his pupil a popular Karen campfire story, part folklore, yet not entirely discounted by even the more advanced Karens.

A baby elephant and a baby tiger were born about the same time, the story goes, became fast friends, and grew up together. One day, however, the tiger announced to his bosom companion that now that he was fully grown he intended to put an end to the friendship. As a matter of fact, he had decided to have his friend for breakfast the following morning. The elephant pleaded and finally, on the basis of their friendship, the tiger gave the elephant six weeks to reap his rice, repair his house and say goodbye to his family. And then he would have elephant for breakfast.

The elephant reaped his rice and repaired his house, and said goodbye to his loved ones. But he was unhappy. He did not want to be a tiger's breakfast, not even if the tiger was a childhood friend. On the day before the six weeks were up, he went to the river, sat down on the bank, and cried. He cried so much that he made the river salty. Along came Grandfather Rabbit, hopping down to the river for a drink. He took a big mouthful of water, then spit it out in surprised distaste. He promptly began berating the poor elephant for making the water so salty. The elephant, by way of apologetic explanation, told his sad story. Grandfather Rabbit, kind and sympathetic, offered his services as an attorney, which the elephant eagerly accepted. Grandfather Rabbit then whispered a plan in the elephant's ear.

Next morning the tiger came trotting up, licking his lips in anticipation of a hearty elephant breakfast. But a strange sight met his eyes. The big elephant was down on the ground and the rabbit was jumping up on top of him in a wild dance. Sometimes he would hop off, lift up one of the elephant's mighty legs (the tiger didn't notice that the elephant was cooperating), or grab hold of the elephant's trunk or tail and turn him this way or that. The tiger was impressed by the strength of Grandfather Rabbit.

"Good morning, Mr. Rabbit," he said, admiration in his voice. "I'm glad you're having fun playing with my elephant, but when you get through just leave him there. I'm going to eat him for breakfast."

"Says who?" asked the rabbit belligerently. "Look, Cheeky-face, I've had six elephants already for breakfast this morning, and this will be my seventh. And if you're still around here when I finish, I might even start on you."

The tiger backed down hastily and galloped off down through the jungle to find himself a lawyer. All of the animals in the jungle, naturally, for they had more sense than to argue with Grandfather Rabbit, turned him down—except one, a monkey. The tiger tied the monkey on his back and hurried back to the scene. But before the monkey could even get started pleading his client's case, the rabbit started talking.

"Well!" he said, heartily. "If it isn't Mr. Monkey with one of my father's tigers at last! I've been wondering when you were going to start paying back those seven tigers my father lent your father. Just tie that one to the tree there and then go get the other six."

Oh, ho, thought the tiger. *So this smart monkey thought he'd trap me and use me to pay off his father's debt, eh? Well, we'll see about that!* He turned and charged off through the jungle, dragging the poor monkey through the bushes and stretching him out so much that monkeys have been slender-waisted ever since. And so Grandfather Rabbit's cleverness saved the elephant.

Eric Hare heard the story through and thought a bit. "Tell me," he said, "in these stories about Grandfather Rabbit does he always win his cases?"

"Of course," said the teacher, "the rabbit is the cleverest creature in all the jungle."

Now it didn't take long for an alert Adventist with a name like Hare to figure out what to do next. From that time on his name was Thara Pa Deh—Doctor Rabbit. He had new labels printed up for every one of his medicines, with his new name and a large picture of a rabbit emblazoned on each. And it wasn't long before his dispensary was doing a whopping business in Bunny Brand medicines.

But that wasn't all. Doctor Rabbit had a trumpet, which he liked to play of an evening, frequently with an audience of Karen children; the Karens love music. And if they would come to hear one trumpet, Doctor Rabbit thought, what wouldn't they do to hear a whole brass band?

And so he called on his friends in Australia to ship him all the band instruments they could get their hands on. When the instruments came he passed them out to the local boys—the tuba to the biggest, trombones and French horns to the medium-sized, and trumpets to the smallest. For days the noise around Ohn Daw was awful. Finally Doctor Rabbit found it impossible to teach his young would-be bandsmen to play whole scales, and he began concentrating on teaching each boy to play just two or three notes. With these few notes, played at the proper time, the band could play a harmonic background while Doctor Rabbit himself carried the melody on his solo trumpet. This they learned to do, and the band began giving concerts.

One day they set out for a village which Doctor Rabbit had never visited before. They walked single file through the jungle trail, each player carrying his own instrument; it was necessary to stop and rest occasionally for the benefit of the tuba player. Finally they reached their destination, only to find the village deserted. The huts were dilapidated and falling down. Everyone was most disappointed. To cheer up the band, as well as himself, Doctor Rabbit placed his musicians in formation, and began the concert anyway, with a few monkeys for an audience. But midway through the first number a most remarkable thing happened. The village was growing arms and legs! From around this hut, from behind that tree, heads, arms, legs, and finally bodies began to appear.

The people of the village, as per Karen custom when their houses rot away, had simply moved out and were in the process of building a brand-new village just a few hundred yards away through the forest. Hearing the soft strains of the mighty brass as filtered through the jungle, they had dropped everything to come to see what was going on. And before long they were out from behind the trees, out in the clearing, squatting around, listening to Doctor Rabbit's brass band. When the people stopped coming, and the crowd was two or three hundred strong, one of the boys stepped forward and told, in native language, some of the early episodes in the life of Christ. The band played another hymn, and another boy continued the story. Finally the whole story had been told. Then Doctor Rabbit put away his trumpet, brought out his Bunny Brand medicines, and began administering to the sick, especially those suffering from the eye sores so prevalent in the jungle. And in that way, with a touch of the old-time medicine show, with a few hymns, a little ingenuity, and a great deal of devotion, Doctor Rabbit brought healing medicine and the word of God to the jungles of Burma. You can be sure that no longer do the Karens shout, *Daw Taka! Daw Taka!* when a Seventh-day Adventist missionary visits their village.

A third of the way around the world, deep in the jungles of Africa, a Norwegian nurse named Petra Hovig had almost the same experience. Alone, except for native helpers, Petra traveled far inland to Liumba Hill. She had come to help the sick of Africa, and she set up a dispensary. But though she and the dispensary waited for the people to come to her for the medical help they so much needed, they waited alone. Nobody came. Like Doctor Rabbit, she went to native villages in search of patients. They did not run from her screaming; she didn't even see them. When she would arrive in a village it would be completely empty. She'd move among the huts, looking for people to help, but there would be no one there; she would cry into the brush, but no one answered. Ten thousand miles Petra Hovig had traveled to aid the sick, and the sick would have none of her!

Petra's only companion was her little hand-wound phonograph; at night at the end of the frusrating day, she'd wind it up and listen to some music. And one night, listening to the mechanical strains from the little phonograph, she got an idea.

Bright and early next morning she went back to one of the villages where the people had fled her arrival. This time, along with her bag of medical supplies, she took her phonograph. She put it down on the ground in the center of the deserted village, cranked it up, and put on a record. Soon the jungle was no longer silent, as the sound of music filled the air. And soon the clearing was no longer deserted as the natives began filtering back through the brush. Their curiosity was simply too much for them. They crowded around the mysterious box whence came the harmonic sounds, looked in it, behind it, under it, jabbering with excitement. Nurse Petra calmly let them look, interrupting only to change the record and wind up the phonograph. And with the hand crank of that little phonograph she unlocked the doors, not only of that village, but of all the villages around. Before too long she was completely accepted in the area, and scores of natives trod the jungle paths to the little dispensary to seek the medical aid that Nurse Petra had come to bring them. Soon the dispensary wasn't big enough, and under the nurse's supervision the natives built neat little rows of huts to take care of the overflow, and to provide a place for those too ill to go back to their homes. Petra now had more work than she could handle, and she began training her own assistants. She started a class for nurses, another for young mothers, and a class in good housekeeping and hygiene. And she taught them the word of Christ. Today, thanks to Nurse Petra's little hand-wound phonograph, the area around Liumba Hill is a far happier place.

Seventh-day Adventist missionaries, or any other white man or woman for that matter, are also welcome today in the New Hebrides in the South Pacific, but that was hardly the case a generation ago, when Norman Wiles and his wife Alma first went to the strange, savage island of Malekula. Here lived one of the most savage tribes in the earth's history, the Big Nambus, heathen cannibals who knew no life but lust and murder. At the time Norman and Alma Wiles went alone and unarmed into this savage island, the Big Nambus were in a particularly bloodthirsty mood, and against white people, for shortly before a British warship had shelled a Big Nambu village in retaliation for a native uprising. Several natives had been killed and wounded.

The Big Nambus seemed to devote their life to fighting; the slightest incident would bring on a clash between two tribes, or even two villages of the same tribe. And when the battle was over, the victors always celebrated in the same way, by feasting on the flesh of the men slain in battle.

"If ever any of God's children were hard to love," Mrs. Wiles recalls today, "it was the Big Nambus. They lived in filth that is simply indescribable. Women were exchanged for a pig or two, and murder was a proud act. Yet, if we were to help them, we had to live among them and love them."

For two years the Wileses struggled to bring Christianity and decency to the Big Nambus. Through their own kindness, and the medical aid they gave the savages, they were beginning to make some inroads, but at a terrific cost to themselves. At the end of two years, wasting away with fever and anemia, they were furloughed back to Australia for a rest. While they were gone the entire island erupted into savage fighting. Norman and Alma had had no time to recover their health, but they hurried back to the island. Norman pushed on through the jungle to the major Big Nambu village, and managed to bring the cannibals together and mediate their differences. But he came back to the mission house shaking with fever. While he was still alternating between burning fever and shivering cold, word of a new outburst of fighting came. The Big Nambus were again killing and eating each other.

Norman Wiles got up from his sick bed and went back into the jungle. Again he persuaded them to cease fighting. But it was at the cost of his own life; only two days after he returned home he passed away, victim of blackwater fever.

Alma Wiles was all alone. The natives who lived around the mission station deserted her, running off into the jungle. She sewed her husband's body into a shroud and tried to dig his grave, but she was too weak. Yet somehow she had to bury her husband and then make her way to the mission station on Atchin Island, many miles down the coast of Malekula and across a narrow strait. Fortunately, that day she saw a small cutter making its way along the coast. She signaled it, and it came in to shore. It was manned by three natives, who dug a shallow grave for her departed husband and stood by while she uttered a prayer for him. They promised to take her to Atchin Island, but night was coming on and they had to hurry. She closed the door to the little mission, dropped a last flower on Norman's grave, and went with the three strange natives to their boat.

After they sailed for an hour or so, a storm came up. The natives could not drive the boat through the driving wind, heavy with rain. They gave up, and put Alma ashore at a point on Malekula far from both the mission station and the strait across which lay Atchin. Then they went on to their original destination, leaving her, bereaved and exhausted, alone in the hostile jungle in the middle of the night.

Finally the storm blew away, the moon came out, and she found a path in the jungle. She followed it to a native village where she was known, and where the natives made her as comfortable as they could. The next day was the Sabbath, and she rested, but not until she had led the villagers in a religious service; Norman would have wanted it that way, she knew. The next day a party of warriors led her halfway to the next village; they dared not, in that time of unrest, cross the boundary line between the two territories. From there she made her solitary way through the jungle to the next village, where the natives helped her and led her halfway to the next village. She followed this same procedure two more times, until she found herself looking across the water to Atchin Island. More natives paddled her across the strait in a dugout canoe, and there, finally, she permitted herself to collapse in the arms of the wife of the missionary on Atchin.

After resting a week Alma returned to Australia, to the home of her parents, who themselves had come out from America as missionaries many years before. She pleaded with the church officials, successfully, to send more missionaries back to Malekula, to carry on the work she and her husband had started. She herself completed nurse's training before returning to missionary work. Later years found her in Washington, D.C., where the church's world headquarters is located, but life in a big city was too tame for the woman who had buried her husband on Malekula. At the age of sixty-five she took the Maryland state nurse's examination, passed it easily, and went to Ile-Ife in Nigeria to resume her work on a new continent.

Although the thousands of doctors, missionaries and medical workers who have gone out into the far corners of the world have sought to bring physical and spiritual comfort to its peoples, there is on record at least one occasion when a Seventh-day Adventist representative deliberately set out to make a patient thoroughly uncomfortable.

The temporarily hardhearted young Adventist was Pastor William Baxter, a flying minister then working with the Seventh-day Adventist hospital and sanitarium at Montemorelos, which serves the people in the remote mountain pueblos of the Mexican state of Nuevo León. In the beginning days of the hospital it was hardly unusual for the mountain people to travel several days and nights by burro-drawn cart, bringing a sick friend or relative to the hospital over the narrow, twisting, rocky trails leading out of the mountains. And then came young Baxter, with his own plane. Almost as enthusiastic about flying as he was about spreading the gospel and healing the sick, Bill Baxter immediately began developing an air lift to serve the people of the remote villages. His plan was twofold. He could fly doctors from the hospital into these villages to hold regular clinics, and he could also fly those patients in need of hospital care in and out. But in order to run this air lift, the villages would have to have landing strips, and these landing strips would have to be dug by hand in that incredibly rugged terrain.

The progress of the work on these air strips reflected the attitude of the village leaders, who would have to get the men out in the thin air of the high altitude to chip and haul rock, day after day, week after week. At one or two villages the work was coming along fairly well, but at the village of Rayones things were going slow indeed. Leopoldo Ortiz, known as Don Leopoldo because of his position as most influential man in the village, was not pushing the work at all. He was even making it difficult for the hospital to secure just one room in the village to use as a clinic when the doctor would be able to come.

One day a rider galloped up to the hospital on a panting, lathered horse. He had ridden from Rayones, across the mountain. Don Leopoldo himself was ill and in agonizing pain! He needed a doctor, and at once.

But the doctors had their hands full at the hospital that day. The only way that Don Leopoldo could be treated for whatever it was that ailed him would be to bring him to the hospital. Bill Baxter thought of that short, rocky runway at Rayones, short and rocky because of the very lack of interest of a man who now needed it most, and grimaced. Don Leopoldo's stomach matched his influence; it wouldn't be easy to take off from that short runway with him on board. But nevertheless, without delay, Bill flew to Rayones, brought his plane down in a tricky landing, and bumped to a stop. The strip was in the bottom of a wide canyon, with high grass and tall trees at both ends. Baxter looked at it, shook his head once more, then walked up the curving trail cut in the canyon wall to the village and Don Leopoldo.

No question about it, the old boy was in great pain. It was, apparently, gallstones. Leaning heavily on Baxter and one of the village men, he was able to walk down to the field. Before helping the groaning invalid aboard, Baxter delayed just long enough to point out the difficulty they were going to have taking off from the short field. If only it was a little smoother, a little longer, he said, it would be far less dangerous. Baxter gave an eloquent shrug. As it was, they might make it . . . and then again they might not.

What little blood there was in Don Leopoldo's face left it. Quickly, before he could back out, Baxter helped him into the passenger's seat and strapped him down. Baxter started the plane, revved up his motor, and taxied as far down the runway as he could. He turned the plane around, gave the engine another check, and looked long and meaningfully at Don Leopoldo. Then he gave the little plane the gas and down the strip they went, bouncing and jouncing, picking up speed. The high grass and the tall trees at the end came closer and closer. Don Leopoldo's eyes seemed to be bugging out to meet them. Closer, closer. And then, at the last split second, Bill Baxter pulled back on the wheel. They felt the tall grasses brush the landing gear. Now came the trees. The plane was fighting for altitude. There was a terrible swishing and a tearing sound as the undercarriage ripped through the leaves. And then they were safe above the treetops, flying serenely.

Baxter looked over at Don Leopoldo, opened his mouth and then closed it. There was no need to say anything further. Don Leopoldo's face was green, and sprinkled with little dots of perspiration. Baxter felt a tiny tinge of remorse; the truth of the matter was that a favorable wind had come up, and he could have cleared the treetops nicely.

He continued the flight without mishap, and brought the plane down to a smooth landing at the hospital field. Don Leopoldo received the excellent treatment that all patients get at Montemorelos, soon got well, and returned to his village. Almost immediately he summoned the men of the village, and put them to work on that runway. Today it's one of the finest air strips served by the air lift. And further, when the doctor makes his periodic visit to Rayones, he has a very nice place for a clinic. It's Don Leopoldo's parlor.

2 *Unto All Nations*

The fourteenth verse of the twenty-fourth chapter of the gospel according to St. Matthew reads: "And this gospel of the Kingdom shall be preached in all the world for witness unto all nations, and then shall the end come."

Surely no other twenty-five words have had such a direct impact on so many of the world's peoples. For the Seventh-day Adventists accept this message literally. To them it means this: when every single living person in the world has been told the good news of the coming of Christ, then the world will end, Christ will come again, and the righteous shall live in happiness forever.

No human endeavor could have a more glorious goal, and to hasten that day when the last man on earth shall have been told the gospel, Seventh-day Adventists have gone forth into all the world. In their case dry statistics tell an exciting tale. They are currently preaching the gospel in 189 different countries (work in Russia and some of the satellite countries is carried on from within), and in 791 languages. Partially to pave the way, the church's medical ministry treats nearly three million persons overseas each year. To augment the spoken word, and sometimes to go where the spoken word can not go, the church's 44 publishing houses publish about 75 books a year, and over 300 periodicals.

The effect of their work can be put another way. Did you know, for example, that virtually every man, woman and child on Pitcairn Island, that far-off pinpoint in the South Pacific made famous by the exciting sea tale *Mutiny on the Bounty,* is a Seventh-day Adventist? Did you know that some of today's devoted Sabbath-keepers once actively participated in head hunting and cannibalism before the gospel was preached to them and they were converted? Did you know that the famous Fuzzy Wuzzies who saved hundreds of Allied soldiers, sailors and airmen in the New Guinea and adjoining archipelagoes during World War II were Seventh-day Adventists working under the leadership of church members? Did you know that on the shores of Lake Titicaca, high in the Andes, there are 114 Seventh-day Adventist schools teaching the three R's, plus the gospel, to the Incas? Did you know that in many countries of the world—Iraq, Formosa, Denmark, Thailand, to name a few—and in many American cities major hospitals were built and are maintained and staffed by Seventh-day Adventists? Did you know that every time you eat a bowl of breakfast cereal you have Seventh-day Adventists to thank? And that although they oppose ornamentation in dress, their leaders nevertheless played a direct role in lifting women's skirts off the ground? Would you believe that in just the past few years miraculous cures and impossible rescues, involving members of the Seventh-day Adventist church and documented by truthful and scientific men, have occurred—and that there can be no logical explanation other than that they occurred through the divine intervention of God?

For many years the only difference between death and life, despair and hope, to uncounted tens of thousands of Indians in the vast Amazon basin was a stout, jovial Nebraskan named Leo Halliwell, and his wife Jessie. The Halliwells were sent to Brazil as a missionary team in the 1920s. Leo made a couple of trips up the Amazon and its tributaries, saw the disease-wracked bodies and the spiritless eyes of the people who lived in that steaming jungle, and determined to help them. Though he knew no more about building a boat than any other man from the Great Plains, in 1931 he designed a small river launch and had it built to his painstaking specifications. He even selected the various types of wood to be used in its construction, from the 400 different kinds of trees that grow in the Amazon valley, some so tough that they cannot be cut with a power saw.

Christened the *Luzeiro* ("Light Bearer"), and stocked with what medicine and foods the Halliwells could beg and buy, the sturdy little launch carried them faithfully through the far reaches of the Amazon for thirteen years. It was then turned over to another team of missionaries, and the Halliwells built another and larger launch which served them until they retired in 1958.

There are no roads in the Amazon valley, and all travel is done on the 40,000 miles of navigable streams. The Amazon itself is unbelievable in its size. It carries one-tenth of all the running water in the world. Oceangoing steamers traverse it all the way to Iquitos, Peru, 2300 miles from its mouth. In the Amazon basin live over a hundred different tribes of Indians, some of whom, like the Panovos, so primitive that they have no homes, eat raw flesh. Others, like the Jibaros, make murder a way of life. Poisonous snakes are everywhere. Should an Indian be bitten in the foot, his only hope for life is to build a fire and char that foot into a blackened stump. Boa constrictors, which kill by squeezing, reach a length of thirty feet; alligators, which constantly attack humans, often reach twenty feet. Electric eels develop a current so powerful that they kill cattle. And perhaps most terrifying of all is the small fish known as the piranha; a school of piranha can strip every ounce of flesh from a living cow in two minutes.

But the biggest killer in the Amazon jungle has been disease, especially malaria. One Sabbath morning the *Luzeiro* was anchored far up the Amazon valley in the peaceful Trombetos River. As the Halliwells were singing their first hymn in their little Sabbath-school ceremony, they saw a man in a canoe coming toward the boat. He was emaciated with disease, and was obviously suffering. He begged the Halliwells to come to his village, where every other person had already died or was dying with malaria.

After they had finished worship, the Halliwells proceeded up to the little village. They went to their guide's home first. In one large room were swung twenty-two hammocks, each radiating out from a center pole, and in each of which lay a sick person. Some were shaking with the chills, others were perspiring in streams. The Halliwells gave each a shot of quinine and methylene blue, then went to the other huts in the village, giving the same treatment. The man who had guided them to the spot asked them please to sing the hymn they had been singing when he first came upon them, and Leo and Jessie happily obliged. They sang to the sick, read from the scriptures, and prayed for them. From there they proceeded to another village which the epidemic had hit even harder. In one hut, of the entire family, they found only one little girl left alive. She had tried to bury the bodies of her parents, brothers and sisters, but weak with fever and only about ten years old, she had been unable to scrape out much more than a shallow common grave. The village dogs had unearthed the bodies of her loved ones, and had dragged them back and forth before her helpless eyes. In this village too, the Halliwells stepped in with medicine and prayers.

That day and the next, they treated over 500 persons.

Up and down the rivers Leo and Jessie ranged, bringing not only medicine, but prayers, songs, hope, and the gospel. From the very beginning they knew that God was with them, for on their first trip up the river they had proof.

As a rule, although people traveling upstream in their canoes would ask to be towed behind the boat, the Halliwells refused; they couldn't possibly accommodate all who asked, and the drag would slow them up on their errand of mercy. But on this first trip, in a stretch of river along which there was no sign of population whatsoever, only impenetrable green bush, Leo suddenly noticed three men in a canoe. They had seemed to come from nowhere. Almost involuntarily Leo threw them a line. One man stayed in the canoe and the other two came on the launch. They were making good time upstream, chatting idly about local conditions, when one of the men suddenly asked the skipper which side of the rocks he intended to go on.

Leo knew that the river was filled with treacherous currents and jagged rocks, but he saw no danger. "What rocks?" he asked.

Instead of answering, the man sprang to the wheel, jerked it from Leo's grasp, and swung it completely around. The little launch turned sharply. Leo looked back, and his heart leaped into his throat. Just a few feet from where they had been, he saw jagged rocks, hundreds of them, a few inches beneath the surface of the river. Those rocks would have chewed their boat to bits, and left them helpless in the water with the alligators and piranhas. Badly shaken but grateful, the Halliwells were profuse in their thanks to the two strangers. A few moments later one of the men said they had reached their destination. They pulled the canoe up to the side of the launch and got in. Leo thought it strange; there was still absolutely no sign of any habitation on either side of the swift, broad river. He made a mental note to see where they went. He turned to the wheel, scanned the river ahead of him quickly, then looked back at the canoe.

It was not there. On the whole expanse of the river there was no canoe, no men, no sign. And suddenly a verse from St. Matthew leaped into his mind:

"He shall give his angels charge concerning thee, and in their hands they shall bear thee up, lest at any time thou dash thy foot against a stone."

Today, thanks to Leo and Jessie Halliwell's pioneering, the Seventh-day Adventist church maintains six launches in the middle and lower Amazon valley, another in the headwaters in Peru, and still another on the Orinoco.

In the islands of the Southwest and Central Pacific the church maintains thirty-eight launches, sea-going boats in which the missionaries and medical workers make their way across the shifting tides and coral reefs, carrying the gospel and medical care from island to island, atoll to atoll. The skippers of the South Sea launches do not find the islands to be the romantic paradises you read about in fiction; they are rampant with tropical diseases of all kinds. Yaws, or tropical ulcers, eat right through flesh and muscles; medical workers have reported treating islanders with bleeding, stinking holes in legs and thighs through which a bandage roll could be passed. They've seen natives hobbling along on their heels, with half of each foot eaten away.

Yet, though the men—and their wives—of the launches seek only to bring relief from suffering and the word of God to the island peoples, they are not always made welcome. On many islands the natives are a bloodthirsty lot indeed. Within recent years, while the people of one island would be singing their hymns in Sabbath ceremonies in little missions, on another island, only a few miles away, the as-yet-unreached heathens might well be feasting on human blood.

And the cruelty! Many a missionary has spent a night in a converted chieftain's house, knowing that at each of the four corners stands the erect skeleton of a man buried alive. It was customary, in building the chief's house, to dig a deep hole at each of the four corners, then order into each one a man to hold the corner pole erect while dirt was pushed in and packed tight around them both. When people treat their own kind in such fashion, it is a small wonder that many of the pioneering missionaries of all faiths were stabbed with spears, beaten to death with heavy war clubs, or even torn limb from limb by the savages' bare hands.

One of the bloodiest of all islands was Mussau, in the St. Mathias group. No white man had ever landed on this island and lived. Occasionally an intrepid trader or anthropologist would visit the island, and never be seen again. From time to time various denominations tried to send missions to the island, but the hostile, devil-worshiping natives made it plain what would happen if they came ashore.

But the very existence of the island of Mussau was a challenge to Gilbert McLaren, the missionary-skipper of the Seventh-day Adventist schooner *Veilomani I.* The barbarity of the natives made it all the more imperative to him to teach them of the existence of a compassionate Christ. And so, one day in 1931, Captain McLaren put out from his anchorage at Rabaul harbor with Mussau as his destination. After an uneventful sail, the vessel dropped anchor directly off one of the villages of the island. In a matter of minutes a dozen war canoes filled with fierce-eyed, rippling-muscled warriors, stern and arrogant, circled the schooner. They shook their spears and war clubs, beat them against the sides of their canoes. "Go! Go! Go!" the warriors cried. Their shouts and gesticulations were terrifying. The warriors themselves came under the influence of their own cries; they were becoming even fiercer with every angry shout.

Captain McLaren frankly did not know what to do. He had known he was coming to a dangerous place, but this was more than he had bargained for. His crew members, converted South Sea Islanders who knew their own people, were beginning to show signs of panic. Suddenly he began singing the good old Adventist hymn "Anywhere with Jesus I Can Safely Go." His voice rang out over the heathen cries, and, one by one, the members of the crew joined in. As they sang on and on, their fears began to leave them, and their voices increased in volume and confidence. And suddenly McLaren realized that this was the only sound in the little harbor. The fierce warriors had ceased their blood-curdling shouts and had stopped banging their clubs against their canoes. They sat silent, and listened.

McLaren and his crew of native boys sang every hymn they knew, and stumbled through some they did not know very well. When they had exhausted their repertoire, they began all over again. Finally the day ended, the sun sank into the sea and the warriors of Mussau silently paddled back to shore, leaving the schooner riding placidly on the still waters of the harbor.

It would have been easy for the *Veilomani I* to steal away under cover of darkness, and don't think McLaren didn't consider it. On the other hand, he felt that only the direct intervention of God had saved him and his boys; the least he could do would be to stay and see what developed. He and the crew members stood a regular, round-the-clock watch that night, and it's safe to say that not a man dozed on his watch. Finally the first streaks of dawn appeared in the eastern sky. Just as the top rim of the orange sun peeped over the horizon, the boy on watch ran to the captain's cabin. "Canoe, canoe!" he cried.

McLaren was on deck in an instant. One lone canoe was approaching the *Veilomani*. In the center of the canoe, attired in full panoply, sat a man who could only be the chief. His paddlers brought the canoe alongside the *Veilomani,* and the chief swung aboard. McLaren welcomed him, and the chief got right down to business. He'd been thinking during the night, and he decided that he had definitely liked the singing he had heard the afternoon before. As a matter of fact, he wanted to hear more of it. Could McLaren teach the people of Mussau to sing like that?

Not a flicker of surprise or relief showed on the missionary captain's face. Of course it could be done, he said, but not overnight. To achieve really fine community singing it would be necessary for the Seventh-day Adventists to put a mission on the island, with a full-time teacher. For the chief's people to sing really well it would be necessary for them to learn to read and write. To drive his point home, McLaren hastily lined up his crew and, even though they knew the words by heart, passed out his supply of hymnals. Then, with the entire chorus making a great production of reading the words, they serenaded the chief again with "Anywhere with Jesus I Can Safely Go."

The chief swallowed the bait, hook, line and sinker. He announced that he would call a meeting of the petty chiefs of the island, a sort of board of directors, and would undertake to sell them McLaren's proposition. After much discussion to iron out the further details, and another hymn or two, the chief boarded his canoe and went back to shore. And the *Veilomani I* lifted anchor and sailed away.

But soon the *Veilomani* returned to Mussau, and this time it brought two Solomon Island teachers, Salau and Oti, dedicated men who were prepared to stay. Again after a great deal of discussion, punctuated with a hymn or two in which Salau and Oti demonstrated their singing ability, the chief permitted them to come ashore.

The bloodthirsty islanders helped them build a mission, and all turned out for reading, writing, religious instruction, and choir practice. Before too long, the terrible island of Mussau was indeed a tropical paradise.

Incidentally, to anyone who knows the South Sea Island natives, and the Seventh-day Adventists who have been working with them for generations certainly do know them, this comparatively quick change from cruelty to kindness comes as no great surprise. The idea that before the coming of the missionaries the South Sea Island peoples lived a carefree and happy existence is completely erroneous. Their pre-Christian life was one of constant misery and fear. No devil-worshiping people are happy, for their worship is based on terror; there is no kindness, no compassion, no love in evil spirits. Sacrifices are not made in a spirit of gratitude, but of appeasement and self-abasement.

When human beings live in fear and misery, the taking of life is not so cruel after all, for death can hardly be much worse than life. Let the most savage murderer discover that worship can be a positive, not a negative thing, that there is a God of love, and he becomes an entirely different person, and a better one.

There is a sequel to the story of how Gilbert McLaren brought this love of God to the people of Mussau. One of the first pupils of the new mission school was a handsome youth named Ite. He showed such promise that when the Seventh-day Adventists opened up a mission in the dread jungles of New Guinea, Ite went along to help. When the Japanese overran New Guinea, it was Ite who helped maintain the morale of the natives and kept up their confidence in the white men who had brought them deliverance from the devils. When the Americans justified Ite's confidence and did return, he was promptly put to work in a large Allied hospital, where for two years he attended to the physical and spiritual needs of the sick and wounded. After the war was over, the Australasian Division of the Seventh-day Adventist church built a fleet of new launches to take the place of those damaged and sunk during the war. The crews were selected from the ranks of the very finest of the native islanders. Ite, naturally, was one of the men chosen. And what a happy coincidence it was that the new launch to which he was assigned bore the name *Veilomani II,* in honor of the *Veilomani I* which had first brought the gospel to Mussau, and which had been sunk during the war.

And now Ite, son of Mussau, helps carry the gospel to other islanders in desperate need of God's love.

All over the South Pacific the Seventh-day Adventists carried on as best they could during the war. Indeed, all over the world, both missionaries and local workers are constantly becoming, in all innocence, caught up in wars and rebellions. Some, like Elder James S. Russell and his wife, have had more than their share. They were en route to Tanganyika in 1941 with their six-months-old daughter, Janet, when their ship, an Egyptian freighter, was shelled and sunk by a German raider. The three were rescued, and taken to Germany on board the raider. Mrs. Russell was eventually released, but Russell was held in a German prison camp for four years. Reunited after the war, Russell and his family were sent to the Middle East, where they were caught in the fighting over the Suez Canal in Egypt. After their evacuation they went on to Lebanon, just in time to be caught in the revolt there.

In revolts and rebellions all over the world, Adventists frequently and involuntarily find themselves in the middle of fighting. One morning in 1957 Bryce Newell, who with his wife and two little girls lived on the mission property on the island of New Celebes in Indonesia, heard the sound of firing and knew the revolution had begun. He did not expect the fighting to come close to the mission, until, that very afternoon, a rebel half-track drove up and took a position in the middle of the school yard. Government forces began blasting at it with artillery and mortars. Between salvos Newell ran out and dug a trench. And for three days, as mortars and shells whistled in, that trench was the Newells' home. They lived in it, ate in it, slept in it, all four of them, until government forces attacked the half-track and knocked it out. Then the Newells were evacuated by government convoy.

During the shelling by the Chinese Communist government of Quemoy, the small island between Formosa and the Chinese mainland, the Seventh-day Adventists sent tons of clothing and food to the people of the island. Wilbur K. Nelson, secretary of the Missionary Volunteer Department of the South China Island Union, felt it necessary to supervise the distribution personally. For days he lived under constant bombardment on the tiny island. Yet he went about doing his work, trying to help the innocent, frightened civilians, his heart going out with pity to the wounded and crippled children. And at night, in the blacked-out dugout, as shells crashed around and the Chinese soldiers in the dugout with him shook with fear, he calmly read the Adventist literature he had brought to the island.

During a lull in the bombing one of the guards asked him: "Why aren't you frightened?"

Nelson smiled. "I'm a Christian," he said.

The soldier thought that over for a moment. "Could I be a Christian too?" he asked.

Again Nelson smiled. "Why not?" He handed over some of the literature, and, as the shells came booming in, watched the soldier begin the road to Christianity and peace.

In times of native revolt, Seventh-day Adventists, both foreign and native, are particularly vulnerable to attacks, for many of their missions, schools and dispensaries are far from the beaten track. One morning Ben Wheeler, a young man from Orlando, Florida, serving as pastor of a church in Kenya, opened up his front door in the morning to see the heads of two of his deacons impaled on poles in his front yard. The dreaded Mau-Mau had been there the night before.

In Madagascar, Henri Droualt, president of the Indian Ocean Union at Tanarive, heard that a native worker in a small remote village had been threatened by rebels. Droualt immediately started to his aid. He hitch-hiked a ride in a truck to a fortified plantation, where all the white people for miles around had come for protection, borrowed a bicycle, then went the rest of the way at night. As he rode along the narrow, twisting road in the darkness, giant bats, which attain a wing spread of six feet in Madagascar, swooped and dived at his head. On two occasions he saw bands of roving rebels, carrying long poles with knives attached to the end, coming down the road, but each time he was able to ride into the underbrush or thickets beside the road, without being seen. Scratched and bruised, he arrived at the native village early in the morning. There he found that in retaliation against the revolt government soldiers had lined up the people of the village and shot over half of them, rebels, loyalists, pagans and Christians alike. It was obviously not safe for the native pastor to remain there. Droualt, with difficulty, finally persuaded him to come back with him to Tanarive. The pastor had a bicycle, and the two traveled just as Droualt had the night before, in the darkness, hiding as armed bands of raiders came by. They skirted two burning villages in both of which every native suspected of having any friendship at all for the white man had been butchered. They passed a plantation whose occupants had refused to leave, saying that they had done no harm to anyone and surely the natives would remember. But their own domestic servants had turned against them and had hacked the man and wife to pieces in their beds. There the native pastor refused to go any further toward Tanarive and safety. With the countryside in such turmoil, he felt it his duty to return to his village and do his best to control his people, even though he was in great danger from both sides. Droualt's protests were to no avail; he sadly watched his pastor disappear into the night, riding back into danger. Then Droualt resumed his own journey, reached the fortified plantation, gave back the bicycle, and from there made his way in comparative safety back to Tanarive.

He had been gone three days, traveling at night through a countryside in which many villages had been burned, and hundreds of persons murdered.

"It was just a routine mission," he reported.

To the west of Madagascar, on the African continent, an American doctor named Jack Hay would probably consider riding a bicycle through the cool of the night a pleasurable novelty. Among the people Dr. Hay serves are the strange, primitive Bushmen who live far out in the Kalahari desert. Dr. Hay visits them by camelback, jouncing across the burning sands. The Bushmen themselves, as a matter of fact, are much like camels in one sense; being nomadic people, when they come to a water hole during the infrequent rains they drink all the water they can hold, puffing up like little black balloons. What they can't drink they store in ostrich eggs which they bury in the sand. They hunt in a primitive but relentless way, simply by tracking an animal down until it wears itself out. They kill it and eat the flesh raw, as much as they can hold. But after going several days without food or water, as is quite frequent in their case, they become just a wrinkled bag of bones. Ignorant and savage, they are persecuted by all the tribes around the desert. Their only friend is Dr. Hay, the American who rides up to them on camelback.

While Jack Hay rides out to treat the pygmies, Nurse Phyllis Standen frequently runs to treat the giant Watusi who sometimes come to her isolated dispensary at Rwankeri in the Ruanda-Urundi Colony just west of Lake Victoria. Phyllis lives all alone in the little cottage which is located, for some reason she has never been able to understand, fully a half mile through the forest from the dispensary. Often at night her giant assistant, six-foot-six Inoki, hammers on her door to tell her of some emergency patient who has just been brought to the dispensary. Phyllis, springing from her bed, tells him to return to the dispensary and begin preparations, that she will be along presently. She dresses in a minute, runs a comb through her brown hair, and then, clutching her flashlight and accompanied only by her little dog Pixie, she begins the half-mile run through the dark forest. Frequently she hears the hyenas howling nearby, sometimes even the stealthy rustle of a large animal moving through the underbrush. No native, she knows, not even the huge Watusi, would stir from his doorstep without the big stick which seems to be almost a part of his arm, yet Phyllis Standen runs through the forest alone, unarmed and unafraid, for she is doing God's work.

Sometimes Phyllis goes into the Ituri Forest to see the shy pygmies who live there, taking with her some salt to lure them to her in order that she may try to find out their ailments and problems and ease somewhat their primitive existence. Sometimes she travels through the exotic countryside, watching the elephants eating the grass by the side of the road, the lions, the hippos, the duck-billed native women, sights rich men pay fortunes to see. At other times Phyllis sees sights that pierce her tender heart. In the highlands, for example, where the days are often cool and the nights downright cold, Phyllis sees men and women muffled to the ears in warm clothing while week-old babies lie completely naked.

And sometimes mothers bring babies to her and she sees terrible infected burns on their stomachs. What has happened, she now knows, is that some days previously the baby cried for a longer period than usual, and the worried mother took her child to the native witch doctor. "The baby has a snake in its stomach," the witch doctor had said, and would then proceed with the standard treatment for such an ailment. He would kindle a fire, let it burn down to white-hot ash. Then he would cut the skin across the baby's abdomen, and rub the hot ash into the wound.

Phyllis Standen leads a happy, productive life in Ruanda-Urundi. She has managed to secure paint for the walls of the dispensary-hospital, has herself hauled out tons of lava from around the little building and replaced it with turf, has planted a native red bush to make neat, clipped, English-type hedges around the front yard. In the dispensary itself, she is training Africans to take care of Africans. Government officials frequently bring visitors from all over the world to the Rwankeri Dispensary to show what this one woman has done.

But Phyllis Standen really believes that she has done very little. "What I really want to do," she said wistfully, "is to teach the mothers of Africa not to burn their babies when they cry."

Away on the other side of the world, in the high Andes, far from where Jack Hay rides a camel and Phyllis Standen runs through the night, Adventist workers use another means of locomotion, one which combines all the features of transportation, dispensary and home.

It's nothing in the world but a dusty panel truck with a big red cross on the side, but, thanks to the young men who drive it and others like it along the high, narrow tracks, it means life and surcease of suffering to the Indians who live in the isolated mountain villages. One of the young American medical technicians who drive these dusty highways is Burton Kepler. He spends each day looking for trouble and each day he finds it. Like the morning when, coming around a hairpin curve at an altitude of 12,000 feet, Kepler had to jam on his brakes to avoid hitting a barefooted Indian who suddenly jumped in front of him.

"Señor, señor, stop, stop!" the Indian was crying, and Kepler had little choice but to do as he was asked. The Indian ran toward him, jabbering in the local language, and Kepler listened attentively. Then he grabbed his satchel, jumped out of the truck, and, leaving it right where it was, followed his guide up a steep, winding trail to a mountain cabin. There a woman, the Indian's wife, lay on a rude pallet, face contorted with pain.

A quick examination told Kepler that this was no case for his small satchel; this woman had to be taken to a hospital immediately. Hearts pounding from the exertion in the rarefied atmosphere, he and her husband got her down the mountain to the truck. Whipping around the sharp curves, from which vertical cliffsides dropped hundreds of feet, Kepler drove to the small Seventh-day Adventist hospital in the village of Chulumani as fast as he dared. And there an American doctor performed the emergency operation necessary to save her life. As she recuperated from the effects of the operation, she was naturally curious why Kepler, the doctor, and the nurses whose efforts had made her well had come to this forgotten spot. Their answers must have been satisfying, for when she left the hospital, the church which had sent the small group out from America was two members stronger; she, and her grateful husband as well, had decided they, too, would become a part of it.

To many Seventh-day Adventists, particularly the doctors who are impatient when they are not out putting their skill and knowledge to work saving lives, there is only one means of transportation: flying. It doesn't even make any difference if the weather is suitable. Dr. Jack W. Provonsha, who currently teaches both medicine and theology at the College of Medical Evangelists, served as a missionary in Alaska, returned to the States to become a doctor, then returned to Alaska. While earning his doctor's degree, Dr. Provonsha also learned to fly, and when he returned to his new home he bought a Piper Pacer. With the plane he could conduct two regular daily clinics in isolated spots in his area, bring seriously ill patients back to the ten-bed hospital run by his doctor wife, Margaret. Dr. Provonsha averaged over 300 hours a year in a region known for the world's worst weather. He flew in fog, he flew in blizzards, but he always got where he was going.

Another of the several Seventh-day Adventist flying doctors is William Richli, who carries on a private practice in both California and the Philippines. Though his Philippine practice is centered in Manila, he likes to go out into the far reaches of the islands and help those people who would never see a doctor otherwise. One time, returning by a two-day boat trip from an island only a couple of hundred miles from Manila, he met a Filipino politician who had used a plane to cover his district and get elected.

"Well," said Bill Richli to himself, "if this guy can do it, I can."

The boat docked in Manila on Sunday afternoon. Two hours later he had bought the only plane available, an old Stinson. On Monday and Tuesday he took lessons, on Wednesday he soloed. On Thursday he took off at sunrise for Masbate, an island across a hundred miles of open sea. From there he flew the 125 miles to his next stop, Tacloban, where he worked a day. Then on to the nearest landing field to the village of Malaybalay, on Mindanao. The field was twenty-five miles from the village. A bus took him for fifteen miles of the journey, and he walked the rest of the way. For the last few miles he took a short cut, walking across country through grass five feet high, in a heavy rain.

Then to Cagayan, flying over the beautiful Maria Christina Falls and detouring around a storm, on across the Mindanao Sea to Cebu, back to Tacloban, thence to Legaspi on the island of Luzon. On the last hop, destination Manila, he ran head-on into a storm over the Gulf of Luzon. He couldn't see a thing, he didn't know how to read instruments, and the plane went into a spin. He had been taught how to get out of a spin, provided he knew which way he was turning, but in the dense fog he had no idea whether he was spinning to left or to right. All he could do was sit calmly, and hope that when he came out of the clouds he'd still be high enough to determine the direction of the spin and get out of it before he hit. Fortunately, he did have enough time, just barely. The next day he learned how to fly by instruments.

Dr. Richli is typical, in miles covered annually, of many other Seventh-day Adventists. The heads of the various geographical and administrative divisions travel constantly, and by air whenever possible.

There is, in addition to airplane, boat, train, jeep and camelback, another popular mode of travel, as Dr. Delmont Emery one day learned only too well. Dr. Emery is a handsome, husky, blond young man, who is living proof that a man can eat meat, drink coffee, and still be a Seventh-day Adventist. His first overseas duty was at Chulumani, on the eastern slope of the Andes, where he had a twenty-bed hospital. Chulumani is 6000 feet up the mountain; below are the jungles where the Aymura Indians suffer the jungle diseases—malaria, parasitic worms of all kinds, amoebic dysentery and tropical ulcers, particularly those ulcers which eat into both skin and mucous membrane, thus frequently destroying the entire side of a person's face. Above Chulumani the respiratory diseases, tuberculosis and pneumonia, are the killers.

Delmont Emery is a friendly sort of guy. While at Chulumani he liked to stroll into the village of an evening, make the rounds of the stores and plaza and talk to people—his Spanish is fluent. Frequently when he'd drop in on a family they'd ask him to eat with them. Although he knew full well that the Indians just had no idea of cleanliness, and that proper table manners in the region called for everyone to dip in the pot with bare hands, he always stayed. Aside from the fact that he liked people anyway, he considered it important public relations to know the people better, and let them know him.

Partly because of Emery's natural friendliness, partly because of his service to the people as a physician, Chulumani was a little island in a surrounding sea of anti-American prejudice. While he was in the area, as a matter of fact, the people of a nearby village stoned the workers of another denomination's mission and drove them out of the region. But in Chulumani the people liked their American doctor. On one occasion he was called to a house where a baby was sick. The baby had amoebic dysentery, and was pitifully emaciated; the parents had waited too long. The doctor did what he could, but it was hopeless, and the baby died. The father, in grief and fury, picked up the dead body of his child, and, holding it in his hands over his head, his weeping wife behind him, walked around the plaza of the village, shouting, "The Yankee doctor killed our child! The Yankee doctor killed our child!"

No one joined in the demonstration. When the angry father went to the police and insisted that they serve a summons on Dr. Emery, a delegation of townspeople called on him and told him either to withdraw the charges or get out of town.

Dr. Emery's natural friendliness paid off in another way, too. Chulumani is also the headquarters of a Catholic order which maintains schools in the area. The three priest-teachers there were all

Dutch, all fair-haired, like Delmont Emery, and all wore long black robes, but no hats.

At Chulumani Dr. Emery and the three Dutch priests were fine friends. The Adventist hospital treated the Catholic students; the Catholic school, which raised its own fresh vegetables, kept the hospital kitchen in good supply. When the younger of the three priests, Father David, wrecked his jeep, Dr. Emery sewed him up and the two became particularly close, working together in many ways. Dr. Emery made regular calls at the school, checking the physical condition of the boys, and Father David would come to the hospital and make the rounds with Dr. Delmont, the priest giving the patients nondenominational spiritual comfort while the doctor attended to their physical needs. Father David was probably the only Catholic chaplain in a Seventh-day Adventist hospital in the history of either church.

Together Dr. Delmont and Father David ranged the area. Sometimes they used the school's jeep, but most of the time they walked, and they walked for miles. When Dr. Delmont was busy in the hospital, Father David made the rounds alone, and tipped the doctor off when he ran across a person in need of medical attention.

Late one night Father David rushed into the hospital and awakened Dr. Delmont. He had just come from a mountain cabin where a woman was in difficult labor, and needed the doctor. The two waited for sun-up, then took off in the jeep, following the winding mountain road, climbing higher and higher into the mountains. They drove for an hour, getting as close to the cabin as they could, then left the jeep on the side of the road and continued on foot. The path wound up the mountainside, and it seemed to get steeper and steeper as they went along. Both picked up sticks to help them with the climb. The sun was now high in the skies, and soon Dr. Emery's khaki shirt was dripping wet. But he was still thankful he was not wearing the long, black habit of Father David; it was sopping with perspiration.

Finally they reached the adobe hut. The woman was lying on the floor. She had been in labor for two days; this was her first child. The neighbors were trying to help. They had wrapped the upper part of her body with long strips of cloth, spiral fashion, and two men were on each end of the cloth, pulling as hard as they could, trying to squeeze the baby out into the world. But the baby wasn't coming. Both young men fell to their knees beside the young woman. As Father David comforted her, Dr. Delmont made his examination. It was immediately apparent that the baby was not in normal position. It was imperative that she be taken to the hospital at once. Dr. Emery dashed out, selected two saplings and cut poles about seven feet long. He took two of the woven Indian blankets, and made a stretcher. And then, one at the head, one at the foot, the two tall, blond young men, one wearing khakis, one a long, black robe, one from Holland and a Catholic, the other from America and a Seventh-day Adventist, one named David and the other Delmont, carried the woman down the mountainside to the jeep.

At the hospital the doctor delivered the baby and soon both mother and child were doing well. That is why in Bolivia today there is a young Indian boy who proudly bears the names Delmont and David.

3 *And Then Shall the End Come*

Certainly no large organization, much less a worldwide movement of the size and influence of the Seventh-day Adventist church, has had a less likely-to-succeed beginning. The church had its beginnings well over a century ago in a belief, shared by many members of several denominations, that Christ would come again, and the world would end, on a definite date: October 22, 1844. The chief exponent of this belief in America, and therefore the first man directly instrumental in the Advent movement, was a phlegmatic New York farmer who took up Bible study at the age of thirty-four on a bet and who never preached a sermon until he was fifty-seven years of age; he described it, perhaps truthfully, as a "cold, dull, lifeless performance."

The next important contributor to the movement was a Yankee sea captain named Joseph Bates, who showed no great interest in religion until his wife slipped a New Testament in among the books he took to occupy his leisure hours on a long voyage. Finally, the one person whose dictates and interpretations formed the very cornerstone of Seventh-day Adventist beliefs, and many of whose voluminous writings are positively believed by church members to have been of divine inspiration, was once a frail child who never finished the third grade and who was not expected to live through her teens. Born Ellen Gould Harmon in Portland, Maine, she married a poor schoolteacher and farm laborer named James White, and is known to history as Mrs. Ellen G. White.

How did three such unlikely persons combine to begin a great religious movement? It began when Farmer William Miller said, in a moment of stress in his thirty-fourth year, "My God!" Miller had by no means led a sheltered life. He had been a lieutenant of militia, then a captain in the regular army, fighting through the War of 1812. He scorned organized religion, rejected the Bible as full of inconsistencies and inaccuracies. He had certainly taken the name of the Deity and had used profanity before, without thinking anything of it. But on this occasion, for no apparent reason, he felt a momentary twinge of conscience. That, according to what he himself later wrote, led to an inner turmoil which ended only when "suddenly the character of a Saviour was vividly impressed on my mind." He became a Christian.

Some of his friends laughed at his new faith. One, in particular, asked him how he knew that there was a Saviour. When Miller replied that the Bible told him so, the friend then asked how he knew the Bible was true. After all, hadn't Miller himself said the Bible was unreliable and self-contradictory?

Miller could hardly deny it. He thought a moment, and then he made his wager. He would make a careful study of the Bible, he promised, and if he could not harmonize all of those apparent contradictions, he would return to his old religion, or lack of it.

For two years, without benefit of any previous theological study, Miller went about his task of attempting to understand the Bible. He put aside his presuppositions, and proceeded to read through it, from the beginning, verse by verse, satisfying himself that he understood each passage before he went on to the next. When he came to an obscure thought or word, he looked it up in a concordance and examined all other references having any relation to what perplexed him. At the end of his long period of study, he was convinced that the Bible was its own interpreter. He did not have to pay off his bet by returning to deism.

During his two-year study, Miller was especially intrigued by the prophetic passages in the Bible, particularly in the Book of Daniel.

The upstate farmer apparently did not know it, but he was by no means the first biblical student to be fascinated by the prophecies of this Jewish courtier to Nebuchadnezzar, King of Babylon, in the sixth century before Christ. Many scholars had written dissertations attempting to interpret Daniel's prophecies before William Miller began his study of the Bible, and others have added to his interpretation after he completed it. Daniel's foretelling of history has since proven to be amazingly accurate. In describing and interpreting a dream of Nebuchadnezzar, Daniel foretold of the nations which would dominate the world. After Babylonia, he said, Medo-Persia would become the leading nation, and indeed the Medes and the Persians, under Cyrus the Great, did become established as the world's greatest empire, and continued its role for several centuries. After Medo-Persia, Daniel predicted, Greece would be the ascendant nation of the world; and so indeed it came to pass, when Alexander the Great overcame the Persians at the battle of Arbela in 331 B.C. Daniel prophesied the breaking up of Greece into four divisions, which duly transpired, and finally, he foretold the rise and the fall of the great Roman Empire. After the fall of Rome, Daniel went on to say, there would be no nation of comparable world domination, and history has so far proven him right.

But of more importance to William Miller and theologians was the prophecy of Daniel pertaining to the 2300 days. Daniel told how the angel Gabriel appeared to him—"And he said until me, Unto two thousand three hundred days; then shall the sanctuary be cleansed" (Daniel 8:14). It is clearly understood in prophecy that the word day means one calendar year. The angel, speaking through Daniel, specified that this period of the 2300 days would begin with the restoration of Jerusalem, an event which was not to occur for another century, in 457 B.C. After this, seventy weeks, or 490 literal years, were to be cut off, leaving 1810 years. During this cut-off period, it was written, the rebuilding of Jerusalem would continue for 49 years; 434 years after that would reach to the Anointed One. History records that just as Daniel predicted, 483 years later, A.D. 27,

Jesus Christ was anointed at his baptism in the Jordan River. At the midpoint of the last seven years of this 490-year period, A.D. 27 to A.D. 34, Daniel predicted the Messiah would be "cut off, but not for himself." In A.D. 31, Christ was crucified, not for himself, but for mankind.

Thus the 490 years allotted to the Jewish nation were finished, and from then on the gospel would go out to Gentiles as well. From A.D. 34, the remaining 1810 years of the 2300 days would reach to A.D. 1844. Everything Daniel had foretold had come true so far; there was no doubt in the mind of William Miller but that in the year 1844 the sanctuary would be cleansed, as the prophet had written. Miller translated Daniel's words literally. The cleansing of the sanctuary, he believed, meant the purging of the earth by fire. But he was far from despondent at the thought of this impending dire event, for he also believed that the end of the world would be marked by the return of Christ. Thus the end of the world would be a day of joy to those prepared for His coming.

For thirteen years, as far as the outside world was concerned, Miller kept his joy to himself. For several years he checked and rechecked his figures, and proved to his own satisfaction that other prophecies had been fulfilled during this period. But even after he was sure he was right, even though he knew he should go out and proclaim his findings to the world, he remained quietly on his farm. There was a good reason: William Miller was shy. He told his wife and a few close friends of his interpretation of Daniel's prophecies, and that was all.

But during that period Miller attended church regularly—he was a Baptist—and paid careful attention to the sermons. He even outlined many he heard which particularly impressed him. Whether he realized it or not, he was preparing himself to speak. On one Saturday morning in the summer of 1831, the opportunity came. A young man rode out from the nearby town of Dresden to say that there was no preaching scheduled that Sunday. Would Miller come and talk to the congregation on his theories of the Second

Coming of Christ? Miller went out to the grove of trees behind his house to think it over, and there he came to his decision. That night he rode in with the young man to Dresden, to be ready to speak in the morning.

Miller was far from an eloquent orator, but his sincerity and the strength of his message must have impressed the congregation, for he was asked to stay on in Dresden during the following week to discuss his theories in greater detail. He agreed, and people came in from neighboring towns to hear him. From then on his lectures were in great demand, at first in the neighboring towns, then throughout New York and New England.

In many denominations, in many countries, clergymen and lay members who had studied the Book of Daniel were also coming to the conclusion that the world would end in 1844. But William Miller somehow became its chief spokesman. Paradoxically, his unscholarly mien, his very lack of pulpit presence, made his presentation even more convincing. To the farmers and small-town folk of New York and New England in the 1830s, here was a man who could be believed and trusted. He was one of them.

Although the prediction that the world was coming to an end was put forward in other countries, it received by far its greatest acceptance in the United States. The new nation, now nearing the half-century mark, was psychologically ripe for a native-born national movement. Most of its people were now third-generation Americans; the old-world customs of their forefathers had been gradually dying out and the ties with the countries of their origin had worn away. They were ready for something new, something national, something they could call their own, and the more exciting the better.

For that was a period of excitement in the new nation, as was evidenced in many other ways. In the presidential campaign of 1840, for example, the year of the famous slogan "Tippecanoe and Tyler too!," mass meetings were held in which whole families came from miles around to shout and sing for not just one meeting, but for day after day. Torchlight processions were sometimes five miles long—whole towns and counties turned out to march in them. The Abolitionist movement was beginning; a Boston mob dragged its leader, William Lloyd Garrison, through the streets of the city at the end of a rope. A man named Sylvester Graham, who advocated nothing more diabolic than the use of whole wheat flour, caused riots when he spoke. Religious camp meetings attracted as many as 20,000 people at a time.

And so the prophecy that the world would come to an end fell upon willing ears. Although its adherents became known as Millerites and their belief Millerism, there was no attempt made to consolidate them into one body; Millerites continued as members of their own denominations. Some accepted the prediction quietly and conservatively, others went to ridiculous extremes. One group of fanatics, taking literally the words of Christ as written in Matthew 18, "Except ye be converted, and become as little children, ye shall not enter into the Kingdom of Heaven," crawled around on hands and knees like little children.

As the day drew near, some persons sold their property and goods. Some farmers ignored their fields, some merchants made no effort to restock their shelves. Yet, perhaps surprisingly, the great mass of believers accepted the approach of the world's end with dignity, and continued to live normal lives. Francis D. Nichol, editor of the leading Seventh-day Adventist periodical, *The Review and Herald,* and one of the great scholars of the church, has, with the painstaking research of the working journalist, explored many of the wilder reports and rumors of the time and found them to have no foundation in fact. The legend that many Adventists bought or made special ascension robes, that others were driven mad by fear and that insane asylums were filled with lunatics as a direct result of Millerism, and many other wild tales have been thoroughly scotched.

Through study of the Jewish calendar used at the time the prophecy was written, the exact date of the Advent had been set for October 22, 1844. The day came. Millerites in some cities and communities gathered together in churches and meeting halls to await the end of the world; others remained quietly at home. The day waned, and night set in, and the hour of midnight arrived, and still Christ had not come. Millerites heard the clocks strike twelve with anguished disappointment, with bitterness, with tearing grief. Wrote an earnest believer named Hiram Edson:

"Our fondest hopes and expectations were blasted, and such a spirit of weeping came over us as I never experienced before. It seemed that the loss of all earthly friends could have been no comparison. We wept and wept till the day dawned."

Another Millerite, Washington Morse, wrote, many years after:

"That day came and passed, and the darkness of another night closed in upon the world. But with that darkness came a pang of disappointment to the Advent believers that can find a parallel only in the sorrow of the disciples after the crucifixion of their Lord. The passing of the time was a bitter disappointment. True believers had given up all for Christ, and had shared His presence as never before. The love of Jesus filled every soul; and with inexpressible desire they prayed, 'Come, Lord Jesus, and come quickly'; but He did not come. And now, to turn again to the cares, perplexities, and dangers of life, in full view of jeering and reviling unbelievers who scoffed as never before, was a terrible trial of faith and patience. When Elder Himes visited Waterbury, Vermont, a short time after the passing of the time, and stated that the brethren should prepare for another cold winter, my feelings were almost uncontrollable. I left the place of meeting and wept like a child."

Perhaps the greater part of the Millerites returned to their own churches, which, indeed, they had never left, and tried to forget the whole episode. But many, the hard core of Millerism, including William Miller himself, could not believe that the prophecy of Daniel was wrong. How could the prophet have foretold so many events with such pinpoint accuracy only to fail in the final, and greatest of them all? They still believed that the Son of God would come again; they had merely misinterpreted the date. They turned once more to their Bibles in a hopeful effort to find some other indication of the date. They gathered at each other's homes and in churches, and pored through the scriptures, discussing every passage. Now the words of Christ himself, as found in Matthew 25:13, "Watch therefore, for ye know neither the day nor the hour wherein the Son of man cometh," proved some solace. How had they dared predict the exact date in the first place, in contradiction to Christ himself?

And in this careful perusal of the Bible, carried on in thousands of homes and churches across the breadth of the growing country, the new students of the Bible found fundamental thoughts and doctrines which had been covered over for centuries. One of these, of course, was nothing more nor less than the Fourth Commandment, which plainly states that it is the seventh day of the week, the Sabbath, which is sacred, and not the first, Sunday. Some of the more industrious students turned to history, and learned that the entire worldwide observance of Sunday was the misguided outgrowth of the well-meaning action of one man, Constantine I, Emperor of Rome. Constantine, one of the leaders of a still-small band of Christians scattered throughout a population in which sun-worshippers were predominant, thought of a clever way to enable these sun-worshippers to come into Christianity; in his decree of the year 321 A.D. he made the sun's day, the first day of the week, a kind of auxiliary holiday. For generations the two holidays coexisted; the seventh day, as commanded by God, was observed as a holy day of solemnity, while Sunday was a day of festival. But gradually, through the perplexing perversity of mankind, the first day came to supplant the seventh, however falsely, as the sole weekly day of Christian observance.

But although the students pored through their Bibles and theological writings, the first satisfying explanation of what did happen on October 22, 1844, was not at first discovered in the scriptures, but in a small paper called *The Day Dawn*. Published by

Hiram Edson, a Millerite leader of Port Gibson, New York, the paper carried an account of his experiences on the morning following the unhappy night of October 22. Seeking divine guidance, he and several friends went out to his barn, shut the doors, and prayed. Comforted, they then set out on foot to encourage other Millerites in the neighborhood. They were cutting across a large field when Edson stopped and the others went on ahead. Suddenly, he reported in *The Day Dawn,* Heaven seemed to open to his view. In his vision Edson saw Christ come out of the heavenly sanctuary, but instead of proceeding to the earth, He entered the second apartment of the sanctuary. As Edson watched, it became clear to him that Jesus had some divine work to do in the most holy part of the sanctuary before coming to the earth.

Then the heavens closed again, and Edson, in wild excitement, ran on to catch up with his comrades and told them what he had seen. Together they decided to publish an account of this vision, and thus it appeared in *The Day Dawn.*

Now Millerite leaders sought a complete interpretation of Edson's vision. It was soon forthcoming; the vision served to point out what had actually been contained in the prophecy all along, but had not been fully understood. A review of the customs and practices of Judaism both in Daniel's day and currently gave validity to the new interpretation.

In ancient Israel the sanctuary was the place where the priests carried on their sacrificial work. It was divided into two apartments, in the first of which the daily services were held. But the second was most holy; only on one day in the year did the priests enter it, and then in order to cleanse the sanctuary from the sins of the people who had come in during the year. This day is still a solemn occasion in the Hebrew religion; it is Yom Kippur.

From Edson's vision, and the ensuing careful study of the scriptures, evolved the belief which Adventists have today. Briefly, it is this: As High Priest of all Christians, Christ did indeed enter the most holy sanctuary on that day, there to complete His mediatorial work before His return to the earth. On this day the judgment of mankind began. Thus Christ will return, but no man knows when. A clear indication of what man must do to hasten the Advent is found in the verse from Matthew: "And this Gospel of the Kingdom shall be preached in all the world for witness unto all nations, and then shall the end come."

To return to history, a copy of *The Day Dawn* fell into the hands of Joseph Bates, who for years had followed the Millerite teachings. Joseph Bates had led a fascinating life. He had gone to sea as a cabin boy, over the protests of his parents, at the age of fifteen. His ship had been captured by Napoleonic forces, and he'd been held prisoner in Denmark. In a series of hair-raising adventures, he escaped and made his way to Liverpool, only to be pressed into service with the British Navy despite his American citizenship. For two years he served on a British man-of-war, protesting, and being severely flogged for it, over and over again. When the United States declared war on England in 1812, young Bates insisted on being classified as a prisoner of war, and was imprisoned with other Americans in the dank hold of an old ship anchored in Chatham harbor. He and the other prisoners were constantly trying to escape. One time, using a table knife, they cut a hole through the hull and eighteen men made their way to freedom. While the British carpenters were plugging up that hole, the prisoners stole some of their tools and cut another on the opposite side. After that Bates and the remaining prisoners were removed to the infamous Dartmoor prison, where they lived a life of starvation, exposure and brutality. Not until 1815, after spending five years in British service and British prisons, was Bates released.

He spent little time at home, shipping out as second mate on a European voyage. By the time he was twenty-five, he was master of his own ship. He was married the following year, and then it was that his wife, Prudence, thinking that he took too many novels along on his cruises, put the New Testament among them. Her effort to turn him to the way of Christ was successful. Over the next ten years, as Captain Bates amassed a comfortable fortune as ship-owner and captain, he also became convinced of the truth of Christianity. He was baptized in the Disciples of Christ church when he was thirty-four years old, and quit the sea a few years later to spread the word of God. As a roving church worker, he traveled almost as much as he had as a sea captain, but on land. He breasted the blizzards of New England and Canada, pioneered into the strange new Western country of Michigan and Illinois, even Iowa and Wisconsin. Captain Bates had a youthful enthusiasm and eagerness. When he heard of a group of members of the Baptist and Disciples of Christ churches in Washington, New Hampshire, who were observing the seventh day of the week as the Holy Sabbath, he set out immediately, by train, stage and foot, to talk to them and find out their reasons. He arrived at the darkened farmhouse of Elder Frederic Wheeler, one of the leaders of the group, at ten o'clock at night, and straightway began pounding on the door. Wheeler got up, welcomed him in, and the two talked all night. Then, again by foot, stage and train, he hurried home. A neighbor and fellow Adventist, seeing him coming, called out, "Hello, Captain Bates, what is the news?"

Without hesitating, the captain replied, "The news is that the seventh day is the Sabbath of the Lord our God."

Bates had traveled so much that he had spent all of his savings. He was down to his last few pennies when, with sudden inspiration, he determined to write and distribute a tract on Sabbath-keeping— "I can go to only one place at a time, but a book can go to many." He was working on it when his wife mentioned that she needed four more pounds of flour to finish her baking. Bates strolled down to the store and got just exactly four pounds of flour, plus a couple of other small things she needed. When he returned, Mrs. Bates was amazed. "You've bought just exactly four pounds of flour?" she asked.

"Yes," he said, "and I spent the last cent I have in the world."

Bates worked on his book a while, then had an urge to go to the post office. A letter was waiting. In it was a ten-dollar bill. "The Lord impressed my mind that you might need money," said the accompanying message, from a fellow Millerite. Bates bought a large supply of groceries, including a barrel of flour, with the money, then walked down to the printers to arrange to have a thousand copies of his tract printed. He didn't have the money to pay for it, of course, but, as he had always said, "The Lord will provide." And, indeed, the money did come in.

About a year after the day of disappointment when the world did not end, Father Bates, as he was known by now, met Ellen Gould Harmon. Neither was particularly impressed with the other; Bates frankly did not believe that the strange experiences she told him about were of divine origin, and Ellen Harmon thought that he, though a gracious and kindly man, put too much emphasis on an inconsequential thing like observing the Sabbath on Saturday instead of Sunday.

Ellen Harmon had had an unhappy childhood. When she was nine a school chum, in a moment of irritation, had thrown a rock at her and struck her on the bridge of the nose. Ellen was unconscious for three weeks, and the injury left her with serious complications; she never went to school again. In her teens she suffered from tuberculosis; her family and friends were sure that her life would not be long. Despite her sickness, her family persuaded her to go along with them to hear William Miller speak on the Advent, but she did not then accept his message.

A few months later, kneeling at the altar at a Methodist camp meeting, she suddenly felt the presence of Jesus in her heart. She was temporarily elated, but another period of sickness and doubt followed, ending only when she dreamed that she was standing before Jesus. Though still timid, she forced herself to attend a prayer meeting at an uncle's house; there she lifted up her small voice in prayer, and, suddenly, her misery and sickness left her and she fell to the floor in a faint. Sometime after that she had two visions. In the first she saw the travels and trials of the Advent people on their way to the city of God. In the second she was told that it was she who must carry the Advent message, in spite of the scorn and ignorance and disbelief she would encounter. Now she was no longer elated by her new-found health and joy in Christianity; she felt inadequate to the task that lay before her; she became depressed and wished she could die. She stopped going to meetings, and remained listlessly in her room. Her friends, concerned about her, persuaded her to come to a meeting at which a kindly old Baptist deacon, John Pierson, known as Father Pierson, would lead the prayers.

While they were praying for her, something like a ball of fire hit her over the heart, and she fell to the floor. She heard an angel repeat to her the words of God: "Make known to others what I have revealed to you."

This occurrence, like many others in the life of Ellen Harmon, was fully documented. Father Pierson had been watching Ellen at the very moment that ball of fire struck. *"I saw it! I saw it!"* he cried. "Sister Ellen, have courage in the Lord. After this night I will never doubt again. We will help you henceforth and not discourage you."

From that time the timid and sickly unschooled girl began her development into a poised, mature and eloquent woman, the mother of a church. She lived for seventy more years. She was a loyal wife, and mother of four children. She traveled the world over, even in her seventies addressing meetings of thousands of followers. She wrote an average of 2000 words a day for the rest of her life; her writings total fifty-three volumes plus thousands of articles and letters. Further, they stand up. Her book *Education,* though she herself never completed the fourth grade, is the basis for instruction in the church's 5000 parochial schools. One of her books, *Steps to Christ,* has sold more than five million copies, in seventy-seven languages. And many of her prophecies, on subjects on which she could have no possible knowledge except that given to her in visions, have been fulfilled to the letter.

One of her most dramatic and startling performances occurred when she was still a frail, teen-aged girl. She attended a meeting of a fanatical wing of self-called Millerites who believed that they had already been saved and therefore needed to do no work whatsoever from then on. The leaders of these fanatics, two men named Sargent and Robbins who had declared that Ellen Harmon's visions were inspired by Satan, loudly proclaimed that she would have no vision in their presence. Suddenly the girl went into a trance. Three times she shouted, "Glory!" then rose to her feet and began to deliver the message of the Advent and God's love. Though she spoke, no breathing was discernible. (Later, during these occurrences, doctors were to hold mirrors in front of her mouth and nose and see no clouding whatsoever upon them.) Sargent and Robbins and some of their followers heckled her, but still her voice rang out, clear and sweet. One of the men, having heard that the devil might be exorcised by the Holy Bible, took a large family Bible from a table and laid it against her breast. She did not quail, but took the heavy Bible and held it aloft with one hand. Then, still holding it high above her head, she leafed through it with the other hand, and, placing her finger upon passage after passage pertaining to the wicked and blasphemous, which she could not possibly see, repeated each passage verbatim. Some of the people present stood on a chair and looked at the verses to which she was pointing. She quoted each one correctly.

The frail girl remained in that position for four hours. The power of the fanatics over the other persons present was broken completely; the people who remained became staunch followers.

Ellen Harmon attended many more meetings, frequently receiving visions in front of large numbers of people. When she was eighteen she married earnest, young James White, and the two went to meetings all over New England and New York together. Now people who knew both the Whites and Joseph Bates tried once more to bring the two together. Bates still adamantly refused to believe her visions and dreams, even though in the meantime

Ellen White had a vision in which she was impressed with the importance of keeping the true Sabbath day and became a Sabbathkeeper, like Bates. But he agreed to meet with the Whites.

During his sea-going years, Captain Bates had become greatly interested in astronomy. Shortly before his second meeting with the Whites he had read of the discovery of a fascinating astronomical phenomenon, a strange corridor of light near the nebula of Orion. Ellen White had no interest in astronomy whatsoever, had never opened a book on the subject. Yet, suddenly, while talking with Father Bates, a vision came upon her, and she gave a vivid description of the strange gap in the sky. From that time on Bates was convinced that Mrs. White's visions were genuine, and he worked closely with her and her husband.

Together with many other early pioneers whose names are household words in the history of the Seventh-day Adventist church, they spread the word, recruited new followers, brought into communication several of the groups of the far-flung Millerites. Though they were desperately poor—James White would go out from time to time to do common labor in order to feed and clothe his wife and children—they managed to sporadically publish and mail a small paper which had great influence in bringing their fellow believers together. At first, as William Miller had done, they sought only to preach their message to members of existing Protestant denominations. But as more and more Adventists joined in the observance of the Sabbath, they were naturally drawn together. Both the Whites and Joseph Bates, along with other pioneers, moved westward with the nation. Eventually they began publishing their periodical, *Review and Herald,* from headquarters in Battle Creek, Michigan. One of America's oldest religious journals, it has been published continuously since 1850.

Gradually, over the mid-century years, the Sabbath-keeping Adventists, as distinguished from Adventists who continued to go to church on Sunday, and the members of a small church known as the Seventh-day Baptists who did not subscribe entirely to the

Advent, began to build churches in many different communities, served by full-time elders. They now owned their own publishing house, for which, as editor, James White was legally responsible. He and some other Sabbath-keeping Adventists began to advocate the incorporation of the church under the state laws in order to maintain their properties. Others felt that such a move would be the union of Christ with Caesar, and preferred the loss of church property to incorporation. A general meeting of interested persons from several states was called in Battle Creek in September of 1860. The question of founding an incorporated church was discussed for several sessions. On October 1 the delegates agreed to become an official church body; the name *Seventh-day Adventist* was adopted as most closely descriptive of the beliefs of the members of the new church.

The following spring the Seventh-day Adventist Publishing Association was organized and incorporated under the laws of Michigan. Later that year, in October, Michigan Seventh-day Adventists met and organized the Michigan Conference, the first formal organization of the Seventh-day Adventist church. The General Conference, top echelon of the new church, was formally organized in 1863.

The first overseas expansion came about quite naturally. American Adventists with friends and relatives back in the lands of their origin—France, Germany, Holland and the Scandinavian countries—began sending word back to Europe of this new religious movement. It became obvious that a messenger should go abroad to follow up the seeds that had been planted there. At a camp meeting in the summer of 1874 Elder John N. Andrews—"the best man among us," as Mrs. White later said—was asked to go abroad. Hearing the news, Elder Andrews, a dour-appearing man, seemed to change before the eyes of the assembly. His face brightened, and his eyes shone with happiness at the challenge. Within a few weeks Andrews sailed for Europe. Because of the unsettled conditions in most of Western Europe following the Franco-Prussian War, he set up headquarters in stable, neutral Switzerland. Soon he brought together the Sabbath-keepers of Northern Europe and the British Isles. Eight years later the first Seventh-day Adventist publishing house in Europe was built at Basel.

At the same meeting which dispatched Elder Andrews to Europe, Mrs. White had a vision in which she saw scenes in countries strange to her, where Seventh-day Adventist publishing houses were turning out literature on the message. She told her husband of the vision, and he asked, "What countries did you see?"

"The only one I can distinctly remember is Australia," she replied.

Australia was literally at the other end of the earth from Battle Creek in 1874. Yet within twelve years a Seventh-day Adventist publishing house was indeed in operation in Melbourne, with readers as far away as New Zealand. Another of Mrs. White's prophecies had come true.

4 Into Life Eternal

Before going on to trace the development of Seventh-day Adventist advances in medicine and education, and to more adventures of the church's workers over the world, you might like to take a look at the Adventists of today.

If you attended a gathering of Seventh-day Adventists, whether at a church, a school, or outing, you would find them not unlike anyone else, at least at first glance. Sabbath-school and church services are similar to Sunday-school and church service in most other Protestant churches. The pastor, or elder, wears an ordinary business suit. The service usually begins with the invocation and announcements. The congregation sings a hymn, the pastor says a prayer, and an offering is taken up. After another hymn, he delivers his sermon, and services close with another hymn and a prayer. Afterward, if it is a fair day, members of the congregation usually linger outside the church to pass the time of day, just as do members of other denominations.

If you looked, and listened closely, however, you would notice certain differences in the services, and in the people themselves. For one thing, in churches which do not have special "cry rooms" for children Adventist services are rather noisy. There's a constant rustle and undercurrent of motion going on during the services, even during the sermon. The reason is simple: Seventh-day Adventists bring their children to church with them. Mothers are constantly hushing their children, taking the smallest to the rest room. No one seems to mind at all.

Another way in which services differ is in the sermon itself. Most pastors are not so much preachers as teachers, and their sermons are directed more to the intellect than to the emotions. Listen carefully to the pastor and you will find that his text bristles with biblical quotations. As he speaks, you hear the rustle of turning pages, as some members of the congregation check every text in their Bibles. Preparing a Seventh-day Adventist sermon is no simple task for the pastor; he knows full well that his congregation contains many listeners who know their Bibles and the tenets of the faith as well as he.

Four times a year the Seventh-day Adventists hold Holy Communion, which again is not unlike the communion services of most Protestant churches. Unfermented grape juice is used rather than wine. Prior to the partaking of Communion, however, the congregation participates in the Ordinance of Humility, a distinctive rite impressive in its simple sincerity. This is the feet-washing service, in which members of the church, in quiet humility, wash each other's feet just as Christ washed the feet of his disciples at the Last Supper. On the Sabbath on which Communion is held, the pastor delivers a short sermon, usually of no more than ten minutes' duration. At its conclusion the congregation quietly arises. The women go into one room off the sanctuary of the church, the men into another. In each room the members pair off informally. A man will usually say to another, "May I serve you, Brother Jones?" The women are less formal; they may pair off without a formal request, or, if they are of the same age, the woman making the overture will probably call her fellow participant by her first name.

As the person addressed sits down in a chair and removes his shoes and socks, his partner in the Ordinance of Humility goes to the table where basins, usually of white enamel, and towels are ready. He picks up a basin filled with water and, bearing it and a towel, returns to his partner and kneels at his feet. Then he proceeds, without levity or self-consciousness, to wash and dry the feet of his brother in the church. As a rule the act is performed in silence, but there may be conversation. It is even possible to overhear, as two men engage in a solemn rite dating back 2000 years, discussion of such modern topics as the relative horsepower of their new automobiles. Conversation, however, if any, is usually along spiritual lines.

When the first man has completed his humble task, he empties and refills the basin and secures a clean towel while his partner replaces his shoes and socks, returning to have his own feet washed and dried. When the ceremony is completed, men and women rejoin in the church sanctuary for Communion. The feet-washing ceremony, incidentally, is not private. In most churches non-Adventist visitors are perfectly welcome to witness the Ordinance of Humility. The participants are neither ashamed nor shy about their participation in this unusual rite; they are proud to be able to emulate one of the most meaningful actions of Jesus Christ.

On any Sabbath after services are over, and the members of the congregation mingle together, you may note subtle distinctions which set them slightly apart. For one thing, although all the people are neatly dressed, and the hair of the young women and teen-age girls has been brushed until it shines, you will see little adornment of any kind—no lipstick, no rouge, no jewelry. Though the fact that they worship on the same day, and observe other customs together, does tend to bind the church members into a more cohesive group than other congregations, you will find no sign of clannishness or extreme piety. As a group Adventists tend to exude more warmth and happiness, even mirth, than other groups. Though perhaps after services their conversation is apt to be somewhat subdued, still from many of the groups comes the sound of chuckles and laughter. There's a lot of physical contact as the women place their hands on each others' arms, and the men shake hands. Adventists are the handshakingest people in the world. It is a manifestation of their warmth and friendliness; they are, after all, all in this thing together.

After the services, most of the people go home for the midday meal. A Seventh-day Adventist home looks no different on Saturday from the way any other home looks on Sunday; the ladies of the houses would find it difficult indeed to forsake making up the beds or picking up around the house a bit. Meals are prepared, tables are set and cleared, and dishes are, if not washed, at least stacked. Yet, nevertheless, somehow, a Seventh-day Adventist home from sundown Friday to sundown Saturday is different. There is no radio or television, no card-playing or dancing (there never is on any of the other six days of the week, either), no trips to the beach, golf course, or places of public entertainment. Yet they do not sit around doing nothing, either. Adventists are nature-lovers; they may well take a walk in the country. They may visit other Adventists, or the sick, or make mission calls. Most Adventists are musical and they may sing or play hymns, or listen to classical music on their high-fidelity sets (many are hi-fi enthusiasts). But it is still a day of rest from secular activities, a day families spend together.

Despite the fact that Seventh-day Adventists by no means fast on the Sabbath, the preparation of meals is made as simple as possible by advance preparation. Indeed, as Dr. Adlai Albert Esteb pointed out in a discussion of Sabbath-keeping, "The word preparation looms large in the mind of any Adventist housewife." Thorough housecleaning on Friday makes it possible, as Dr. Esteb says, for "God to walk through our home and find it cleaner on Sabbath than on any other day." After such preparation, it is easy to tidy up a bit on the Sabbath.

Keeping the Fourth Commandment is not just a one-day operation, for the Seventh-day Adventists take its wording literally—"*Remember* the Sabbath day to keep it holy." And so, all during the week, in many homes, members of the household remember the Sabbath by preparing for it. Many housewives prepare the Sabbath meals on Friday, wash the Sabbath dishes on Sunday—after rinsing and stacking them. The idea of remembering the Sabbath and preparing for it all during the week can be carried into year-round activities. Just as Mrs. Esteb, for example, prepares the Sabbath meals during the week and places them in the deep freeze, so does she frequently bake two dozen or more pies at a time for fall and winter holidays during the summer when fruit is in season. It's simply a matter of planning.

It is quite possible to be a good Seventh-day Adventist without going to extremes on the Sabbath. Jesus Christ pointed out that the Sabbath was made for man, and said, "It is lawful to do well on the Sabbath." He asks specifically the question: If your ox should fall in a pit on the Sabbath, would you not pull it out? When emergencies arise, His followers think nothing of attending to them as best they can; they are simply pulling their ox out of the ditch.

Most Seventh-day Adventists take the same attitude, thoughtful but not extreme, toward many other facets of everyday living. Take a simple problem that comes up in many homes: whether or not to look at television, when and for how long. Again in the words of Dr. Esteb, "We do not give a blanket taboo to television any more than we would taboo the automobile or the printing press or the radio or any other modern invention. It's not in the instrument, but in the use made of it. The same printing press that prints a Bible can also turn out some very licentious literature. So television, like any other invention, can be used for good or evil purposes. We advise discrimination and discretion in choosing programs on both radio and television. And we ought to bear in mind the fact that even though some programs might be good, we might well be spending our time at something even better. After all, good things can become the enemy of the best things!"

And so, actually, it all comes down to the value and importance of time. Time is one of man's greatest God-given talents—why waste it on inferior activities? Is it the purpose of living to be entertained by television or any other medium, or to think and grow and keep in pace with discovery?

Despite this somewhat negative attitude toward television, the church itself is by no means above utilizing this new medium to extend its message. The Seventh-day Adventist program *Faith for*

Today, begun in New York in 1950 over ABC-TV, is one of the oldest shows on television. It is telecast not only throughout the United States, but also in such countries as the Philippines, French Morocco and Iceland. Its customary format contains not only extremely good music and a brief sermon by its founder, Pastor William A. Fagal, but a dramatization of some engrossing human experience. Until recent years the actors were all unpaid amateurs, often including Pastor Fagal himself, his wife Virginia, and their two children; just about any capable performer willing to rehearse for a week was welcome. Sometimes casting was a bit difficult, as on the occasion when an actor was needed to portray a drunk coming out of a monumental binge, but it always worked out all right. The role of the drunk, on that particular occasion, incidentally, was admirably performed by an Adventist minister who had never touched a drop in his life.

In spite of the success of *Faith for Today,* many Seventh-day Adventist leaders believe that time can be spent to better advantage than looking with bugged-out eyes at a video screen. This attitude is applied by many Seventh-day Adventists to many activities other than television. Carl F. Hartman, a young pastor who was converted to Adventism in his late teens, remarked that not long after he had determined to devote his life to the Seventh-day Adventist ministry he went to a movie, as he had been doing most of his life. "But I was in my seat hardly five minutes before I realized I just wasn't happy," he said later. "The movie was perfectly acceptable, and I had no other express duty to perform at the time. There was no reason, I had felt as I bought my ticket, why I shouldn't go in and look at a movie if I wanted to. But yet I just didn't feel happy. And finally I realized that surely, somewhere, there was something I could do that would be of greater benefit to both me and mankind than sitting in that theater. Just on the basis of sheer enjoyment, I knew I'd be happier doing something than just sitting there. So I got up and left."

To people outside the church, many of the demands the church makes on its members' personal lives are difficult ones. As Hartzell Spence wrote in an article on the Seventh-day Adventists in *Look* magazine, one of the series called "The Story of Religions in America," "It is not easy to be a Seventh-day Adventist." Indeed, this is very true—to the person who is not a member of the church. A strict belief in the tenets of the faith is an absolute requirement. Seventh-day Adventists believe steadfastly that the earth was created just as the Book of Genesis says it was. Hence the church rejects completely the theory of evolution, as well as the theory, taught by many geologists, that the age of the earth can be measured only in eons of time. Seventh-day Adventists have no difficulty whatsoever in accepting the Creationistic theory. Not only does the Bible say so, and they are taught from early childhood to believe the Bible, but their teachers and professors in Seventh-day Adventist schools and colleges, all adherents to the Creationistic school, and many learned scholars, give many intellectual reasons why this is a more adequate explanation of the origin of earth and man on a purely scientific basis.

Ask the average woman which of the Adventist taboos she would find most difficult, and the chances are she'd reply, in a plaintive voice, "Well, I really don't see why a little lipstick could possibly hurt. I'd just hate to be without it."

To the girl born and raised in the church, however, the foregoing of cosmetics is really not such a great cross to bear. She has been taught since early childhood that her face, as part of her body, is a temple of God; it needs no further adornment. It doesn't bother her at all not to smear lipstick on God's temple. This does not mean, however, that she is any less feminine. Go to any girl's Sabbath-school class in a fairly large city and, although you'll see faces devoid of cosmetics, you'll also see a dozen different hairdos. It's quite possible, even in the Seventh-day Adventist church, to eat your cake and have it too.

There's no question but that people of other denominations who are converted to Seventh-day Adventism from adolescent years through adulthood do find the transition a difficult one in many ways. Just as it is difficult for a woman used to cosmetics and ornamentation suddenly to eschew them, so it is difficult for a man to spend a quiet Saturday with his family or to accept without reservation the belief that the whole world was shaped in a day, or that dinosaurs lived on the earth 4000 years ago, and perished when Noah found it impossible to take them with him on the Ark. It is difficult, too, for people who have built their meals around a solid meat course practically all their lives to prepare and eat meatless meals.

The evangelists of the church recognize these difficulties, and usually emphasize the positive advantages of their faith rather than the negative taboos. Even these thoughtful advisors, however, can do little when it comes to the problem of many converts, that of convincing their families that they are doing the right thing. It would probably not surprise many Americans to learn that in some lands across the seas young men and women have been brutally mistreated by their own families and cast out of the home on becoming Seventh-day Adventists. This maltreatment is not entirely restricted to other lands, however. Even in America, even among other Protestant sects, the announcement of a young man or woman that he or she intends to become a Seventh-day Adventist may occasionally bring forth a storm of protest from parents and other members of the family.

"When my family learned that my fiancé intended to become a Seventh-day Adventist, and had interested me in the church," a young woman said, "my mother told me never to come home if I saw him again, and my father threatened to shoot him if he came on the property. I chose my husband and my faith, and after several years my family relented and accepted us both back again. I had always been close to my father and mother, and those years away from them were bitter ones. But I was lucky compared to what happened to another girl I know. She was only in her teens, and had no place to go if she left home. Her parents were mean to her in many little ways. Her father ground up pork, which is expressly forbidden by the Bible and which we, of course, do not eat, and added it to every dish placed upon the table. The girl refused to eat it, and was near starvation before kind neighbors took her in. During that time, too, her parents deliberately made work for her to do on the Sabbath, and punished her when she didn't do it. Why was there this prejudice against Seventh-day Adventists? I really don't know, unless it's simply because people don't know what we believe and why we believe it, and in their ignorance consider us odd and queer."

In spite of prejudice and persecution, church membership is growing steadily and rapidly. In the past ten years the number of members has grown by 33 per cent.

Today, world headquarters, the coordinating body of the denomination located in Washington, D.C., is known as the General Conference.

The world field is divided into thirteen areas called divisions, each with its own elected officers and departmental secretaries. They are North American, Australasian, Central European, China, Far Eastern, Inter-American, Middle East, Northern European, South American, Southern African, Southern Asia, Southern European, and U.S.S.R.

Each division is composed of two or more Union Conferences, also with officers elected every four years. There are, for example, ten Union Conferences in the North American division.

A conference is composed of a country, state or province, according to size and Adventist membership. The North American division contains sixty-one conferences.

Individual congregations elect their own officers—deacons, deaconesses, departmental leaders, and clerk and treasurer. The pastor of the church, who is referred to as Elder or Pastor, never Reverend, is appointed by the conference.

Over all this the General Conference sits comfortably, with a firm, businesslike organization and clear administrative lines. It occupies a new, efficiently planned building in Washington's Tacoma Park Section, which has become almost a Seventh-day Adventist community. Hard by General Conference headquarters are the large Tacoma Park church, the Washington Sanitarium, Washington Missionary College, the offices of *The Review and Herald,* several other periodicals and a large publishing house, and a cafeteria. Grocery stores all stock vegetarian food like meat substitutes and soybean milk powder.

The president of the World Conference is elected in the general session of world delegates held every four years. The current president is Reuben R. Figuhr. Chief executive of a multi-million-dollar enterprise, Elder Figuhr came up the hard way, beginning as a young pastor in the Oregon Conference, serving as a missionary in the Philippines for ten years, then becoming successively president of the Philippine Union, president of the South American Division, and vice-president of the General Conference. Figuhr is probably one of the world's few top administrators who can issue directives in Tagalog as well as in Spanish, German and English. A slender man with a stern visage, the president nevertheless gets a twinkle in his eye when he tells of the time his career nearly terminated before it began. He was a Wisconsin farm boy, a long way from home, when he got off the train at Gaston, Oregon, to attend Laurelwood Academy. He arrived unannounced and no one met the train. The boy set out for the academy on foot, carrying his heavy suitcase. After walking along the dusty road for three hours in the late summer heat, he was on the verge of turning right around and going back home to Wisconsin. But just then down the road came a pretty girl about his age.

"Is it much farther to the academy?" the boy asked.

"Oh, no, you're almost there," she said, with a smile as encouraging as her words. Furthermore, she added, she was a student there, too.

"I thought that a school with such young ladies in the student body would be well worth attending," Elder Figuhr says today, with a grin. "And I was right." And so Reuben Figuhr picked up his suitcase and trudged on again, along the road which led not only to Laurelwood Academy, but to the eventual presidency of the church.

As for the girl with the warm smile, she is now Mrs. Figuhr.

Under the president come the twelve general departments and their heads—Education (Erwin E. Cossentine), Home Missionary (J. Ernest Edwards), Medical (Theodore R. Flaiz, M.D.), Ministerial (R. Allan Anderson), Public Affairs (Marvin E. Loewen), Publishing (George A. Huse), Radio-Television (Elmer R. Walde), Sabbath School (Gerald R. Nash), Self-supporting Institutions (Wesley I. Amundsen), Statistical (Henry W. Klaser), Temperance (William A. Scharffenberg), and Youth (Theodore E. Lucas).

The functions of most of the departments of the General Conference are obvious from the title itself. But others, such as the Temperance and Public Affairs departments, encompass more than the names signify. Elder Scharffenberg, a stocky, exuberant man, not only preaches and teaches temperance but travels about the world as a sort of one-man poll. In scores of cities he has asked one hundred men on the streets, one hundred women, and one hundred men in drinking establishments just why they do drink. He has found five basic reasons. The first, to which a total of 57 per cent of his interviewees subscribe, is social pressure—a simple matter of conformance. The second reason is that alcoholic beverages are more available as a thirst quencher than anything else. (It is one of Scharffenberg's dreams to have someone put up machines which vend orange juice on streetcorners all over the world.) The third reason people drink is to find escape from incompatibility at home or in business, and the fourth is addiction. Finally, Scharffenberg finds a surprising amount of fine men and women who are totally unaware of the potency of alcohol. "I really don't think these people would drink at all if they knew the truth," he says.

Rarely does anyone object to Scharffenberg's interrogations; most people answer willingly. In Perth, Australia, one man, stopped on the street, became so enthusiastic over Scharffenberg's project that he dragged him to his own favorite pub and lined up his fellow habitués for questioning. "It was a most pleasant afternoon," Scharffenberg reported later. "Everyone wanted to buy me a beer."

Scharffenberg is not an advocate of prohibition per se, remembering too well the last time it was tried. He prefers education as the means by which alcoholic consumption can be curtailed. He would very much like to see a curtailing of the number of liquor outlets. In France, for example, where drinking is almost universal, there is one liquor outlet for every 87 people. ("I was in a restaurant in Paris where the menu contains sixteen pages of alcoholic drinks, but you couldn't get one glass of orange juice.")

In Norway, on the other hand, where there is only one outlet for every 3000 people, there is far less drinking.

"And I definitely feel that there should be some form of prohibition on liquor advertising," Scharffenberg said. "I simply can't understand the wholesale promotion in magazines, newspapers and other media of a narcotic drink that pulls people down."

Scharffenberg also has run an official tabulation on the percentage of smokers in various cities of the world. He bases his figures on a total number of 5000 persons observed on the streets between the hours of 5:30 and 7:30 P.M. In Moscow he noted that 8 of 100 men were smoking, and only 2 women out of the total. In Copenhagen he observed 18 men out of a hundred smoking; in London, 23; in Paris, 31; in Washington, 25.

"In three-fourths of the world people neither drink nor smoke," he said. "It's a sad but interesting fact that the other 25 per cent is in Christian lands."

Scharffenberg is the leader of an international movement to desocialize the serving of alcoholic beverages. Over the world he has secured the signatures of eighty-four men of cabinet rank or above to pledge that they will not serve alcoholic beverages. One of these men is the president of his country, Dr. U Ba of Burma. Scharffenberg's department publishes a handsome slick-paper magazine called *Listen.*

Many other departments also circulate periodicals. The Religious Liberty department publishes an equally handsome magazine called *Liberty.* One of its objectives is education against all Sunday blue laws. At first glance this would appear to be born out of a purely selfish motive, inasmuch as the church does not recognize Sunday as a religious holiday. However, the church's objection to blue laws are broader than this; Seventh-day Adventists would not advocate Saturday blue laws either, for the church is opposed to the principle of coercion of the individual to conform to any rules dealing strictly with religion. It follows the principles laid down by Roger Williams three centuries ago, that while the last six commandments deal with man's relationship with man, and should well be covered by law, the first four commandments deal entirely with man's relationship with his God, and should not be legislated by a government of man. Thus, even though members of the Seventh-day Adventist church are both devout Christians and patriotic citizens, they definitely oppose laws such as those, for example, which would require the seeker of public office to be a Christian. This, they feel, is tantamount to man's attempting to place himself in the position of God.

Thus the General Conference headquarters buzzes today with activities which can hardly be classified as strictly of a religious nature. Certainly the church has extended far beyond the wildest dreams of its founders both in scope of its activities and in geographical extent. When the church was organized, with delegates from a handful of states, in the little town of Battle Creek a century ago, to detached observers it appeared that there was little if any prospect that the church would ever extend around the world.

New members plunge as eagerly into church work as the old. They know before they come in that this is no pie-in-the-sky movement, that belief alone will not bring salvation and happiness, but that they must work to accomplish it. Even so, merely accepting the teachings of the church may bring a large measure of relief. To cite one example, the church interprets the scriptures to mean that the world will end by the direct action of God Himself, and not by the hand of man. In short, the Adventists can cast off the fear that atomic war will destroy the earth. It will be cleansed by God, and by God alone, and in this cleansing the true believers will not be harmed.

Some of the formal beliefs of the church today, based on literal interpretation of the Bible, include the following:

Jesus Christ is the Son of God, preexisted with God the Father, was born of a Virgin and lived as a man among men, died on the cross as an atonement for the sins of mankind, rose, and ascended into heaven. There he intercedes as High Priest as the lives of men are called into judgment; only through Christ is salvation possible.

Christ will come again, and His Coming will be literal and physical, visible to all mankind.

God, through Christ, created the earth and all life on it, just as the story of Creation as given in Genesis says. Thus neither the world nor the life on it evolved over a period of time; in other words, the theories of evolution and geological uniformity are false and scientifically inadequate. Seventh-day Adventist schools and colleges teach the Creationist doctrine, on both biblical and scientific grounds.

The Ten Commandments reveal the will of God, and are unchangeable precepts binding upon all men. But salvation cannot be assured merely by keeping these laws, but through Christ. The Fourth Commandment, pertaining to the sacredness of the seventh day, is to be obeyed literally, from sundown Friday to sundown Saturday.

Baptism is by immersion, and is a rite in which only those of sufficient maturity to understand its meaning should engage.

Holy Communion is open to all who confess Christ. It is held four times a year in connection with the Ordinance of Humility, or washing of the feet.

Adventists today are quite positive that they know the exact future of the world. Their belief is based entirely on the words of the Bible. The church, ever a leader in the dissemination of literature, has pamphlets, available for the asking, which set forth their beliefs in detail, substantiated thoroughly by biblical passages. Without going into this substantiation, this is what Seventh-day Adventists believe will happen on and after the Second Coming of Christ:

At some time in the future—and Adventists believe that the hour is near—Christ will come again. He will not come invisibly, in secret, but will appear personally and publicly, to be seen by the entire population of the world. When Christ comes, there will be both wicked people and righteous people living on the earth, and wicked and righteous people lying dead in their graves. Each of these four classes of mortals will be affected in a different way by the coming of Christ. The righteous-living will ascend into the clouds, translated into immortality without passing through death, to be taken at once to join the Lord in heaven. The righteous dead will be raised from their graves, made incorruptible and immortal, and, with the righteous living, will be taken to heaven.

The wicked living on earth at the time of Christ's return will suffer instant death. They will remain in death, along with the wicked already in their graves, for a period of 1000 years. During these thousand years the righteous, both those alive at the time of Christ's return and those dead, will be living and reigning with Christ in heaven.

During this period there will not be one living soul on earth; it will be a dark and desolate wilderness. Satan, during this period, will be completely powerless. He will be unable to reach either the righteous, for they will be in heaven, or the wicked, for they will all be dead. But at the end of the millennium will come the time for the resurrection of the wicked. Now Satan will have in his army all the myriads of men and women who have lived and died in wickedness since the world began. With this mighty army he will attempt to overthrow the Kingdom of God, centered in the Holy City, which descends to the earth at the end of the millennium, but he will not succeed. He and his army will be destroyed completely by fire. The wicked will not live on in hellfire, but will be completely and eternally dead.

This fire which destroys Satan and the wicked will also cleanse the earth. The world will be restored to the beauty of the Garden of Eden, and will become the permanent home of the redeemed of all the ages. This new world will be an earthly paradise. Its beauties are beyond imagination, for, as the Bible says, "Eye hath not seen nor ear heard, neither have entered into the heart of man, the things which God hath prepared for them that love Him." The whole world will be fertile and there will be no pestilence. Though there will be the same beasts which abound in the world today, their natures will be completely transformed. "... The wolf also shall dwell with the lamb, and the leopard shall lie down with the kid ... and the lion shall eat straw like an ox." The people, the righteous who will have returned to the earth, will be without any infirmities whatsoever. There will be no sick, no blind, no deaf, no lame. It will be paradise, forever and ever.

With such a reward in sight, it is no wonder that the Seventh-day Adventists willingly eschew such minor pleasures as lipstick and rouge, tobacco and liquor, dancing and card-playing, and are happily eager to work to speed that glorious day when Christ will come again.

5 The Right Arm of the Church

In an age when the scientist is king and cynics his courtiers, there is a natural disinclination to believe, as do the followers of Ellen G. White, that her visions and prophecies were truly of divine inspiration. Even during her early life, in a far less skeptical period, some of her contemporary associates who had left the church claimed that her visions were merely the hallucinations of a neurotic female. Over the years since her death, however,—at the age of eighty-seven in the year 1915—more and more of her predictions have come to pass, and much of her counsel on living is now known to have a solid and scientific foundation. Some of her pronouncements, viewed from the world of the sixties, were simply amazing. If Ellen G. White was not divinely inspired, then certainly she was a far more remarkable woman than her early years and education would indicate.

Of all her visions, none have proven true with such dramatic vindication as those pertaining to medical science. Almost a hundred years ago, Mrs. White uttered concepts, in complete contradiction to what was believed to be sound medical knowledge at the time, which have been completely accepted by the medical profession today. But although in one sense Mrs. White was far ahead of her time, in another she merely went back to early Christian times, before a strange and pagan theory was brought into the Christian religion.

The beginning of the Christian religion marked a marriage between two fascinating cultures. The ancient Hebrews had believed that the soul and body were inextricably combined. They believed that a soul went to heaven in the same body it had occupied on earth, although they had no exact explanation for the disintegration of that body after death. When Christ, and the Christian religion, were born, the new faith moved first into Greece. The New Testament, of course, is translated from the Greek, yet the Hebrew influence is plain therein. Greek scholars, for example, comment on the peculiar sentence structure in the writings of the Apostle Paul. The Greeks themselves found him hard to understand; he wrote, you might say, with a Jewish accent.

The Hebrew body-and-soul concept was new to the Greeks. They had believed that the body was nothing; it was the soul alone that mattered. Looking upon the body as a thing apart, and with their cultural eagerness, the leading Greek savants, as typified by Hippocrates, had begun to make great strides in the anatomical and scientific aspects of medicine. Their findings, combined with the gestalt concept of the Hebrews, might well have led to a golden era in medicine. But just as the men of science were beginning to find their way, a teacher of rhetoric named Augustine and a follower of Mani became converted to Christianity. Though he cast off Manichaeanism and became a devout Christian—indeed his influence on Christianity is thought by many to be second only to that of St. Paul—he nevertheless retained one of the principles of that strange Persian faith. Somewhat similar to the earlier teachings of the Gnostics in the first century, this was that the spirit is good, but that matter, or the body, is evil. The soul represents God; the flesh represents the devil.

The followers of St. Augustine accepted this with an aesthetic joy. An immediate result was the termination of the Roman bath; the warm water was perforce, by the very sensual pleasure it gave, a thing of evil. Far from taking care of their bodies, St. Augustine and his followers thought it a proof of faith to deliberately neglect their health, even castigate themselves. The early saints believed that by punishing their own bodies they were striking at evil. And so the healing art, which had been on the verge of emerging into full flower, now went into a centuries-long eclipse. Even during the early years of Ellen G. White, some vestiges of this attitude remained. Fever was considered a sign of too much vitality; to subdue it the body was bled, purged and poisoned with calomel.

The importance of diet to the body was unknown. The biblical adjuration to eat a variety of whole grains had been forgotten or ignored. The diet of rural people in America during the greater part of the nineteenth century was based on pork, white corn pone, and bread made from flour ground to white starch and further devitalized by saleratus. From the last fresh vegetable in the fall, to the first stalk of rhubarb in the spring, people existed on pieces of salt pork swimming in grease, sopped up with corn pone. For Sunday dinner, and for three meals a day every day in the week for those who could afford it, the groaning board was the order of the day. Food was brought on in courses, with a heavy soup, several different kinds of meats, as many starches as were available, different kinds of breads, and heavy desserts like rich pies and puddings. If anybody was criticized for his diet it was the light eater; the idea that eating too much food might be unhealthful was too ridiculous even to consider.

Most men chewed tobacco, spitting constantly. Women's long dresses brushed the streets, and the floors of their homes as well. There could have been no more efficient way to spread bacteria; babies crawled the germ-laden floor and popped things into their mouths; the infant mortality rate was fantastic. It was a wonder that many of the children, particularly those of the middle and upper classes, had been born in the first place. In fashion at the time was the wasp waist, created by pulling the corset strings in cruelly tight. Squeezing the figure in so tightly resulted in forcing those organs above the waistline up into the diaphragm of the chest, while the organs below the waistline were pushed down. The reproductive organs, of course, were crowded together. In an autopsy performed on one woman of fashion it was found that the wasp waist had almost bisected her liver; it resembled a dumbbell.

As for the doctors of the period, in most cases they relied on what was known as the sheet iron of medicine: strychnine, calomel and opium, frequently all at the same time. The shotgun dose, as the administration of all three simultaneously was known, was actually probably the best way to administer them; when combined, the three poisons had a tendency to neutralize each other.

This, then, was the situation when Ellen G. White, with little formal education and sickly herself, came upon the medical scene. One day in 1863 she and her husband, with a party of Adventists, went by wagon to a tent meeting thirty miles north of Battle Creek. At a family meeting in the home of a local church member, Mrs. White led the small group in prayer. Elder White, who was carrying a heavy load, was in poor health and depressed. Mrs. White laid a hand on his shoulder and prayed for him. Suddenly she was taken off in vision. An entire program of hygiene and healthful living was presented to her in this vision. Though this program would hardly seem exciting today, it was revolutionary at that time. For it dealt chiefly with temperance in eating, drinking and the administration of drugs, and with the beneficial uses of water.

"When we tax our strength, over-labor, and weary ourselves much, then we take colds, and at such times are in danger of diseases taking a dangerous form," she wrote following this vision. "We should encourage a cheerful, hopeful, peaceful frame of mind, for our health depends upon our doing this." Though this advice seems obvious today, at the time it was revolutionary. Psychosomatic medicine, which recognizes the influence of the mind on the body, was at that time still generations away.

It was revealed to Mrs. White that it was a sacred duty of the Seventh-day Adventists not only to take care of their own bodies, but to tell others of the benefits of health. A few months later she issued a small pamphlet entitled *An Appeal to Mothers,* with basic but sound advice on the care of infants. Six months after her first vision on health, she experienced another. During this time she produced several pamphlets on health, one of which advocated a vegetarian diet. She specifically condemned pork. In her earliest writings on diet, Mrs. White stressed the importance of whole grains in the diet. Decades before the days of whole-grain cereals, whole wheat bread, and enriched bread, Seventh-day Adventists were frequently referred to with scorn as "bran eaters."

By no means were all of Mrs. White's medical theories unique to her at that time. Other persons were beginning to think about health, and were making suggestions ranging from the medically sound to the ridiculous. Skeptics have attempted to refute the divine origin of her health visions by saying that she could merely have parroted these early medical spokesmen. Had this been true, she certainly showed a medical knowledge far more advanced than that of the medical profession of her day, for she demonstrated remarkable selectivity in choosing which spokesmen to quote. Sylvester Graham, for example, who had advocated the use of whole grain flour some years before, had also preached earnestly on the danger of salt in any amount to the human body. Mrs. White also advocated the use of whole grains, but she advised the use of salt in moderation. And some faddists had condemned the use of all drugs and serums; Mrs. White did indeed adjure against the use of "drugs which poison" but yet she herself was vaccinated against smallpox.

Whether she received knowledge in vision or not, Mrs. White's medical advice was far ahead of its time. Further, it has proven to be sound. There is no need to point out here that the value of whole grains, green vegetables, and moderation in eating—particularly of greasy foods and rich desserts—has long since been accepted by the medical profession. But much of her medical writing dealt with less obvious medical topics. She spoke of "the electric currents in the nervous system" long before the electroencephalograph was developed. Long before Freud, Jung and the other pioneers in psychiatry, she wrote, "Few realize the power that the mind has over the body. A great deal of the sickness which afflicts humanity has its origin in the mind and can only be cured by restoring the mind to health. There are very many more than we imagine who are sick mentally."

Before the birth of Sister Kenny, whose hydrotherapy cure proved of such great value in the treatment of post-polio patients, Seventh-day Adventist doctors were specializing in hydrotherapy, as advocated by Mrs. White.

Long before the medical profession advised sufferers of heart disease to cut down on cholesterol-bearing animal fats, Mrs. White advocated nut foods to take the place of flesh meats, and stated that "the oil, as eaten in the olive, is far preferable to animal oil or fat."

Only recently has the phrase "population explosion" come into popular usage, and planners of the future have become actively concerned about feeding the increasing masses of people who will populate the world of tomorrow. We know that it takes at least four pounds of grain to produce one pound of meat, and that this pound of meat contains toxic substances not found in grain. There will obviously come a time, if the population of the world continues at its present rate, when mankind will not be able to afford the luxury of this one-for-four ratio.

And yet Mrs. White wrote, a century ago: "The life that was in the grains and vegetables passes into the eater. We receive it by eating the flesh of the animal. How much better to get it direct, by eating the food that God provided for our use."

Mrs. White brought about many other advances in medical science in an indirect way. In a vision on Christmas Eve, 1865, it was revealed to her that Seventh-day Adventists should have their own medical institution. Nine months later the Western Health Reform Institute was in operation. However, for several years, Mrs. White and the Seventh-day Adventist board which administered it were not entirely pleased with its administration and operation.

The largest contributor to the enterprise had been a Battle Creek farmer and broom maker named John Preston Kellogg. Kellogg's oldest boy, John Harvey, had been a sickly youth who was not permitted to enter school until he was nine years old. He made up for lost time by slipping out of bed at night after his parents had retired in order to read and study. He went to work in his father's broom factory at the age of eleven, at the offices of *The Review and Herald* at the age of twelve. At first he swept out the place, but after only a few months he began reading proof; he found so many errors that he was placed in the editorial department to stop them before they were committed.

Young Kellogg's ambition was to be a teacher. The one thing he did not want to be was a doctor; once he had peeped through a window at a minor operation being performed in a private home, and the sight had sickened him.

But Mrs. White had marked well young John's industry and intelligence. His ambitions, both positive and negative, were tossed out the window when she decided it was he who would be the chief of staff of the hospital. He dutifully went off to New York to study medicine at the Bellevue Hospital Medical College. Nor did he live lavishly while he was away from home; at the beginning of the year he bought a barrel of graham crackers and a barrel of apples, and they constituted his fare for the ensuing months. The diet must have gone well with him, for he gained seventeen pounds on it. But he often wondered why he could not buy simple items to add to this monotonous diet, such as cereals already cooked and ready to eat.

In 1876, when he was twenty-four years old, Dr. Kellogg became medical superintendent of the Western Health Reform Institute. He later coined his own name for it, "Sanitarium," and from then on it was known as the Battle Creek Sanitarium. John Kellogg may have entered the medical profession with reluctance, but it soon developed that Mrs. White had chosen wisely. According to Dr. Dunbar Smith, until recently medical superintendent of the Battle Creek Health Center which today carries on the traditions of the old "San," Dr. Kellogg was not merely a genius, but a genius in many fields. As a diagnostician, he was superb; as a surgeon he was even better. During one period, at a time when a patient undergoing an abdominal operation had a bare 40 per cent chance of survival, Dr. Kellogg performed sixty consecutive abdominal operations without a casualty.

In the field of nutrition Dr. Kellogg was also peerless. He not only made important studies in the field of nutrition, but developed new food products. The entire breakfast food industry is directly attributable to his work. He also developed noncaffeine drinks like Postum, and meat substitutes of the types eaten by millions of vegetarians today. Although he was not interested in business, he still managed to organize over thirty corporations. And though he didn't really care much about money, he nevertheless managed to net about three million dollars on the side from his food products alone.

Dr. Kellogg was a mechanical genius, too. The universal dynamometer, which he invented to test muscular strength back in the Eighties, is in official use by the United States Army today. And the vibrating reducing couches which have recently enjoyed a huge sale are very much like the vibrating chairs and couches which are on exhibit in the Battle Creek Health Center today—and which were invented by Dr. Kellogg.

As an educator, Dr. Kellogg founded and administered a medical school, a nursing school and an undergraduate college. His medical school graduated 800 doctors. Under his guidance, Seventh-day Adventist medical work earned its traditional appellation, the right arm of the church.

Finally, Dr. Kellogg retained his mental powers into respectable old age. At the age of eighty, when Glenn Curtiss, the aircraft manufacturer, gave him a huge estate in Florida to use as an institution, Dr. Kellogg found he was required to pass the Florida state medical examination in order to run the medical institution. Although it is conceivable that medical science had undergone some changes in the sixty years since the doctor had been a medical student, he nevertheless passed the exam with a high grade. Ten years later, on his ninetieth birthday, the doctor donned a pair of shorts and tennis shoes, ran until he was gleaming with sweat for the benefit of the cameramen, then did some tricks on his bicycle. He died a year later, quietly, after a three-day illness.

During his lifetime Dr. Kellogg wrote a score or more thick volumes on medical subjects. Often he would operate all day, dictate all night, catch an hour's sleep, and begin the schedule all over again. On one occasion, when his publishers moved a deadline up on him, he dictated for twenty solid hours, and not one correction had to be made in his copy. Nor did this frantic schedule seem to interfere with his family life. Dr. Kellogg and his wife, although they had no children of their own, took into their home forty-two children to raise. Several of the children were legally adopted, and nearly all turned out very well. The doctor had his own ideas of discipline. Once, disgusted with the table manners of a nine-year-old boy who had come to live with the family, he told the child that he must be an animal inasmuch as he ate like one, and banished him to the barn for the night.

But Dr. Kellogg spent that night in the barn too, so the child wouldn't be alone and frightened.

People came from all over the world to the Battle Creek Sanitarium. At one time the San had 2000 employees caring for 3000 guests at a time. To heat the water used in the elaborate series of water treatments, the big furnaces burned fifty-five tons of coal a day. At night Dr. Kellogg answered health questions in the huge auditorium, and then the guests participated in the Grand March, frequently led by such visitors as John D. Rockefeller or Henry Ford. The tradition of the Grand March is still carried on in the Battle Creek Health Center, incidentally. As a white-haired lady pounds out the resounding chords of the Grand Assembly March, two lines of patients march briskly in intricate patterns over the big gymnasium floor. Dancing, like meat, alcohol and tobacco, may be prohibited at the sanitarium, but you can never say that the patients don't get enough exercise.

Of all his accomplishments, it is the foundation of the breakfast food industry for which most people probably remember Dr. John Harvey Kellogg today. When only twenty-six, he introduced a health food called granola, a combination of toasted grains, to his patients. But this was somewhat crude and Dr. Kellogg sought ways to improve it. His decision was hastened by the fact that one of his patients, munching on a piece of zwieback, broke her false teeth and demanded that Dr. Kellogg pay her ten dollars for them. One night he dreamed of a way to make flake foods. Early next morning he hopped out of bed, boiled some wheat until it was soft, then rolled it out paper-thin. Baked in the oven and crumbled, it became wheat flakes—or bran flakes, or, if made of corn, corn flakes, call it what you will.

One day there arrived at the Battle Creek Sanitarium a middle-aged man in a wheelchair, named Charles W. Post. He was thinking primarily of a return to good health, but, as a born promoter with a constant eye out for something new, he couldn't help wheeling his chair into the laboratory and talking with Dr. Kellogg's assistants.

One of the products Dr. Kellogg was cooking up at the time was something he called "Minute Brew," a beverage made of toasted grains to take the place of coffee. Post suggested to the doctor that they go in together on marketing it for the general public, but Dr. Kellogg rejected the offer. Post, however, continued to go into the laboratory to watch the progress being made. Dr. Kellogg's younger brother, W.K., who was supervisor of the hospital, doing just about everything there was to be done for the princely sum of six dollars a week, came running to the doctor with the fear that Post might steal the formula and market the brew himself.

"Let him, by all means," the doctor laughed. "Anything that will get people to drink less coffee is all right with me."

Post did indeed do exactly that; he brought out a coffee substitute called Postum. Then he and his little daughter Marjorie, later Mrs. Joseph E. Davies, wife of the ambassador to Russia and owner of the world's biggest yacht, performed some Kellogg-like experiments in their own kitchen, and came up with a crunchy cereal not unlike granola, Dr. Kellogg's first cereal food, which Post dubbed Grape Nuts. Then came Post Toasties. Post had marketed his first package of Postum in 1895; in 1903 his personal fortune was estimated at $10 million, and it didn't stop there. His company was later merged with others and became the cornerstone of the great General Foods Corporation.

The doctor's brother, W.K., saw Charlie Post getting rich, and although the doctor didn't care, W.K. did. At the age of forty-six, worn to a frazzle by his brother's ceaseless demands, believing himself to be an old man, he pulled out of the sanitarium and, with a businessman who had come to the San as a patient, started manufacturing Corn Flakes on his own. At first it was a bitter struggle, not only to make the new, little company a success, but to keep his older brother from taking over. Finally, after some years of almost ceaseless work and some brave business decisions for a man who thought of himself as old and tired, his Corn Flakes—"The Original has this signature—W. K. Kellogg"—began to take over. His company, too, became a giant in the industry.

One other great accomplishment of Dr. Kellogg's, this one brought about working with Mrs. White, was in the reform of women's dress. Dr. Kellogg gave medical authority to what Mrs. White had already received in vision, that the wasp waist deformed the human body, and that sweeping skirts comprised an excellent method for the distribution of germs. As Mrs. White wrote, "The shackles of a slavery worse than any political despotism holds one-half of civilized humanity in a durance more galling, more enervating and more deplorable than Egyptian bondage."

Though the two were fervent believers, they were not bluenoses. Mrs. White had not left her femininity behind when she espoused the church. She knew that it was not enough merely to preach against fashion; before women would discard the current mode, they would have to be given something attractive and appealing in its place. And so, while Dr. Kellogg's *Health Reformer* warned of the dangers of the current style, Mrs. White designed and distributed patterns for a sensible, yet attractive, style of dress which gradually replaced the wasp waist of fashion. It might be interesting to note that this woman who decried cosmetics and ostentation in dress, nevertheless advocated, and successfully, the lifting of women's skirts a full six inches or more so they would no longer sweep the dirt.

But the relationship of the Seventh-day Adventists and Dr. Kellogg did not remain serene. The energetic, driving little doctor was bound to step on somebody's toes sooner or later. In 1901 the church fathers suddenly awakened to the fact that they were maintaining twenty-two medical institutions, that of the 3500 professional church workers 2000 were engaged in medical fields. Plainly there was an imbalance here; the right arm of the church had grown completely out of proportion. So had Dr. Kellogg's own self-esteem; he became a little hard to live with. In 1907 the church and Dr. Kellogg came to an official parting of the ways, although the doctor never entirely gave up his Seventh-day Adventist beliefs and was buried from the church.

The medical school Dr. Kellogg helped found was first moved, then closed. But at the very time it was closing, in 1910, Mrs. White was advocating the foundation of another denominational medical college. Thus the College of Medical Evangelists, located in Loma Linda and Los Angeles, California, came into being. It is today one of the world's most respected medical institutions.

6 The Temple of God

Ellen G. White's medical writings of almost a century ago still live on in the diet and health practices of millions of people around the world. The Seventh-day Adventists must certainly be among the healthiest peoples in the world today. A good part of their time and effort is devoted to maintaining physical health; in some homes the attention to diet borders on faddism. But they have a good reason to preserve their bodies in cleanliness and health, a reason which comes directly from the Bible. As is written in I Corinthians 3:16, 17: "Know ye not that ye are the Temple of God, and that the Spirit of God dwelleth in you? If any man defile the Temple of God, him shall God destroy; for the Temple of God is holy, which Temple ye are."

The Seventh-day Adventists have proven an amazing fact: People who believe that their bodies belong to God take better care of them than those who believe that their bodies are their own.

All Seventh-day Adventists shun alcohol and tobacco, and the great majority eschew coffee and tea and follow a lacto-ovo-vegetarian diet, or vegetarian diet bolstered by eggs and milk. In many respects the members of this faith comprise one big happy family, but in the matter of diet they range from the meat-eaters at one extreme to those who will not touch even eggs or dairy products at the other. "I might remark that I know not whether meat-eating causes high blood pressure," Francis D. Nichol once said in a speech at the College of Medical Evangelists, "but I do know that the discussion of it does.

"From the earliest days of our history the controversy has continued. From those at one extreme has come a heated blast of pharisaic judgment, from the opposite extreme a chilly gale of cynical laughter. The heated air meeting the cold front has produced a heavy condensation and fog, so that too many of our membership see the whole subject of health but dimly through these distorting vapors."

However, although most Adventists can laugh at themselves, there does seem to be a solid scientific background, as well as a biblical reason, for a meatless diet. According to the Bible, before the Flood man ate only grains. Anatomically, the digestive organs of man are indeed more closely akin to those animals which eat grain than to those which eat meat. The process of elimination is carried on in every minuscule portion of the body of any animal; toxic poisons are constantly being produced, to be picked up by the blood and carried away for elimination. There is no question but that at the moment of slaughter these toxic substances are preserved in the carcass, and, when eaten, add to the elimination load of the body which intakes them. Meat-eating Adventists say the increased toxicity is slight; the vegetarians say that it is not slight in the first place, and in the second, even if it were, those who take into their bodies, the temples of God, any amount of poison contravene the teaching of the Bible. It is true that the toxic material can be washed out of meat, but when this is done the flavor is also decreased. It is also true that much of the cholesterol content found in meat can be trimmed away with the fat, but by no means all; even lean meat contains sixteen per cent of oils rich in cholesterol.

"You can't make a person grow taller or faster by feeding him a vegetable diet, but there is no question but that he will live longer," says Dr. Harry W. Miller, who has served the church and his fellow man through medicine for six decades, and who is recognized as one of the world's great experts in nutrition. "The vegetarian protects himself, through his diet, from cardiovascular diseases, from nephritis and diabetes, from mental degeneration and brain weakness."

Dr. Miller spent years in China—in a later chapter we will see some of the excitement of the early days in the Far East through his eyes—and observed the Chinese carefully in respect to diet. They are basically vegetarian people, through circumstance rather than choice; during Dr. Miller's decades in China he saw little meat available to any Chinese, and almost none to the great mass of people. In the south of China the people eat rice, Dr. Miller noted, and in the central and northern portions they eat wheat and corn, but all through China the staple is the soybean. And Dr. Miller saw many Chinese in their seventies and eighties still active, still with strong solid teeth. For years Dr. Miller experimented with soybeans and finally, by cooking them under pressure, getting rid of the tough fibers, adding sugar and vegetable oil and homogenizing the remaining mixture, he was successful in making a palatable soybean milk. He and his son operated a soybean milk company in Shanghai, with routes all over the city, for years.

In controlled experiments with animals Dr. Miller found that soybean milk was far superior in nutritive content to cow's milk. His most impressive results, however, came about inadvertently. Chinese mothers, beset by poverty and with more children than they could feed, would frequently bring their newborn babes to the Seventh-day Adventist clinic in Shanghai and simply leave them. There was nothing Dr. Miller and his staff could do but put the babies in the hospital and feed them.

Frequently there was not enough cow's milk to go around, and, in desperation at first, Dr. Miller had no choice but to feed these infants soybean milk. He noted that the children did fine. On the occasions when limited quantities of cow's milk were available, it would be given to a selected group of children while another group remained on soybean milk. Careful observation of both groups revealed that the children on a soybean milk diet were far healthier.

"Soybean milk contains more protein and more iron than cow's milk," Dr. Miller explained. "Cow's milk is superior only in calcium, but this superfluity of calcium is unnecessary to the human infant. The young calf must grow its entire skeleton in about six months, and it needs this much calcium. But the human takes fifteen years to reach his full growth and doesn't need to have this prodigious amount of calcium pumped into him. Tens of thousands of babies have been raised on soybean milk, particularly those allergic to cow's milk, and they are far better off than other babies. If they continue life as vegetarians, they will have a far greater chance of living many more productive years than those partaking of cow's milk and meat."

Dr. Miller is world-famous as a surgeon, having performed some 6000 thyroid operations alone. He has built and run hospitals in several different countries. But he feels that his greatest contribution to medical science and the welfare of the world's people has been through his work in the field of nutrition, helping the children of the past three generations who have been able to take advantage of his work, and of all the generations to come, to better health and longer, happier lives. Incidentally, he believes that in soybeans lies the hope of feeding the world in future generations. For years the United States has been exporting skim-milk powder to underprivileged nations, in many of which the people are not used to milk, do not like it themselves, and do not want to feed it to their children. Yet we continue in our well-meaning attempt to change the dietary habits of whole nations.

There must come a time when no nation can be so lavish with its foodstuffs. A cow must be fed eight pounds of soybeans to produce one gallon of milk; those eight pounds of soybeans would go much further in feeding people than the one gallon of milk. The most feasible answer to malnutrition all over the world, as worked out by the United Nations staff of nutritionists, lies in four meals of vegetable origin, from cottonseed, peanuts, sesame seed and soybeans, and one from fish. Doctor Miller maintains that the soybean offers the most in nutrition.

Nonvegetarian families, when considering shifting to a vegetarian diet, ask, quite reasonably: But if we don't eat meat, then what *do* we eat? How do we get our protein, how do we build our meals? The Seventh-day Adventist nutritionists are fully aware of the doubts and indecision of the public on the question of vegetarianism, with or without dairy products and eggs, and have published several guides to proper meatless eating. The Battle Creek Health Center, which, like other Adventist hospitals, seems to feed its non-Adventist patients in a most satisfactory manner, puts out a forty-two-page book containing some fifty recipes for meatless dishes which have found such favor with the patients that they have asked for them.

A small loose-leaf booklet prepared for use in home health education classes under the direction of the medical department of the church and entitled *Food, Health and Efficiency* gives not only recipes, but a complete explanation of what the human body requires and what foods provide this. As the chief food value in meat lies in its protein content, it might be well to see what *Food, Health and Efficiency* has to say about protein, in brief.

First of all, proteins are absolutely essential to life, health and efficiency. Proteins are necessary for growth and for repair of the parts of the body that wear out, and have other functions as well. Without sufficient protein the young do not grow, adults become weak and tired, and all are more susceptible to disease.

It's not difficult at all for any person to obtain plenty of protein from a meatless diet, whether with or without dairy products and eggs. Anyone eating legumes such as peas, garbanzos, lentils, soybeans and other types of beans, cottage cheese, nuts and eggs, whole grain cereals and bread and milk will certainly get enough of the right kinds of protein in his diet. Gluten and other prepared high-protein foods are excellent adjuncts.

Most Seventh-day Adventist housewives, however, in addition to these simple dishes, prepare more complicated dishes which can be mighty tasty. And this is certainly in keeping with the advice of

Ellen G. White, for although she condemned elaborate preparations and overeating, she nevertheless advised all women to learn the science of cooking in order that they might make simple and nourishing food appetizing. She once wrote, "It requires thought and care to make good bread. For there is more religion in a good loaf of bread than many think."

When you sit down to something like a pecan loaf, or cottage cheese patties with Italian sauce, or any of a number of dishes made with gluten or commercial high-protein foods with sauces or gravies, together with vegetable dishes, brown bread, fruit and nuts, it is difficult to remember to be abstemious.

An interesting thing about the service of food in a typical Seventh-day Adventist home is the way everyone, father and children as well as the housewife, is interested in and frequently comments on the specific properties in the food that is on the table, as well as making certain that he eats some of every dish. Seventh-day Adventists, in short, actually work at eating; each person is aware that his body represents the temple of God, and is careful to stoke it properly.

Their careful observance of this and all other rules of health produces measurable results. Just a few years ago Dr. Ernest L. Wynder of the Sloan-Kettering Institute, believing that cigarette smoking was a cause of lung cancer and seeking a scientific way to prove it, hit upon the idea of comparing the incidence of lung cancer in a group of Seventh-day Adventists with that of a controlled group of non-Adventists. He worked in Los Angeles, where thousands of Adventists live in the smog along with everyone else, and used patients admitted to Seventh-day Adventist hospitals, of which the majority are not church members, for his study. The control group of non-Adventists numbered 8128; the Seventh-day Adventist group, 564. Of the Adventist group, 70 per cent had never smoked, while the rest had smoked in varying degrees before joining the church. Only 3½ per cent had smoked at all in the five years previous to the study, and only half of 1 per cent had taken a drink since becoming an Adventist. Other than smoking and drinking, the Seventh-day Adventists differed from the control group only in that they ate less meat and drank less coffee and tea but more milk.

First Dr. Wynder, working with the control group, determined the proportion of cancer sufferers to the whole. He included in his study forms of cancer which are believed to have no connection with smoking. Projecting these figures into the group of Seventh-day Adventists, he found that the normal expectation of cancer would be as follows:

He would expect 17 cases of cancer of the colon and rectum, and 22 cases of cancer of the prostate. Among females he would expect 24 cases of cancer of the breast. Among both males and females he would expect 10 or 11 cases of lung cancer and 11 cases of cancer of the mouth or throat.

Those were his expectations. This is what he found:

The colon and rectum cases numbered 17, the exact amount expected. Cases of cancer of the prostate numbered 24, two more than expected. Cases of cancer of the breast numbered 25, one more than expected. But where the study had indicated that he would find 10 or 11 cases of cancer of the lung, he found only one, and this was a man sixty-two years old, newly converted to Seventh-day Adventism, who had formerly smoked a pack of cigarettes a day for twenty years. Where figures had indicated an expectation of 11 cases of cancer of the mouth or throat, he found one case of cancer of the lip, and that in a person who had been overly exposed to the sun, another possible cause of this type of cancer.

Further, Dr. Wynder found that the same general pattern held true for heart disease. The Adventists had far less incidence of cardiovascular disease than the control group.

In recent years the Colorado Health Department made a study on tooth decay in children in all the schools in the state. When the reports came in, it was found that the pupils of three schools, one in Boulder, one in Denver, and one in Grand Junction, showed, in several age groups, less than one-half the amount of tooth decay of children in all the other schools in the state. It so happened that all three were Seventh-day Adventist parochial schools. To health workers, these results were intriguing and exciting. Why were these children blessed with teeth just twice as good as other children living in the same neighborhoods? No completely satisfying scientific answer was ever found, but an investigation revealed that the Seventh-day Adventist children's dental health was coincident with their low intake of refined carbohydrates, such as soda pop and candy, between meals. Most of the Adventist children, the investigation showed, were given three solid, nutritious meals a day, and they ate those meals instead of picking at their plates. Thus they had less occasion to eat between meals than the other children, and when they did have a between-meal snack, it was more likely to be fruit than candy or cookies and soft drinks.

Professional health workers will tell you that lack of motivation is one of the biggest problems they have to face. School nurses can suggest proper diets to parents, but they cannot make these parents carry them out in their kitchens, nor can they force children to eat properly in their homes even if the correct food is placed before them. Nor is this restricted to children.

"How many times," says Joyce Hopp, director of Health Education for the General Conference, "have I been in attendance at meetings of professional health societies and heard scientific reports on the correlation between smoking and lung cancer through a haze of cigarette smoke! And do you realize that there are still tens of thousands of children in the United States who have never received polio shots despite all the publicity and campaigns to encourage parents in this regard? Quite frankly, our Seventh-day Adventist children, as well as adults, do indeed enjoy better health than their neighbors. It is entirely because this religion builds in motivation for good health. I just wouldn't know how to teach children proper health rules without this motivation. Further, our teachers probably do a better job in health instruction than the teachers in the public schools. It's not that public school teachers don't want to do their job properly, but that many of them just don't know how to go about getting all the information they need. But I can, and do, go to our own Teachers' Colleges and reach the student in her preparation to become a teacher. The latest information on health is available to our teachers, and they take full advantage of it."

The non-Seventh-day Adventist visitor to one of the church's missions or sanitariums anywhere in the world may well notice, late in the morning of his second day, a peculiar drowsiness. It is a strange, sleepy lethargy that simply can't be fought off. It can be downright embarrassing, even frightening. If you were not told what the trouble is, it might well take you a few days to figure it out. The answer is simply this: You didn't get your morning's coffee, and your body is crying out for its customary dosage of caffeine. Seventh-day Adventists do not undergo this strange feeling of languor, because they are not addicted to caffeine in the first place, but even so, they have their own methods of pepping themselves up.

One method is simply to get a little more oxygen in their lungs. The entire body must have oxygen, delivered by the blood from the lungs, but the cells of the brain are most sensitive of all to a lack of oxygen. Yet few people use their lungs, through deep breathing, to take in a full supply of oxygen. Getting a quick pick-me-up from this life-giving gas is easy, even without a whiff from an oxygen tank. Several times a day, in the open air, or in front of an open window, stand up with your hands on your lower ribs. Breathe in slowly and deeply until you feel these lower ribs begin to push out—it will take practice at first to utilize the muscles of the lower ribs to full capacity. After you feel that you have taken in all the air you can possibly hold, then breathe in again. Tuck your fingers under your ribs and give them a little tug.

Now let all the air out, pushing in with your hands on your lower ribs to help, then breathe in deeply again. Do this five or six times, several times a day, and you'll get one of the greatest stimulants of all, a full quart of oxygen.

At the Battle Creek Health Center, Dr. J. D. Henriksen gets all ambulatory patients out on the porch at seven-thirty in the morning, and, in a charming Danish accent, leads them through a series of breathing exercises which tone up the body as well as supply it with oxygen. It's a wonderful way for anyone to start the day. First, stand with feet together, hands at the waist. Swing one leg forward in a slow kick, then down, breathing in on one swing, out on the other. Repeat several times with each leg. Now swing one leg to the side, breathing in on one swing, out on the other, again repeating several times with each leg. Finally, swing each leg backward and down.

Next, standing with feet apart and arms stretched out from the shoulder, bend to the left, swinging the right arm over the head while you inhale, then repeat to the opposite side while exhaling. Repeat five times, then five more beginning on the right side.

Next, stand with the feet apart and arms at the side. Swing your arms up forward to a horizontal position while you take a deep breath. Now squat down, dropping your arms to the sides and exhaling. Repeat several times.

Now stand with feet apart and arms at a forty-five-degree angle from your side. Twist your head and body to the left while breathing in, letting the arms wrap around your body loosely, then swing to the right while exhaling. Do this five times, then begin on the right side for five times more.

Finally, stand with feet apart, body bent forward, arms hanging down. Swing your arms and body up to a straight upright position while breathing in deep, bend backward, bending the knees, then swing forward and touch the floor with your hands while breathing out. Do this several times, and now you're ready to face the day.

If you want a real tonic, try a cold mitten rub. Do this in a warm room, incidentally, and never when your body is cold. Dip a rough washcloth in tepid water and wring it almost dry. Rub first one forearm until the skin is pink, then the upper arm. Then dry your arm.

Next morning, with the water a little cooler, get both arms pink. Next day get the water a little cooler still, and add the chest. Next day add the rest of your body, the day after that one leg, and the final day, rub yourself all over. As you let the water get colder and colder you find that you are actually ready to add ice cubes to the water, dipping the washcloth in frequently. If you get chilly, dry each section after you finish. If you get tired after the first couple of stages, proceed more slowly.

The benefits of the cold mitten rub are due to solid medical facts. What you are doing is stimulating the blood vessels in the skin, opening them up to their full capacity, which in turn pushes the blood back into the heart with increased vigor. In addition to toning up your entire body, it actually helps increase your resistance to both colds and cold.

Adventist medical experts advocate full use of water. Taken internally, there's simply nothing like it. Two glasses of warm water in the morning—it would perhaps be wise to begin with less and work up—comprise probably the best laxative known to man. Remember to drink two more glasses of water, cool this time, in midmorning, two more in midafternon. This is one of the best recipes for good health in the lexicon of medicine.

Water applied externally can do wonders too. You don't need aspirin for a sore throat; try instead a throat-heating pad at night. All you have to do is wet a cloth, put it around your neck, and cover it with a wool sock. The blood will rush to your throat to warm it up. When it has performed its mission, the circulation in your throat will return to normal, the wet cloth will get it cool—and the blood will surge back again. This will keep up all night—the wool sock, of course, prevents evaporation—and will carry away the soreness while you sleep. Hot salt-water gargles during the day will add the finishing touches.

Do you have headaches? Well, aspirin is good, but hot water is better. Draw hot water, as hot as you can stand it, into a container or your bathtub. Then sit down and put your feet in it. Be careful at first; it can make you dizzy. But after twenty minutes of this your headache should be much relieved. What has happened is that the blood which was congesting in your head, its pressure causing the ache, has hurried to your feet to cool them down. Proof of the pudding is the dizziness many people experience; this is caused by the blood leaving the brain too fast.

Suppose you have an infection somewhere—a cut finger or toe. Put it in hot water for two minutes (or place a cloth dipped in hot water on it, if you prefer), then in cold water for thirty seconds. Repeat for twenty minutes. The hot water causes the blood to rush to the infection, carrying white corpuscles to fight it, and the cold water causes the blood to rush away, carrying with it the cause of the infection.

These are merely some of the simple remedies which will make life easier. Many such, in addition to the full remedies of medical science, are used in Seventh-day medical institutions all over the world. In some countries, particularly the Near and Far East, and in Denmark, for that matter, the Adventist hospitals are by far the largest and the best; there are 107 in all. The church also supports 114 clinics and dispensaries, some deep in the jungle, some on remote islands, some high in the mountains. Seventh-day Adventists have so well proven themselves to be excellent hospital administrators that government and private agencies have called upon them to build or administer large institutions. Thus when Chiang Kai-shek had the first large and modern hospital built on Formosa in 1954, he called in Dr. Harry Miller, who had already established four large hospitals in continental China, to supervise the construction and organization. Dr. Miller was seventy-four at the time. When the Kettering Foundation decided to provide land and building facilities for a $7,500,000 200-bed hospital in Dayton, Ohio, Eugene W. Kettering called upon the Seventh-day Adventists to operate it. He showed the community leaders of Dayton why he had chosen the Adventists by flying a large group of them to the Adventist sanitarium in Hinsdale, Illinois. They came away convinced.

The church does not mind calling upon its own members to aid in its hospital work. In 1957, A. W. Sherman, a prosperous building contractor in Omaha, Nebraska, was asked to go out to the Far East to supervise hospital construction there. He was offered the princely salary of just about one-fifth his average income in Omaha, but he didn't hesitate; he simply shut down his business and went. Since then he has supervised the construction of a new hospital wing and nurses' dormitory at Bangkok, built a 150-bed hospital at Rangoon, and has advised the local people on plans and construction of churches and schools all over the Far East, in Singapore, Sumatra and Sarawak.

Not only has Sherman taken a great cut in income, but he has added immeasurably to his stock of headache material. In Bangkok, for example, the native workers made their own bricks right there on the job; they resembled burned pieces of toast, warped and crooked. The bricklayers worked on scaffolding made of bamboo tied with vines, and their helpers carried the mortar to them in pans balanced on their heads. Sherman was not only a contractor, but a foreman for every operation. Wherever he went he was followed by a little band of interpreters, for workmen on the job spoke Thai or any one of four Chinese dialects; even so, it was frequently easier for him to brush the interpreters aside and show his workmen what he wanted by doing it himself. He was constantly being amazed by the equipment used to build these new modern edifices. Carpenters used bow-type drills, similar to those used by Boy Scouts to make fires. In place of rock-crushing equipment, workmen sat around chipping away at large stones with small hammers. But in spite of the equipment limitations, the end result was a good, solid construction job. At last reports, the challenge, interest, and constant discovery were such that Sherman had no immediate intention of returning home and becoming prosperous again.

In many parts of the world hospital administrators must be as resourceful in the operation of their hospitals as Sherman is in the building of them. Dr. Otto Hauser, medical director of the Seventh-day Adventist hospital at Surat, India, found his ingenuity stretched almost to the limit in the great flood of September, 1959. The Tapti River overflowed its banks, and the hospital grounds became a swift-flowing, dark brown sea. To evacuate patients from the low-lying charity section of the hospital, across the surging flood, Dr. Hauser worked out a rope-and-pulley arrangement by which patients could be hauled to safety. Nurses and staff members commuted between their hostel and the hospital by hanging onto the ropes.

And then the lights went out. This did not faze Dr. Hauser one bit, however; he simply took a quantity of large bottle caps, filled them with castor oil, and dropped in twists of absorbent cotton. Hospital life went on as usual, illuminated by castor oil lamps.

Would you like to take a look at a Seventh-day Adventist hospital abroad? Perhaps one of the busiest is the Bangkok Sanitarium. The hospital has a large staff—radiologist, pathologist, internist, surgeon, thoracic surgeon, obstetrician, and residents and internes—as well as nurses, the faculty of the nursing school and administrative workers. They all live in a large walled compound in the center of the city. As Bangkok is the crossroads of the East, and people—church officials, doctors, missionaries, occasionally governmental officials—are constantly passing through, one of the wives of the hospital staff serves each week as hostess, assigning visitors to bed and board. Sometimes the compound has so many visitors that it may be necessary for some to sleep in one home, eat in another. It is usually the duty of the business manager to meet the incoming dignitaries at the airport, make up his work that night.

The 200-bed hospital itself is located in a five-story building, a large and efficient operation tucked away in the middle of an old Eastern city. By contrast, on the Island of Bhuket, several miles away, there is a small 10-bed hospital, located in a shop donated by Chinese merchants. One American doctor is in attendance, assisted by Thai nurses from the Bangkok Nursing School. One of its guests in recent years was Vice President Richard M. Nixon, who, on his return to the States, commented publicly on the impressive work of the Adventists in the Far East, and the pleasant reception he had been accorded there.

A strange phenomenon in many countries is the reluctance of girls to enter the nursing profession, even though it would vastly improve their lot in life. In Japan, for example, a feeling still persists that nurses are all women of low moral character.

The same impression also persists in Latin American countries. In the beginning days of the School of Nursing at Montemorelos, in Mexico, the school year would begin with only a handful of girls, for even Mexican families barely above the peon status would disapprove of their daughters working for a living. When a pretty girl named Adha Sano, from a family which could hardly be termed well-to-do, appeared at the school, she brought with her the word from her father that he did not expect her to actually do any work. The director of the school, Miss Marguerite Peugh, wrote back that the nursing could not be learned without working. She saw to it that Adha scrubbed such things as bedpans and laboratory equipment over and over until she got them clean. It wasn't that Adha was unwilling or lazy; she just simply had never had to wash a dish in her life.

Miss Peugh was both teacher and nurse, but her two duties never conflicted; she frequently performed both at the same time. Often she would be teaching a class when the student nurse on duty, faced with a situation she could not handle, would come running in breathlessly for help. "Well," Miss Peugh would say to the class, "come on, we'll learn something new today."

And, followed by the class, she would proceed to the ward, and show both duty nurse and students what should be done.

There is no question but that this mode of teaching, ranging from the repeated washing of equipment to actual bedside demonstration, was effective. For one thing, Adha Sano, the little girl who couldn't wash a test tube, went on to become one of the hospital's finest nurses.

She has been in charge of surgery at the hospital for many years, handling hundreds of major cases with efficiency and dispatch. For a year she served as acting director of the School of Nursing, teaching others to do what she had once been unable to do herself.

"She was even tougher on the poor kids than I was," Miss Peugh reports with a smile.

7 And They Went Forth....

From Battle Creek in the last two decades of the nineteenth century the new, small church began sending out tenuous lines to other parts of the world. John Andrews had been sent to Europe, a delegation to Australia. In 1883, a persistent Adventist persuaded a reluctant sea captain in New York harbor to take on board some church literature and distribute it at ports of call. The captain flung the entire package onto a wharf at Georgetown, British Guiana, washing his hands of the whole deal. One old man picked up one wind-blown copy of the Adventist paper, took it home, and there a woman saw it and borrowed it. From that one copy a small group of Sabbath-keepers sprang up in British Guiana.

These tiny lights in far-off places had been ignited under the impetus of the headquarters of the church in America. Its entry into the next foreign land came about in an entirely different way. One morning a letter from far-off South Africa arrived at church headquarters. In it was the amount of $250, and a request for a missionary.

How had the word gotten to South Africa? Either through the mysterious workings of God, or a strange set of coincidences indeed. A young man named Pieter Wessels, reading his Bible, had noted that baptism should be by total immersion. He asked a deacon of his church about it, and was told that such things weren't important; he might as well, the deacon added sarcastically, observe the Sabbath on Saturday. A few days later, Pieter saw one of his brothers hitching up his oxen on Sunday and chided him for it. The brother jokingly remarked that he was doing no wrong; the Sabbath was the seventh day of the week, not the first. The two remarks, both pertaining to the seventh-day Sabbath, set Pieter to thinking. He looked into his Bible again, and became convinced that what the deacon and his brother had said in jest was no joking matter in the scriptures. He persuaded his family to begin keeping the true Sabbath and they were later joined by a neighbor named Van Druten. Thus, out in the Transvaal, a small group of Dutch farmers began remembering the Seventh Day, completely unaware that in America a whole new church had been formed with the true observance of the Fourth Commandment as one of its cornerstones.

One Sabbath day, Van Druten, walking down the dirt alley of a diamond-mining camp near Kimberley, saw a man sitting outside his tent reading his Bible while all the other workers were at the mine. Curious, the Dutch farmer asked the miner why he was not working with the others. The miner was an American named William Hunt who had come to the minefields from California where he had heard a Seventh-day Adventist lecture; it had impressed him, and he had obtained some literature which he had brought with him to South Africa. He showed one of the tracts to Van Druten, and the Dutch farmer's jaw dropped in amazement. So he and Wessels were not alone in the world, after all!

Armed with the literature, they convinced other farmers to join their small group, scraped together the $250, and requested a missionary.

The church, receptive to the challenge, sent out its first missionaries to Africa. They set up headquarters in Capetown. Soon there was a school, an orphanage and a sanitarium. Hardly was this first mission established when the British opened up a whole new area to homesteaders in what is now Southern Rhodesia. Elder A. T. Robinson, the leader of the mission, saw a great opportunity for the church there. He called on Cecil Rhodes, premier of Cape Colony, and asked for permission to set up a mission in the new land. Rhodes took a dim view of missionaries; he maintained, with some reason, that they brought the natives little material benefit. Robinson, however, likewise with some reason, replied that Seventh-day Adventist missionaries worked differently from some of the others. He began explaining a plan for educating the natives and readying them for coming industry. As he talked, Rhodes reached for a piece of paper, and started writing. Robinson hesitated, thinking he was talking to deaf ears; Rhodes looked up and, impatiently, said, "Go on, go on." Robinson continued to outline his program and when he had finished, Rhodes handed him a sealed envelope.

"Hand this to Dr. Jamieson when you get to Bulawayo," he said.

Robinson knew that a Dr. Jamieson was the administrator of the new country far to the north, with headquarters in the frontier town of Bulawayo. Though he had no idea of what was in the envelope, he put together an expedition—one of the members was Pieter Wessels—with a covered wagon drawn by sixteen mules, and started on the six-weeks journey from Kimberley to Bulawayo. There they delivered the sealed envelope to Dr. Jamieson.

The administrator opened the envelope and read the message. Then he looked up. "How much land do you people want?" he said.

Wessels, who was acting as spokesman, hesitated. What had the note from Rhodes contained? "Well, uh, Doctor," he said, "we ought to have 12,000 acres, but it would depend upon the terms on which we get it."

"Terms!" Dr. Jamieson sputtered. "Heavens and earth! Rhodes commands me to give you all the land you can make use of. Do you want better terms than that?"

And so the Seventh-day Adventists pegged out 12,000 acres in the deep bush of Matabeleland.

The church sent a new group of missionaries to man this mission. One was W. H. Anderson, a senior at Battle Creek College who was permitted to graduate two months early in order to marry his sweetheart and catch the boat for Capetown. Anderson and his bride, with a group of other missionaries, went by railroad to the end of the line, at Mafeking, and from there started on their six-hundred-mile journey into the new territory in a covered wagon drawn by a span of sixteen oxen. Two days later they had gone ten miles. They traveled at night, rested and fed the oxen by day. By the fourth day it was necessary for Anderson to go out and hunt wild game for food; members of his party, fortunately, were not vegetarians. As they traveled, Anderson got an idea of what he was going to face in Africa. While out hunting one day, he rounded a turn in a path and came across a strange scene. A native boy was lying on his back, held down by two grown men. Another man was knocking the boy's front teeth out with a rusty spike and a stone. The youth had reached manhood; this was his tribe's way of celebrating it.

After a journey of six weeks Anderson and his party reached their destination in Matabeleland, set up a rude school and tiny church and got a farm underway. Other missionaries came in, only to be wiped out with malaria, but the Andersons somehow managed to pull through and the mission persevered.

Some years later, with the Matabele mission well in hand, Anderson was invited by King Lewanika, king of the Barotse tribe, to bring a mission much deeper into the interior of Africa. Anderson set out on foot to look over the situation. He walked to the Zambesi River, crossing it near Victoria Falls, then on to Kalomo and Monze. He pegged out a 5,000-acre farm, then returned for his family. His trip had taken four months. He had walked over a thousand miles, had lived almost entirely on what his rifle procured—and had gained eighteen pounds. He had also earned the name by which he was known throughout southern Africa for the rest of his lifetime, *U Vulindhela,* the trail-blazer.

But the real journey came when he started out for the new mission with his family—wife, little daughter, and even his stepmother—over a wild, roadless terrain in a wagon drawn by eighteen oxen. The first day they made a total of five hundred yards. At the end of a week, after averaging a mile a day, they came to a bed of sand two and a half miles across. The wheels of the heavily laden wagon sank deep into the sand and the eighteen oxen couldn't budge it.

Anderson left a native boy to guard the wagon, and carried the load of nearly 4000 pounds, in repeated trips, across the two and a half miles of sand.

"In such experiences as these," *U Vulindhela* wrote later, "the romance of missions disappears."

After the sand the little party entered the thick bush, infested with ravenous beasts—lions, leopards, hyenas, and wild dogs. When they camped a ring of fire was kept blazing around the oxen, wagon and people. One morning the tracks of a huge lion were found just fifteen feet from where the Anderson family had been sleeping on the ground; the jungle king had obviously stood there for some time before moving on. Another morning, as they began the day's trek, a bold lion followed them closely. Anderson had to set the prairie on fire behind him to discourage the uninvited fellow-traveler.

After two adventure-packed months of travel the Andersons reached their destination, a barren farm site. The trail-blazer had hardly climbed down off the wagon before native children began coming in from the area around clamoring to go to school, even though it was a school without buildings or books. Anderson could not resist their eagerness to learn, and although neither the teacher nor the pupils understood a word of each other's language, he began teaching them.

There was another problem; *U Vulindhela* had to spend much of his time hunting in order to keep his family and pupils eating. Hearing that a trader who lived forty miles away had some grain, Anderson inspanned his oxen and started out. On the way, lions got in among the oxen in broad daylight, killed two, and scattered the rest. When he arrived at his destination he found that the trader, a man named Gruges, had gone out hunting and would not be back for a month or six weeks. *U Vulindhela* went to the barn and loaded the wagon with all the grain it could hold, leaving word for Gruges to come and get his money when he returned from his hunting expedition. Back at the mission, he sent a note to headquarters at Capetown (it was a ten-day round trip to the nearest post, and mail came once a month) requesting the money. Next month he received word that there was no money. Shortly after Gruges appeared, and Elder Anderson calmly wrote him out a check on a bank in Bulawayo, five hundred miles away. The moment Gruges left, Elder Anderson and his wife fell on their knees and beseeched the Lord to touch the hearts of the brethren in Capetown—for that check was worthless.

Some months later Elder Anderson received his bank statement from Bulawayo. On the very day before the check had been presented for payment the money had arrived at the bank for deposit. Trader Gruges never knew that a missionary had slipped him a rubber check.

While *U Vulindhela* and his fellow missionaries were getting started in Africa, across the Atlantic an Adventist couple was cruising the coast of Central America, performing dentistry and spreading the word. A party of physicians and teachers entered Mexico, centering their work in Guadalajara. Gradually the work spread through Mexico and the islands of the West Indies, down into the countries of Central America and northern South America.

In the Pacific one of the church's most amazing missionary ventures was taking place. The strange little island of Pitcairn, settled by some of the mutinous crew of the famous ship *Bounty* after a perilous trip across the open sea from Tahiti with their native wives, has always had a romantic appeal to people the world over, and the Seventh-day Adventists were no exception. During the 1870s Elder James White had sent a package of literature to Pitcairn, but he had no way of knowing that it ever reached the little island so far off the shipping lanes. And then along came a Seventh-day Adventist named John I. Tay. At the age of sixteen he had read *The Mutiny on the Bounty* and had developed a deep interest in Pitcairn Island. There had been no way for him to get there, and he lost interest. He was a middle-aged man, living in San Francisco, when his health began to fail and he was advised to take a sea voyage. His destination, he resolved, would be Pitcairn. He had no money, so he signed on a ship bound for Tahiti as ship's carpenter—receiving no pay whatsoever in return for not having to work on the Sabbath. He reached Tahiti in a month, and there he learned that it might be years before he could pick up a ship which would pass by Pitcairn. John Tay, as many an Adventist had before him, prayed. Just four weeks later, a British man-of-war put in at Tahiti, on the way to Pitcairn. When the ship left, Tay was on it.

On Pitcairn, Tay found to his amazement that when he began speaking to the islanders about the Seventh-day Adventist message they were familiar with what he said. That package of literature sent out years before had arrived, and some of the leaders of the 130 people on the island, all descendants of the original landing party, had looked it over and been impressed. However, they had been hesitant to embrace the new faith, with its many differences in religion from their own. Tay spoke at prayer meeting, visited the people in their homes, began Bible studies with a group which grew larger every day, spoke at Sunday services—he did not go to the pulpit, but stood in his pew—and spoke again at the next prayer meeting. When he paused, a voice suddenly came from one of the islanders.

"I will keep the Sabbath," he said. Another repeated the words, and another. On the following Sabbath the bell rang for church at ten o'clock in the morning, and everyone on the island attended. On Pitcairn Island the Sabbath has been kept ever since.

But when a boat put in at Pitcairn five weeks later, and John Tay left for home, he was still not satisfied. He felt that the islanders still had much to learn about the Seventh-day Adventist religion. Furthermore, on the way from Tahiti to Pitcairn he had touched in at various islands in the South Pacific and had seen that there was much need for missionaries, doctors and teachers. When he arrived in the United States, and told Seventh-day Adventists of the great opportunity that awaited the church on Pitcairn and the other islands of the South Pacific, a wave of enthusiasm swept Sabbath-keepers all over the nation. The idea of a Seventh-day Adventist missionary ship to take the gospel to those remote islands was born spontaneously, but it was the children of the Sabbath schools who put the project over. Nearly every child worked hard to raise money in some way or another, selling pies, cakes, candy—one little boy sold fifteen dollars' worth of popcorn balls. With the money they raised the ship was built, and to the children went the honor of naming the vessel; their overwhelming vote was *Pitcairn.*

Though built a hundred years after the mutineers had destroyed the *Bounty,* the *Pitcairn* was even smaller. The early missionaries who volunteered to venture across the great Pacific in this little ship were brave men and women indeed. There were six of them, John Tay, Elder E. H. Gates of Ohio, Elder A. J. Read of New England, and their wives. After the thirty-six-day voyage to Pitcairn, they were required to show even more bravery. For the only way to enter Bounty harbor is by long boat, through the pounding surf. The missionaries and their wives transferred to the islanders' long boats, each thirty-six feet long and manned by a score of sturdy rowers. The long boats approached the heavy waves guarding the harbor carefully, then, at just the right moment, the helmsman of each boat gave a quick command, "Lay to!" The men gave a mighty pull on the oars, and sent their craft skimming through the surf between the two black rocks guarding the harbor to the quiet waters of the bay.

Once on shore, what a wonderful welcome the visitors received! The islanders brought out oranges and pineapples, the most delicious in all the world. Services were held in the chapel, and they all sang the wonderful old hymns and even some of the school songs. Both Pitcairn Islanders and the Seventh-day Adventists were happy people, secure in the blessings of the Lord. That first day was a joyous one, and it was followed by many more, culminating in the glorious Friday afternoon, just before sunset and the beginning of the Sabbath, when Elder Gates and Elder Read baptized sixty-four of the Pitcairn people and received them into the Seventh-day Adventist church.

After leaving Pitcairn, the missionairies sailed on to Tahiti and other South Sea Islands. The Tays remained in Fiji to carry on the work from the capital city of Suva, where John Tay lived only a few more months. Elder Read and his wife remained at Norfolk Island, which had been settled not too many years before by the overflow population of Pitcairn. Then Gates returned to Pitcairn, remained for a year, establishing a school. The *Pitcairn* brought many new missionaries and doctors to the South Seas, and American couples from quiet homes all across the country found themselves in such places as Tonga and Rurutu as well as Australia and New Zealand. By 1900, the Seventh-day Adventists of Australasia were so well organized that they formed their own conference. Since then most of the missionaries sent to the islands of the South Seas have come from Australasia itself.

One of the great missionaries to the South Seas about the turn of the century was a dapper, bearded little sea captain named Griffith Francis Jones, still revered in the memory of many islanders as "Jonesie." When still in his twenties, an ambitious young seafarer of no particular religious bent, he had been pacing the deck of his ship one morning when he saw a piece of paper blowing about. He bent over, picked it up, and was just about to give the crew a dressing down for not keeping the decks clean when his eye happened to notice what was written on it. The piece of paper was a torn portion of *Present Truth,* a Seventh-day Adventist paper published in America, containing a few paragraphs of the Advent message. Later, ashore in England, the captain happened to see another piece of paper on the street, and picked that up, too. It turned out to be a torn page from another Seventh-day publication. The captain had been considering leaving the sea for a life of service to mankind. The coincidence of the two pieces of paper decided him, and he resolved that his service would be under the auspices of the church which published them. With his wife Marion he went across the Atlantic and half of America to the Seventh-day Adventist academy at Keene, Texas, and from there they went to the Pacific.

In the Seventh-day Adventist launch *Melanesia,* little Jonesie, "the man with grass on his face," and Marion sailed to islands which no white man, or woman, had ever visited before. In the Solomon Islands, inhabited by devil-worshippers and one of the blood-thirstiest places on the face of the globe, the missionary couple set up their first mission at Viru, on New Georgia. Arriving at dusk, they said their prayers and turned in on the deck of the little vessel, rather than in the stuffy cabin. During the night they were awakened by the stealthy swish of paddles. They were barely on their feet when a long war canoe scraped the side of their boat, and a dozen huge, battle-scarred warriors, gripping heavy war clubs, scrambled aboard. Captain Jones and his wife knew only too well the fate of previous white visitors to this area; they had been clubbed to death, perhaps eaten. But the little man of God did not hesitate. He stepped boldly into their midst, and began speaking. Such a powerful but calm voice coming from a man who came barely to their shoulders impressed the savages, and they let him continue. He told them he was there to teach their children, to minister to them in times of trouble and sickness. When he finished, the warriors huddled together. Then they squatted calmly on the deck, as their spokesman stepped forward to deliver their verdict. Captain Jones and his wife would be welcome at Viru.

Once a South Seas trader remarked, "the worst punishment I could think of to inflict on my worst enemy would be to banish him to the Solomon Islands." When Captain Jones arrived, the islands were far from a tropical paradise. Malaria was rampant. Nearly every native had some kind of skin disease. Every child seemed covered with suppurating yaws, large running sores. Visitors left pus-stained footprints on the *Melanesia's* deck. A form of ringworm was particularly persistent in the Solomons; sufferers with the disease would sit on the deck and scratch so hard that the scales would fly in all directions. But perhaps even worse than their physical discomfort was the constant fear in which the natives lived. Their entire life was governed by devils, evil and cruel spirits which, the natives thought, were all around them. But gradually, as the Joneses healed the Solomon Islanders' sores, taught them to sing the rich Christian hymns, taught their children to read and write and care for their bodies, the natives cast off their bondage to the devils, and found peace and happiness with God.

There has been much criticism in recent years of those missionaries who, narrow-minded and apparently under the impression that Christianity and Western civilization are synonymous, sought to change many of the natural customs of the natives as well as their religious beliefs. The Joneses, and other Seventh-day Adventist missionaries, never attempted to transform the natives into puritanical bluenoses wearing woolen suits on the Equator. They brought word of a loving God, a God of forgiveness. Some years after the Seventh-day Adventist missionaries had extended their work throughout the Solomons, a new commissioner set out to find for himself what the missions had accomplished. His tour was occasioned by complaints from traders to the effect that the missionaries had taken their happy, heathen customs—their devil dances, their betel nut, their pig feasts, their idol worship—away from the natives and had left them nothing in return. And although the traders didn't say it, they were also finding the natives much less easy to swindle.

The missionaries felt that the natives themselves could testify to the state of their current condition better than anyone else. When the commissioner arrived he was greeted by several native men and women, wearing clean white singlets and *lap-laps* (a *lap-lap* is a short white wrap-around skirt which has replaced the fringe of dirty leaves the natives used to wear, but which is still cool and comfortable), who willingly answered the commissioner's questions. Said one, in perfect English: "Please, sir, do not ask us to go back to our old heathen practices, and please do not think that we were happy with them. Oh no, sir. When dancing heathen dances we were never really happy, for we were frightened of the devils we were trying to pacify. When we went head-hunting, we were fearful that others, with the same thought in mind, were head-hunting us; we spent sleepless nights. Our worship was wicked, our idols were devils who told us to do bad things. We knew no love, no joy; we had no hope, only fear, both of our devils and of each other. We were sick in mind and body.

"Then the missionary came. Now we are healthy. Now we know the true great God, we have hope, we are clean, we love one another, and we love Jesus. Oh, sir, do not say we were better back there. We do not want to go back. Now we have hope, love and happiness."

The commissioner went away, convinced.

The functions that natives participate in today are every bit as much fun as the old orgies were mistakenly thought to be. As evidence, here is an announcement of a recent church get-together on a South Pacific isle.

KAM! KAM!

MAN MARI PIKININI

OLOGETA KAM!

LUKIM PIKSA

HARIM TOK

GUDFELA MUSIK

OLOGETA BOLONG BUK TAMBU [WELCOME]

SUNDAY NIGHT

The early missionaries themselves found not only joy in their work, but frequently laughter and humor. Even dire adversity sometimes turned out to have its funny side. On one occasion when at a mission in the Solomons, Mrs. Jones was stricken with a tropical fever. She became so weak that the captain was convinced she could not last the night. Wanting to give her a proper burial, and being a methodical man, he planned to make a coffin for her out of the only planking on the island, the floor of their tiny living room. He measured the floor area carefully, and made a careful sketch of the coffin in order to utilize every piece of flooring.

But Mrs. Jones recovered, and it was no longer necessary to tear up the floor. Sometime later, while cleaning up, she found the sketch. From then on she frequently teased the captain, much to his embarrassment, about planning her coffin before she was dead. Not every woman is able to turn her own near-death into a family joke.

We will talk more about the adventurous missionaries in the South Seas and their wives, but in keeping with the pioneering theme of this chapter, let us jump to the present. For even in these times, Seventh-day Adventist work is going on among peoples just as savage, if not more so, than the Solomon Islanders Captain Jones first faced. One of the places in the world where mission work of great danger is being carried on today is New Guinea, a vast area (New Guinea is, after Greenland, the world's largest island) of sharp mountain ridges covered with dense jungle growth. Even in the seventh decade of the twentieth century tribes of savages who have never seen a white man continue to be found in New Guinea. They live marooned in small, steep valleys between the ridges, unaware that the oceans exist, much less lands beyond them. They do not even dare to walk to the top of the ridges which bound their tribal area; such is their own fear and suspicion that they know that showing themselves to the tribe in the adjoining valley would mean an instant attack.

Yet into this perilous country goes, unarmed and on foot, a former surgical nurse of the British Navy named Leonard Barnard. Just recently, after walking three weeks through the jungle, he came across a strange, primitive tribe with a mode of living hitherto completely unknown to the outside world. These people are tree dwellers; they live in huge two-story houses, built high off the ground and occupied by as many as sixty persons. Each story is segregated; the men live on the top floor, the women on the bottom. The people are so primitive that they do not bury their dead, but merely throw the bodies out of the house and leave them lying there. Each tree house is ringed by piles of bones and decomposing bodies, and the stench is appalling. Yet despite their primitive ways Leonard Barnard walked among these people without fear, and, although he could not speak to them—there are over 300 dialects in the region—he made it known to them through his actions and his little black bag of medicines that he was their friend.

There is a good reason why many of the natives of New Guinea are cannibals; they have eaten just about everything else that lives in their own tribal area. There are portions of New Guinea in which there are no mammals, no fish, few birds; even the last of the snakes were killed and eaten long ago. The people subsist on roots like taro; to them a successful missionary is a man who can grow better yams, mangoes and bananas. And Barnard is a successful missionary.

Though formally trained to do only minor surgery, there have been times when Barnard has performed major and unusual operations. On one occasion the chief of a primitive tribe he was visiting for the first time came up to him with a painfully distended buttock the size of a big kettle. He had been in a battle with the tribe on the other side of the ridge, the chief pantomimed, and had been struck with a fishhook type of spear which had broken off inside him. Although fully aware of the difficulty of the operation, Barnard calmly proceeded to remove the spear tip. "I felt that Christianity was on the spot," he explained later. He operated and found the hook encased in a cyst containing over a pint of pus. Barnard removed spear tip and cyst, drained the pus, and the chief recovered completely. From then on Barnard was a welcome visitor, bringing the word of God to another of the primitive tribes of New Guinea.

Dr. C. E. Weniger, dean of the church's Theological Seminary, has visited New Guinea on separate occasions and seen the result of Barnard's work. He saw tribesmen come in the dispensary, emaciated, swollen of stomach, hair filled with vermin, their faces evil and sinister, and dull eyes reflecting their negative animist religion based entirely on fear, and wearing only a fringe of leaves filthy with their own excreta. On his return a year later he saw these same men, and what a change! Now their bodies were healthy, a reddish undertone coloring their black skins. The stinking fringe of leaves had been replaced by a clean *lap-lap*. And from the sparkling eyes of each shone forth a new man, a man confident and happy, living in Christian hope.

While John Tay, who first brought the teachings of the Seventh-day Adventists to the South Seas, was dreaming of Pitcairn, a humble sheepherder in California named Abram LaRue was dreaming of China. He was past middle age, he was uneducated, he knew no medicine and he could not speak a word of Chinese. Nevertheless, he managed to get to Hong Kong, and from there to China. He paved the way for others to follow. About a year after Captain Jones first went to the South Seas, the General Conference sent a party of two medical missionaries, Drs. Harry W. Miller and Arthur C. Selmon, with their wives, deep into China. They went by ship to Shanghai, by riverboat to Hankow, then to the end of the railroad, Sin-Yang-Cheo. There they left their heavy equipment and walked for three days across country, pushing their personal necessities and some medical supplies in wheelbarrows, to their destination, a town called Sin-Tsai-Hsien on the Sah-Ho River, in the province of Honan. They immediately set about gaining the confidence of the local people, learning the complicated Chinese language, dressing in Chinese fashion, the men even shaving their heads and growing queues. After a trial period they decided that they definitely wanted to remain, and the two men went back to Hankow for their heavier belongings and silver money to live on, as paper money was nonexistent. To bring all this back overland by wheelbarrows would be nearly impossible, so they went by river, the long way round. The Sah-Ho River is shallow in some places and a boat would run aground on the sandbars. Consequently they built a long raft, made of hollow bamboo poles roped together and about the size of a large living room, and proceeded on it downstream to the railhead, Sin-Yang-Cheo.

They had a glorious trip, floating down the Sah-Ho past green trees and rice paddies in the spring. They traveled by day, tying up in the middle of the river by night as a protection against the robber bands which ranged the countryside. They went on by rail to Hankow, where they bought medical supplies, transshipped them from the railroad to the raft at Sin-Yang-Cheo, then proceeded up the river to the mission. Going up was not so glorious, for they, with four helpers, had to pole the raft all the way. Soon their hands were so badly blistered that it was necessary to bandage them.

Midway on the trip back a delegation of Chinese met the raft at a river landing with the plea that one of the doctors treat the wife of the chief magistrate of a nearby village. Dr. Miller took his little medical bag and, led by the delegation, walked across the fields, on raised paths through the flooded rice paddies, to the village. There he treated the woman for some minor malady; it took more time to be properly thanked by her husband than it had to perform his medical duties. He cut the ceremony as short as possible because he had told Arthur Selmon to leave without him if he was not back by one o'clock in the afternoon. Finally he was able to get away, and he set out alone for the landing. Rain had started falling, and the narrow path between the rice paddies was slippery underfoot; he kept losing his footing and falling off. By the time he got to the river, the raft was gone.

There he was in the middle of China, all alone, soaking wet, with no money, and speaking only a few words of Chinese. When he saw a group of men approaching he received them with mixed feelings, for although he was glad to have companionship, he was fearful for his life; if they proved to be bandits, they might well cut his throat with perfect equanimity just for the little black bag he carried. The men turned out to be police rather than bandits, but Dr. Miller soon found he was little better off. They took him back to the village, and threw him into jail. The little dirt-floored cell was filled with opium smokers, and the fumes made his nose puff up. It was a miserable night.

Next morning there was a great furor and hullabaloo; the chief magistrate had learned that the man who had saved his wife had spent the night in the city jail. Dr. Miller was rushed with great fanfare to the chief, who apologized profusely, then turned over to him his own personal sedan chair with eight bearers. The chief magistrate assigned another group of men to run along beside the sedan chair, some carrying umbrellas to shade Dr. Miller's august personage, others carrying strings of money to pay the bearers when they reached their destination, others to protect the money-bearers and to see to it that the money was placed in the proper hands. The odd procession jogged along across country and through several villages, in each of which the entire population came out to make obeisance to the pale panjandrum in the sedan chair. Years later, Dr. Miller was to travel in special trains furnished him by the ruler of all China, Chiang Kai-shek, but the trip by sedan chair was to remain in his memory as by far the most delightful journey of his life.

Dr. Selmon and his helpers poled the raft around a bend in the river to find Dr. Miller waiting in the sedan chair, shaded by the umbrellas. Dr. Selmon reported he had not passed an uneventful night; for while Dr. Miller had been languishing in his cell with the opium smokers, Dr. Selmon had had his own share of adventure. He and his four helpers had waited several minutes past the appointed time and had then gone on. At sundown they had found a stretch where the river was both wide and deep, and had anchored there. In the dead of night they were attacked by some twelve or fourteen bandits. It was a dark, rainy night, and the bandits waded out from each side of the river above the raft, to the deep water, then silently eased themselves into the current and came down on the raft with quiet stealth.

Fortunately, Dr. Selmon had been on watch. He heard them wading into the stream, and awakened the four helpers. When the heads of the bandits began bobbing up around the sides of the raft, Selmon and his boys were ready, poles in hand, and began beating them off. Dr. Selmon hesitated when it came to hitting a man on the head with a pole, for he was not only a man of medicine, dedicated to patching up heads rather than opening them, but also a man of God. While he hesitated, a hulking brute of a bandit with a knife in his teeth got a hand-hold on the side of the raft and heaved himself aboard. Dr. Selmon hesitated no longer. He swung his pole with all his might and hit the bandit on top of the head. The bandit crumpled, fell back into the river, and the water closed over him. No longer a neophyte in the art of self-defense, Dr. Selmon went to help his boys, flailing away with abandon. In that way, five men beat off a dozen. There was no way of knowing how many would never emerge from the water alive.

Back at Sin-Tsai-Hsien, the two adventurous doctors calmly renewed their practice and their study of Chinese. From there Dr. Miller and his wife went to the walled city of Shang-Tsai-Hsien. Dr. Miller and his wife enjoyed their work there immensely, until both became ill with sprue. Mrs. Miller died, and Dr. Miller returned to the States to recover. For several years he was medical superintendant of Washington Sanitarium in Washington, D.C., where he remarried. But the call of China was strong, and with his second wife, Ethel, he returned. They built a new, shiny sanitarium in Shanghai, as fine as any institution in the world. Among their patients was the wife of Soong Yao Ju, known in America as Charles Jones Soong, one of the most influential Chinese of all time. They became friendly, and Madame Soong helped the Seventh-day Adventists get a publishing plant started right in the Soong compound. One of the Soong daughters, a bright child named Mei-Ling, loved to play in the yard of the publishing house; she later married an army officer named Chiang Kai-shek. Dr. Miller and his fellow workers established an interesting pattern in China. Through their sanitarium they reached the most influential Chinese, and established contacts which enabled them to carry on their work more efficiently. In a sense this was much like the educational policy in the United States, where the Adventists first established colleges, then academies; by the time they were ready to start parochial schools, teachers were trained and ready. It frequently pays to begin at the top.

Dr. Miller was not content in Shanghai; he wanted to penetrate into the wilds of Manchuria and Mongolia. His wife and another young woman went to Mukden, in Manchuria, to see if they could raise $30,000 to establish a hospital there. At the time Chang Hsih Chang was the absolute ruler of Mongolia. He was known as the Young Marshal; the Japanese had had his father, the Old Marshal, assassinated in hopes that the son would be more tractable. When Mrs. Miller and her companion saw the Young Marshal and told him of their hopes, he cried expansively, "Thirty thousand dollars isn't enough—I'll give you a hundred thousand."

The young ladies found themselves in a quandary. They were authorized to raise only $30,000. They sent for Dr. Miller to solve their dilemma, and he came, traveling two days and three nights on the primitive railroad. When he arrived, he was ushered in to see the Young Marshal immediately, past people who had been waiting for days, and after some discussion Dr. Miller permitted the ruler to donate the larger amount for the hospital. The Young Marshal put a car with a driver at his disposal, and Dr. Miller selected several acres of beautiful wooded land— "Take all you want," the Young Marshal had said—"for the new hospital." Hardly had it been completed, unfortunately, when the Japanese came in and took it over. The staff of the hospital, as well as the Young Marshal himself, had to flee.

The Young Marshal took up residence in the walled compound in Shanghai, with a staff of forty people, including guards, and a full general named Ta'en in command. He also had an American advisor and an Australian advisor, as well as three doctors, who worked shifts around the clock in constant attention on the Young Marshal, for he was a hopeless drug addict.

But was he so hopeless? It developed that he had had an ulterior motive in his generosity to the Seventh-day Adventists; perhaps they could cure him of his addiction. He propositioned Dr. Miller, and the doctor agreed to try. Fortunately, he knew the ways of the Chinese. He insisted that the Young Marshal issue direct orders to General Ta'en that the Marshal himself was not to be obeyed; if the Young Marshal demanded dope from the general, the general was to refuse. Dr. Miller told the Young Marshal that an enema would be the first step in the treatment, and administered it. Shortly thereafter the Young Marshal was out cold; Dr. Miller had laced the enema with a powerful anesthetic. While the Young Marshal was unconscious the doctor carefully searched his bed. Packets of opium and heroin were tucked away everywhere; the Young Marshal was taking no chances.

Dr. Miller also knew that the three physicians were dependent on the Young Marshal's addiction for their livelihood, and would sneak narcotics in to him at the first opportunity. He called them together, explained the Young Marshal's desire to be rid of dependence on drugs, and pointed out to them their great responsibility in this matter.

"I know that none of you would countermand the Young Marshal's orders," Dr. Miller said, "but it goes further than that. For if some irresponsible person should happen to comply with his demands, unfortunately the blame would fall on you. Therefore, for your own good, you must be extremely suspicious of all strangers, for if the Young Marshal does obtain any narcotics, you three will most certainly be beheaded."

That was the last seen of the three physicians. Now Dr. Miller felt it was safe to begin the treatment. One of his weapons against addiction was sodium amytol, which he administered when the Young Marshal was in the most agonizing throes. Another weapon was prayer; Dr. Miller sought divine guidance constantly during the treatment period. And finally he used his own hands, for at times the Young Marshal was like a raging lion and Dr. Miller had to subdue him forcibly. One time, when Dr. Miller was trying to force a sodium amytal tablet into his mouth, the Young Marshal came down hard with his teeth on Dr. Miller's forefinger and thumb. When, in the short space of just one week it was all over, when through the joint miracles of medical science and prayer the

Young Marshal had been completely cured of his addiction, he noted the bandage on Dr. Miller's fingers and asked him what had happened.

"You bit me," Dr. Miller said grimly.

The Young Marshal looked at the bandaged thumb and forefinger, at the doctor, and then grinned. "Well, at least I got the better of you one time," he said.

In gratitude the Young Marshal insisted on giving Dr. Miller a personal gift, over and above the amount he had given the sanitarium for the doctor's full services. He wrote out a check. It was for $50,000. Doctor Miller's salary at the time was exactly $25 a week.

Doctor Miller knew that he should give the $50,000 to the church. Instead he built a new hospital at Lanchow, from the ground up. It was a completely nonprofit institution, and Dr. Miller never got a penny out of it. But ever after, he admitted, his conscience hurt him for indulging his own desires with that money, and not giving it to the church.

The doctor's initiative helped to build a total of twelve sanitariums in China, all of them the finest institutions possible. Among his many patients were today's Communist leaders. When the Communists overran China in 1949, the church hoped that his influence would help save some of these institutions, and although he was then in America, he agreed to go to China to try. He was on the last plane to land in Shanghai from the West; he stepped out of it while the motors were still running and it immediately took off again. The Communists entered the city almost immediately after and Dr. Miller did, indeed, get along well with them, at first. They abolished graft, vice, opium and established order on a businesslike basis.

Unfortunately, under the Communists the situation soon became intolerable. Dr. Miller was persuaded to leave China on the last boat. From then on his ties were with Nationalist China. In 1954, he was asked by Chiang to build a sanitarium in Taiwan which is now the leading medical institution there. For this work he was given the highest medal of the Chinese government.

Although the Seventh-day Adventist missionaries and doctors all over the world encountered problems, probably on no continent were conditions as difficult and dangerous as in South America, where other missionaries had preceded the Adventists by three centuries. Some work had been done in South America in the early 1900s but the great pioneer in this forbidding land was a young man from Cleveland, Ohio, named Fernando A. Stahl. He is still remembered in Bolivia, Peru and Ecuador today by the title he earned there, "Apostle to the Indians."

Stahl found the Indians of those countries in a deplorable condition, living in squalor and ignorance, addicted to drunkenness and to chewing coca leaves. Just getting close to them was difficult enough; they never bathed or changed clothes. Children were sewn into their garments, which were never changed until they rotted off. Over the centuries they had acquired the thinnest veneer of civilization from the early Catholic missionaries; strangely, this smattering of religion, blended in with their own paganism, led them to resist, as fiercely as any primitive tribe on the globe, the Seventh-day Adventists who had come to help them. The early missionaries and their first converts were derided and reviled, stoned and beaten. What happened to Juan Huanca, a native convert, was an example of what all Seventh-day Adventists could expect. Huanca refused to join in the drunken revelry of his people, and, to teach him a lesson, his own tribesmen beat him until he was semiconscious, then poured raw liquor down his throat. Only through long weeks of faithful nursing by Dr. Stahl and his wife did he survive. Others were not that fortunate.

But the Stahls persevered. They did not shrink from the filthy creatures, but put their hands upon them, brought them through serious illnesses made worse by their own lack of hygiene, taught them to bathe, to wash their clothes, and to clean their huts. And gradually they built up a small, faithful core of Indians who had found the love of God.

One of these men was a big, strapping member of the Campa tribe named Pasquale, also known as Capitán. Pasquale had himself been a heathen, but some terrible tragedy of which he could not bring himself to speak had led him to leave his tribe. Somehow he had stumbled into the mission at Metraro, on the eastern slope of the Andes, and had there found peace. Other Campas had also come slipping through the jungles to the mission to become good church workers, and finally Stahl and another American, V. E. Peugh, determined to lead an expedition into the jungles whence they had come and set up missions along the rivers. Looking at the map, they planned to journey down the swift tributaries leading to the big Ucayali, then downstream to the island city of Iquitos. Between the two areas of civilization lay wild jungles where only one white man had previously dared to go; he, a Catholic priest, had been killed by the Indians.

The half-breed slave traders who worked the area would be equally dangerous. Their business methods were simple; they'd hide outside a village until a mother and child came near, then kill the mother and take her child. Each child was worth several dollars in the slave market; the traders would naturally stop at nothing to prevent missionaries from coming into the area and interfering with their lucrative enterprise. In spite of the dangers the arrangements for the expedition went forward. Plans were to drop off several trained native workers along the upper reaches of the rivers, where the dangers were not so great, to organize missions. Stahl and Peugh, the leaders, had long, sturdy canoes built for the journey. They packed them with foodstuffs, but the most important item was medical equipment. They took quinine for malaria, medicine for hookworm, which caused the Indians' stomachs to blow out like balloons, drugs for the eye diseases prevalent in the region, disinfectants and surgical tools.

Stahl had high hopes of using this equipment, particularly in one certain village. Two years before a more enlightened headman named Yum Pecari, from far down the Ucayali, had made his way up to the mission and pleaded with Stahl to come there to help his people. The village, Yum Pecari had said, was located about two miles back from the river. When Stahl had expressed doubts that he could find it, even if it were possible for him to go there, Yum Pecari had promised to move the whole village to the banks of the river, in plain sight. For two years Stahl had been hoping he would be able to visit the village that would move itself for his coming.

The trip began uneventfully. The party stopped off at the first villages and left native workers. But soon they were in the real wilds, two white men with Pasquale and a few frightened Indian paddlers in two canoes. The swift river ran through heavy jungle growth in the hilly country, dark and foreboding. One morning, after they had been paddling only an hour or so, Peugh heard a distant roar. As they went on swiftly downstream the roar became louder and louder. They were approaching the famous Cascades, hard by Pasquale's native village.

As the sound of the rapids grew louder, an obvious change came over Pasquale. He seemed both eager and apprehensive. They rounded a small bend in the river, and there, still a few hundred yards away, they saw high stone cliffs rising on either side of the river. Through that narrow gorge the entire flow of water tumbled.

"At the head of the Cascades," Pasquale suddenly said, "is the mighty whirlpool." He shuddered, then seemed to make a decision. He beckoned the other canoe to come closer and stood up in the bow.

"Let me tell you what I have never told before," he said. "You must realize that in these villages, far from the light, the people believe in evil spirits. They do not know sickness and disease; when a person becomes ill the only possible explanation is that someone has bewitched him. And so the witch doctor is called, to determine who it is that has called for the evil spirits.

"The witch doctor is the most powerful man in the tribe. Once I lay ill. The witch doctor was called. He gathered my family together, said his magic words, performed his magic ritual, then he whirled around thrice with his arm outstretched. When he stopped, he was pointing at my little daughter. So it was she who had bewitched me! The tribe took my little daughter and tied her to a tree. The witch doctor handed her a stick, and with it she made marks in the dirt in front of her. If the evil spirits went away during the night, she would be released. But the next morning I was still sick. I pointed my finger at her. And they took my little daughter out into the jungle and chopped her body into a thousand pieces. But still I did not recover. And again the witch doctor came and again he whirled, and this time he pointed at my wife. The tribe tied her to a tree, and she made marks in the dirt, and still I did not recover. And so I pointed my finger at her, and the tribe took her to the high rock you see there and threw her into the whirlpool. Finally I did recover, and I thought about what I had done." Now Pasquale was weeping. "I fled my village and went into the jungle. Much later I found myself at the mission. There I learned the love of God. I repented my own sin, and became ashamed and sad for the ignorance and cruelty of my own people!"

Pasquale had held the men's attention as he talked, and no one had noticed that the canoes were drifting with great speed to the very whirlpool into which Pasquale's wife had been thrown. Suddenly—"Look out!" someone cried, and they began paddling as hard as they could to the bank. It seemed that they would be pulled into the vortex of the whirlpool, but just above it was a large tree, the overhanging branches of which extended out into the river. They dropped the paddles, clutched the branches, and pulled the canoes. They had escaped the whirlpool by inches.

A few feet back from the river bank they found a small clearing in the jungle. As they stood about in it, thanking God for their deliverance, out of the jungle stepped a tall, imposing Indian. He wore a headdress of brilliant macaw feathers, stuck in a bamboo ring which fitted down over his head. Around his shoulders was a stole of bright feathers. He stood, rigid, imperious. Peugh, as leader of the expedition, stepped forward and extended his hand in greeting. The tall Indian ignored him. Pasquale came forward, approached the chief, then wheeled and stood with his back to him. The chief turned and stood with his back to Pasquale. The white men later learned that this was the standard form of greeting among the Campas; when strangers from two villages meet in one of the narrow jungle trails, each solemnly turns his back on the other. If no blow on the back of the head is forthcoming, each man then knows it is safe to pass. Peugh and Stahl emulated Pasquale's example, stepping up to the chief, then turning their backs. No blows were struck, and they presumed the chief was friendly. He motioned them to follow him, and they did, each man carrying his medical equipment. The chief led them along a narrow path winding up across the face of the cliff, around the falls, then down an equally precipitous cliff on the other side to the chief's village. It seemed completely deserted; neither man saw any sign of life. The chief led them to the center of the village, turned to them, and then, as if seeing them for the first time, stretched out his hand in greeting. With that action, men, women and children poured out of the huts of the seemingly deserted village and surrounded the missionaries, crying, in the Campa dialect, "Here are the doctors!" Somehow, in the mysterious way of the jungle, the village had known they were coming.

The two missionaries looked around them and were appalled. They had seen tropical diseases, but they were not prepared for the terrible things they saw in that village that day—malaria, tropic ulcers, sores of every description. Most of the people seemed emaciated; it was learned later that they had eaten all the monkeys in the region, and now existed on a diet of yucca root and the native green, bitter bananas. But what was most appalling of all was the condition of the people's eyes. Their eyes were puffed out, lids stuck together. Many people were completely sightless and obviously in great pain.

"You take the eye cases, Brother Peugh," Stahl said, "and I'll take the rest." Each walked to a tree on opposite sides of the village, hung up his canvas roll of medical equipment so that it hung down, exposing the instruments and medicines packed inside, and, then and there, went to work.

They had intended to spend one day at the most at each village; at the Cascades they spent two weeks. There was that much work to be done. The days settled down to a routine of treating the sick. Each morning began the same way; when the sun was barely up, Pasquale would awaken them by reaching under their mosquito netting and gently tugging on a big toe. One morning after they had been at the village a few days six Indians from the next village down the river materialized out of the jungle. They brought a warning: At their village the witch doctors had persuaded the men to lie in wait for the missionaries and, when they came up on the river bank, to slaughter them. The six men had risked death at the hands of their own people to come and warn the missionaries; now, their message given, they slipped quietly back into the jungle whence they had come. Peugh and Stahl did not consider turning back; they had come too far, and there was too much to be done in this forsaken region. But each wrote a letter to his wife back at the mission, giving them final instructions on what to do if they never returned. One of the villagers, who was desirous of seeing Metraro anyway, agreed to make the several-day journey through the jungle to deliver them.

While Peugh and Stahl were treating the sick of the village, the paddlers went up to the head of the Cascades and released the empty canoes into the river, hoping they'd come through the gorge intact. Both craft were buffeted to splinters. The villagers then turned to and made a raft of balsa logs, pegged with hard wood saplings, on which they could continue the journey down the Ucayali. On the day of departure the chief and Pasquale advised against getting an early start, and they did not start out until an hour before noon. They drifted, paddled and poled for over an hour, then came to another swift rapid. The water was rough and foamy, but there appeared to be no rocks. Pasquale told them not to touch a paddle or say a word as they went through the rapids. They let the raft drift into the chute, and felt themselves being suddenly carried along on the swift current as though on wings. The raft was bounced and tossed, but made the run through the rapids safely and came out into the still water below. Again Pasquale made elaborate gestures for silence, pointing for emphasis to the right bank of the river. There sat the village where the ambush awaited them. But in the whole village they saw not a sign of life. They drifted on past in broad daylight, every man holding his breath, then came to another swift rapid. Just as they entered it Peugh looked back. Every hut in the village seemed to be disgorging armed men, waving their spears and shouting. But the warriors were too late; the raft entered the rapids, and soon the village was out of sight.

Then the reason for this delayed departure from the Cascades became obvious. It had been carefully timed so that they would pass by the village at siesta time.

They floated on down the river, through the jungle, for three days without seeing another sign of habitation. On toward the end of the third day, however, Stahl began looking around him eagerly. He had begun to notice the landmarks Yum Pecari, the chief who had sought his aid two years before, had told him about. In late afternoon they rounded a bend to see, directly before them, a large promontory. On its high banks stood hundreds of Indians, waiting. The moment they saw the raft they began shouting and waving. Through the mysterious communications system of the jungle, the villagers had learned the missionaries were coming, and were on hand to greet them. They ran out into the river, grabbed the raft, and pulled it ashore. Again the two medical missionaries went to work treating the terrible jungle sores.

Next day was the Sabbath, and they put aside their medical work to hold Sabbath services with Pasquale and the paddlers as the villagers observed and listened with respect. While they were singing a hymn, a naked savage, carrying a long knife, suddenly burst out of the jungle and ran toward one of the paddlers. The people of the village surrounded him immediately, disarmed him, and were going to kill him then and there, but the naked savage kept crying out to the man he had headed for originally. Suddenly the Indian from the mission gave a glad cry and ran to the intruder. It turned out that the two were brothers who had been separated many years before. The savage was released and he and his brother went off and talked happily together for some time. After the happy reunion they came to Peugh and Stahl. The savage had been spying on them, he confessed, when he had recognized his brother. He was one of a group of Campas hired by the slavers of the region to kill the entire party. But when his brother had told him of the wonderful things the two missionaries had done for the Indians, both in Metraro and along the Ucayali, healing the sick, bringing them the love of God, he resolved to warn them. Now he promised to tell his fellow would-be assassins the truth he had learned, and assured the missionaries that they could travel in safety from then on. Then he said goodbye to his brother, and slipped back into the jungle whence he had come.

The missionaries did not doubt his good intentions, but whether he would be successful in persuading his fellows to call off their murderous mission was another matter. Every night from then on, when Peugh turned in, he knelt outside his mosquito netting and uttered the prayer that David had said when he was hunted by the Philistines: "Now I lay me down in peace and sleep. For thou Lord only maketh me to dwell in safety."

He felt it to be most appropriate.

Whether because of prayer or the paddler's brother, the rest of the trip was made in safety, at least from human adversaries. Nature was not so considerate, for now it was April, and the rainy season. Each day, as flood-swollen tributaries poured into it, the river grew higher and higher. The Ucayali was a huge river now, in some places several miles wide. Once, trying to make up time by traveling at night, the raft ran into some obstruction in the darkness and everyone was thrown off. Somehow they all managed to scramble back on board, but much of their equipment was lost. Another time, at a particularly wide point in the river, they were caught in a wind storm which whipped up ocean-high waves. A swift river came pouring into the Ucayali on their left, and where the current met the wind-driven waves there was turmoil. The Indians sobbed and wailed, and the missionaries prayed. Though the huge waves swept across the raft it did not capsize, and somehow they came through all right.

"You simply can't imagine the Ucayali in flood unless you have seen it," Peugh said later. "The water was dirty brown and surged forward in great undulations. It took everything before it. Sometimes, before my very eyes, a huge promontory of many acres would suddenly crumble and simply disappear. In the ugly brown water we could see alligators, and we knew that whole schools of the deadly piranha lurked beneath the surface."

Finally they arrived at Iquitos, where they received their final reward for the trip. A tribe of Indians from far back in the jungle had heard of the good they had done on the way, and sent a delegation to Iquitos to present them with a token of their appreciation. It was a shrunken human head.

They purchased land in Iquitos for a mission, and Stahl and the Indians stayed on to help get it started. Peugh returned to Lima, traveling by river steamer to the end of its run, then a launch, then a smaller launch, then a canoe, then by muleback on the seven-day trip over the Piches trail across the Andes. Finally, after hitch-hiking a ride on a truck and proceeding the rest of the way by train, he reached Lima, his destination.

That was just one trip of one party during the pioneering days in South America. Other missionaries were having the same adventures the length and breadth of the continent. The very name of one tribe of Indians bears mute testimony to the dogged pioneering determination of the Seventh-day Adventist missionaries. Sometime during the 1880s a chief of an Indian tribe which lived far back in the interior of British Guiana had a dream. In this dream the full story of Christianity was revealed to him. He was told of the creation of the earth, the Sabbath, how Jesus Christ had died for the salvation of man and how He would come again in glory. Someday, the dream revealed, a man with a book would come and teach his people more of this way of life. In the meantime, the chief made sweeping reforms, abolished human sacrifices, and he and his people observed the Sabbath. But the old chief died before the last part of his dream came true; he never saw the man with the book.

An occasional explorer or prospector who made his way into the distant country brought back word of these strange Indians who kept the Sabbath and hoped for the arrival of the man with the book. O. E. Davis, president of the British Guiana mission, heard about them and wanted desperately to reach them. But they lived hundreds of miles away, through jungles infested with wild beasts and huge poisonous snakes, over wild rocky rivers. He had no one to send, nor the money necessary for such an expedition.

Finally, however, Davis decided that if he had no one to send, the only answer was to go himself. He set out for the tribe in a dugout canoe, but came down with fever and had to return. A year later he tried it again, this time taking into consideration all he had learned on the previous effort. He took with him an interpreter and carriers, went up the river to the falls, around the rapids, then through the jungle on foot. Again he contracted jungle fever, but he kept going. And this time he reached the tribe. The Indians received him with joy and wonder. There was no doubt; he was the man with the book.

Through his interpreter, Davis taught the Indians the full story of Christianity. He even taught them to sing, and, because the interpreter was not up to translating hymns into the Indian language, he taught them to sing them in English. Thus, hundreds of miles from the nearest white man, Indians who could not speak one word of English were nevertheless singing hymns in that language. As the weeks went on, Davis realized that the fever he had caught on the way was getting worse and worse. He took to his hammock to conserve his strength and carried on his teaching from there, crowding more and more lessons into each day. One morning he knew he could last no longer. He called his Indian friends around him for one last session. They prayed together, he in their language, then sang together, they in his. He bade them be faithful and carry on the teachings of Christ, and then he died. The grieving Indians wrapped his body in a shroud made of bark. They buried him and built a shelter over his grave.

More years passed and no missionary came to them, but the tribe kept the faith; an occasional prospector reported hearing them singing, in English, hymns like "Shall We Gather at the River." The British Guiana division tried desperately to raise funds to send and keep a missionary among them, but it was too expensive an undertaking. The years went by, but the officers of the division did not forget; one day they gathered together and uttered a special prayer for the mission. The very next day a check for $4,000, contributed by an anonymous donor for that very purpose, arrived. A. W. Cott and his wife, both of them nurses and teachers, went into the area. They healed the sick, opened schools, and taught not only the word of God, but agricultural methods and home economics. Today, deep in the jungle of British Guiana, a tribe of Indians lives on a higher level of Christian civilization. They are known the world over as the Davis Indians, after the determined man with the book who lies forever among them.

8 *And Preached Everywhere. . . .*

Here is the story of another mission. It is located in one of the most barren, yet strangely beautiful areas of the world. In almost the center of this seeming desolation two mighty formations of red rock rise up from the reddish sand of the desert floor, each with sheer cliffs rising hundreds of feet to a flat tableland of several acres. If you look sharp you will see, high up on the side of one of these rock faces, the little cluster of buildings which make up the Seventh-day Adventist mission. There's a little one-room schoolhouse built of rock, and a white frame clinic, both dwarfed by the huge sheer cliffs rising directly behind them.

Just a mile or two from the mission a solitary native hut squats, almost invisible, on the desert. It resembles an igloo made of red mud. One day strange wailing sounds began coming from the hut, faintly audible even at the mission. The Adventists looked at each other and nodded. The natives were having a sing, presided over by the medicine man. The child of the owners of the hut was seriously ill, and relatives and friends from miles around had gathered to appease the evil spirits which had brought illness to the child. Inside the hut the sing went on and on, as the medicine man traced drawings in the sand floor. But despite the singing, despite the pictures, the baby boy grew worse. A cute little fellow, just seven months old, with a cherubic round, brown face and sparkling buttons for eyes, he was slowly wasting away.

In the hut, too, a controversy was raging. The husband had

learned some of the white man's way, even his language. On the Sabbath, when a small group of natives gathered in the home of the doctor of the mission, it was this very man who translated the doctor's words as he led the services. And he, who loved his son, wanted to take the little boy up to the clinic so the white doctor could care for him. But the wife was adamant. This was none of the white man's business, she cried. Anyone could see that her baby was in the grasp of evil spirits, and only the medicine man could drive out those spirits.

But after the sing had been held and the child was worse, not better, the father persuaded his wife at least to let the doctor come and look at their baby. He set out swiftly, striding up to the clinic in the thin, mountain air, found the doctor, and asked him to come. The doctor sighed with relief; he had been waiting and hoping. He had learned through the grapevine that the child was ill; and had wanted to go to him, but he knew the situation in that family and knew he could not go unless invited. Now he picked up his little black bag and hurried to the hut with the grief-stricken father. There he found not only the sick child and the mother, but the medicine man, who had been hastily summoned. Only after a prolonged argument was the doctor permitted even to look at the baby. That was all he needed to make a diagnosis; the doctor had seen too much of this before. The little boy had a serious case of dysentery. It had already gone on too long; now he was in desperate need of medication.

The doctor told the father the true situation, and the father translated his words to his wife and the medicine man. Again there was a long conversation in the difficult language the doctor could neither speak nor understand; only after an hour of pleading did the mother and medicine man permit the doctor to treat the child. But under no circumstances, the medicine man warned, could the child be taken from the hut, nor could the doctor come again. The doctor did what he could, and left medication for the mother to give the baby after he had gone.

This one treatment was not enough, and the mother threw the medication away. The baby got worse and worse. One medicine man after another, five in all, were brought in to draw pictures and lead the weird chant in an effort to appease the evil spirits. Each charged the grief-stricken parents the equivalent of $150. But still the baby worsened, and now the mother wanted to take the baby over the rutty roads to the medicine man of another tribe, a hundred miles away. The father went to the trading post to try to borrow the money. The trader, who also knew the situation, refused to lend it and pleaded with the father to let the mission doctor cure his son. Once more the father persuaded his wife to let the white doctor come, and again the white doctor was waiting and hoping.

This time he and his wife, a nurse, together trudged to the little hut; both were sickened at what they saw. The once happy, gurgling little boy was now lying weak and helpless, gasping for breath. Mutton grease and charcoal had been smeared over him, blocking his pores completely. Their hearts went out to the tiny, frail, emaciated little lump of humanity, dying so needlessly of an illness that could have been cured. They both tried to explain to the mother that the baby's only chance for life would be found in the clinic where he could be properly cared for. Both promised to devote all their knowledge and efforts to save her baby, even though, they frankly admitted, too much time had gone by; if the baby survived at all, it would now be largely through the compassion of God.

The baby's parents went outside the hut to discuss the situation. Suddenly the mother turned on her husband and ran back into the hut, furious and hysterical. She kicked both the doctor and his wife. She spat on them. They took her abuse in silence, for they had volunteered of their own free will and love of God and His people to come to this strange land with its strange customs, and it would do no one, least of all the sick baby, any good for them to speak harshly to her. For a full two hours more they pleaded with her to let them take the child to the clinic as she alternately sobbed and abused them. All the time the father sat with the comatose child in his arms, big tears streaming down his round, brown cheeks. Finally the mother permitted the doctor and his wife to take the child to the clinic, but by then it was too late. Though they did all medical science could do, and though they offered up their heartfelt prayers, the baby had no resistance left, and quietly passed away. The father himself dug a shallow grave, the baby was prepared for burial by switching his little woven shoes so that each was on the wrong foot, and the wasted little body was laid away.

Where and when do you think this weird little tragedy occurred —in some far-off pagan land among strange people many years ago? No, it happened right here in America, in the year 1959, at the Monument Valley Mission in southern Utah. The "natives" were Navajo Indians. The doctor was Lloyd Mason, who had given up a lucrative practice in California to help the Navajos find health and happiness in the word of God.

Just a few years before, but many years after missionaries of all denominations had first blazed a path of righteousness and mercy into distant lands, two Seventh-day Adventists, Marvin and Gwen Walter, had come into this strange, forbidding area of rugged, sharply rising mountains and barren wind-swept flatlands, the home of some 80,000 Navajos. They saw the ravages of malnutrition and tuberculosis; they saw eyes crusted over with an opaque film resulting from the sand-filled winds; they saw babies and adults dying from diarrhea and dysentery caused by ignorance and filth. Harry Goulding, who had set up a trading post in the area before it had become a reservation, gave the Walters ten acres of land on which to build a mission. At first the Walters operated out of a trailer, driving a four-wheel-drive jeep to the isolated *hogans* of the Navajos. Although neither was a doctor, they had both done their best, and they finally won the confidence of so many Navajos that they could no longer handle the large numbers of people who came to them for help. And so the Walters, having pioneered in the strange, rugged country, moved on, and the church sent in a doctor and his wife to administer to the sick, a teacher to help the children learn what they could in the few days of the year that even the youngest could be spared from their tasks at home. After several doctors had taken over the mission for brief periods, Dr. Mason and his wife volunteered for just one year.

"But although we received about one-sixth the income to which we had been accustomed," Dr. Mason said, "when the year was up we found our work had been so rewarding, so thrilling, that we just couldn't leave. Tragedy is extreme on the desert; there are no moderates. Many of us come in with the impression that the Navajos are stoical, unfeeling, but when we get to know them we learn that they can cry just as big tears as some of us white people. This is a land where the doctor carries a pick and shovel as part of his equipment. We are called in too often when it is too late. We bury the patients we cannot save."

During their stay, the little stone clinic has been expanded to a full hospital, small but complete. Today, Navajos come in to the clinic from fifty, even one hundred miles away. Over a hundred babies are born in the clinic each year; their mothers, often actually in labor, are brought in over the rocky desert roads by pickup truck, sometimes even on horseback. Occasionally an entire family comes in for treatment. Recently a party of a dozen Navajos—men, women and children—made their way to the clinic in a three-day journey from an outlying village. They had two donkeys, and they all took turns riding. At night they camped under the stars. They all enjoyed the trip immensely, with the possible exception of the sick person, a woman suffering with a disorder of the gall bladder.

Children come in to school from miles around as well. Unfortunately their attendance is sporadic, for it is the children who act as sheepherders for the small flocks of sheep which graze on the scrubby little bushes of the desert. Even so, from this one-room school attended by children from six to twenty have come forth youths who can read and write in English, and do arithmetic. The

Navajos, incidentally, when given an opportunity, prove to be extremely intelligent. They are particularly good at mathematics.

The mission is supported by the church, of course, but it can hardly allocate to this one mission a disproportionate amount. Additional help comes from individuals all over the country. Almost every day during the summer, many tourists visit the mission. Some of them are doctors, who fill up their automobiles with medical supplies of all kinds before leaving home. Others, who have never heard of the mission before but who can see the work that is being done there, leave a few dollars. Many, back home again, can't get the picture of the little clinic and its silent, uncomplaining patients (and Navajo children are the most appealing in all the world) out of their minds, and mail in another contribution. In 1959 the Pacific Union Conference, in whose area the mission is located, asked every member to give a dollar to the work. There are 75,000 adult members in this conference; many denominations would have been more than happy to receive a contribution from half its members. Instead, well over $100,000 was forthcoming. Thus the members of the Seventh-day Adventist faith carry on their work, not only in the romantic field of foreign missions, but among the original, forgotten Americans at home.

No matter to what strange new corner of the earth, what long-forsaken island, desert or high mountain valley the Seventh-day Adventist church has penetrated, isolated pockets of humanity with new challenges are constantly being discovered. In seeking to bring the gospel to the last man on earth, it makes no difference to the Adventists whether that man is at home or abroad, or lives among the people least likely to listen. A few years ago, in India, Irvin and Mildred Sorensen, an American missionary couple, heard of a tribe of gypsies who lived far out in a wild region. Known as the Lombadis, and apparently akin to all gypsies the world over, the tribe had been completely overlooked by other missionaries, but to the Sorensens the challenge was too great to let the oversight continue. It took them two days' journey by horse cart from the nearest town, over a mountain range onto a wild plain, to reach the gypsy village. When they drove up into the center of the village, composed of mud houses thatched with brush, the men came out to see them, but the women stayed inside. It was, perhaps, just as well; though the Lombadi women are beautiful, and each one likes to wear a dress of colorful material, it just so happens that she wears that same dress, without ever removing it, for a year.

The Sorensens found the gypsies to be happy people, given to dancing all night to the wild beat of the drums. The women part their long black hair in the middle with silver ornaments on the side. They wear bracelets from the wrist to the shoulder, tinkling bells on their ankles, rings on their toes. The Sorensens lost a little appreciation of those tinkling bells, however, when they learned what their wearers were capable of. One of the gypsy women, they learned, had seen a boy riding a bright, shiny bicycle, and coveted it. She called the boy to her, and plunged a knife into his throat. Looking furtively around, she saw someone coming down the road from a distance. To hide the evidence of her crime, she calmly stepped over the dead boy lying on the ground, so that her full skirts covered him. There she stood, holding the bicycle, until the people had passed by. Then she left the scene with the bicycle. The gypsies who told the Sorensens of her exploit thought her quite clever.

Though it was a most difficult and unreceptive place in which to preach the gospel, nevertheless the Sorensens persisted. They showed the gypsies simple rules of hygiene and cleanliness, persuaded them to have separate quarters for themselves and their animals, to clean their hands before cooking. But in spite of the Sorensens' best lectures, the women showed no desire to bathe. Most missionaries learn early that the best results are gained by showing rather than telling, and that native people do not like to be constantly ministered to, but like to do little things in return. And so Mildred bravely put both of these tenets to the test. She remarked wistfully that she'd love to have a bath; the next thing she knew the women were happily making arrangements for the event. Water was heated, a big kettle was made ready, and the Lombadi women all participated in the washing, under Mildred's direction. It seemed like fun, the women talked and giggled over it, and before long one of the older, and perhaps dirtier, of the women received a repeat performance on herself. She lived through it, and another, then another, of the gypsies underwent the experience. And that's how today, in a gypsy village far in the interior of India, bathing has become socially acceptable, thanks to an American girl named Mildred Sorensen.

Sometimes the Lord's work is carried on in strange ways by His pioneers. In the city of Cebu, on the island of Cebu and capital of the state of Cebu in the Philippines, the early missionaries had started a small congregation; now, in the days of the republic, the congregation wanted to build a church. It would be an evangelistic center, a handsome showplace.

Building a Seventh-day Adventist church in Cebu proved to be no easy matter; the predominant religion is Catholic and the elected city officials took a dim view of the project, fearful that the majority of the people would object. But the congregation went ahead with its plans. Through an individual it quietly bought a large, commanding lot right across the street from the state capitol. The building committee had carefully checked the law and learned that there was no ordinance against building their church; when the lot had been safely transferred to the church, they openly sought a permit to build from the city hall. They were refused. But, the committee protested, how could they be refused? It wasn't against the law. Well, hedged the city clerk, the law was going to be changed.

The congregation was stymied. They sent to division headquarters for help, and shortly after an American missionary named J. R. Spangler appeared on the scene. Bob Spangler, a large, black-haired young man who'd have made an excellent finagler for a shady enterprise if he hadn't chosen to serve the Lord instead, turned to his

Bible for aid. He found therein the story of the widow who wanted justice and besought the judge repeatedly until she gained it. Bob decided to follow her procedure. He and a committee from the congregation visited all the city council in their homes, receiving from each the same answer, "Come back tomorrow." That's exactly what they did, day after day after day. After two weeks of that, the mayor broke down and told his secretary to give them the building permit. That was just fine until Bob read the fine print; it proved to be only a temporary permit. It could be rescinded at any time, even after the church was erected. Spangler gave back the permit. The congregation gathered together in a prayer meeting to pray for their church.

Apparently the city fathers were now becoming a little uneasy. A few days after the prayer meeting, Cebu's number one citizen, Congressman Sergio Osmena, son of the former president of the Philippines, left the national capital to come home on an emergency visit. He met privately with Bob Spangler and assured him that it was the city's intention to keep the area across from the state capitol clear of *all* buildings; and that erection of a Protestant church would be "unthinkable." Now it just so happened, he went on, that he was the owner of a nice lot, even larger, in another part of the city. Wouldn't Spangler like to trade? Bob said thanks, but the church was very fond of the lot it had.

The Congressman gave up that line of attack. He suggested that the building committee of the church meet with the city council, and Spangler accepted the invitation heartily. The meeting began with some polite conversation, and then the mayor suggested that they all have a drink. The building committee politely refused. The mayor passed around long, luxurious cigars; the Seventh-day Adventists politely refused. Hors d'oeuvres of tiny slices of toast spread with shrimp paste were passed around; again the church committee smiled—and refused.

This was too much for the mayor. "What *do* you do?" he cried. The church committee went into a huddle, agreed on their desires and made them known. The meeting then continued, with the city council eating hors d'oeuvres, drinking tall drinks, and smoking cigars, while the Adventists had soda water and peanuts.

It soon became obvious that the city council, and the Congressman, were not themselves prejudiced against either Protestantism or the Seventh-day Adventist church, but feared retaliation at the polls if they permitted the structure to go up under their administration. They made one suggestion after another; after each one the church committee would bow their heads, pray for guidance, then look up and refuse it. They were perfectly sincere in their actions, but at the same time, it made for excellent stalling tactics. "This is immoral!" Congressman Osmena burst out at one time.

One of the oldest of the councilmen, a wise and tolerant man, finally came out with what his confrères were thinking. "This is a strong Catholic city," he explained seriously. "What do you think would happen to us if a Protestant church was erected right across from the state capitol?"

"I don't think anything would happen," Spangler said, equally serious. "But if that's really what's worrying you, I can provide an easy out. You just flatly refuse us the permit. Then, under the statute of religious freedom of the Constitution of the Philippines, we will appeal your decision, all the way up to the Supreme Court, if you like."

That is just exactly what the city fathers would not like. They could see the headlines in the paper now, spread all over the republic—CEBU COUNCIL OVERRULED BY SUPREME COURT ON RELIGIOUS FREEDOM.

There was more silence. Then the mayor leaned forward. "Look," he said. "Will this building you intend to erect look like a church? I mean, will it have a steeple on it? Will it have bells? Will the name Seventh-day Adventist be prominently displayed?"

Bob Spangler rubbed his hands together under the table. It just so happened that the congregation had all agreed that they did not want a churchlike structure, but rather an evangelistic center, a handsome but nonsecular edifice with a large auditorium which non-Adventists would feel free to enter. "No, it won't," he said to the mayor. "Tell you what we'll do—we'll draw up four or five sketches and whichever one you approve, that's the one we'll build! There'll be no further argument! Agreed?"

Before the members of the council could think twice, they did indeed agree. After that it was a simple matter for the committee to have one sketch drawn of exactly what they wanted, and a few more drawn of what they knew the city council would not want. At the next meeting Spangler and the committee solemnly spread out all the sketches before the council, stepped back, and let the city fathers make their own free choice. The council looked at the sketches deliberately drawn for their disapproval and shuddered. With a sigh of happy relief they unanimously chose the sketch the building committee had also approved. Everybody shook hands all around, and celebrated the event with more tall drinks, long cigars and soda water. The permit was issued, the center was built, and the mayor, who also happened to be a prominent member of the Knights of Columbus, formally opened the building at the dedication ceremony, and urged his fellow townspeople to visit it often.

Only then did the city attorney, who had sat quietly through all the proceedings, come up to Bob Spangler. "Señor Spangler," he said, "I would like to shake your hand. You ought to be an attorney, not a preacher!"

Bob grinned. "When Christ sent forth His disciples," he said, "He told them: *Behold I send you forth a sheep in the midst of wolves: be ye therefore wise as serpents, and harmless as doves.* We have tried to follow His advice."

To pioneering missionaries, head hunters and wild beasts may be difficult, but red tape is impossible. When a man or woman is willing to spend long, hard hours healing the sick and educating the ignorant with his only reward the salvation of those people, selfish and bureaucratic regulations can make even the most devout Seventh-day Adventist come close to forgetting brotherly love. One of these men was Dr. J. Gordon Reynolds, and one of these women was his wife.

Dr. Reynolds, a graduate of the College of Medical Evangelists, had long wanted to work in Mexico, and Mrs. Reynolds wanted to go with him. A small hospital was made available to him in Obregón, in the state of Sonora. Although it was difficult for just any American to go into Mexico and set up practice, for Dr. Reynolds, at the outset, it was comparatively easy. At that time the Mexican state of Sonora and the American state of Arizona, which have a common borderline, had a reciprocal arrangement by which each honored the other's license to practice medicine. Dr. Reynolds took the Arizona state examination, passed it, received his license, and was thus also licensed in Sonora. He went to Obregón and began the practice of medicine.

Obregón, in the early Thirties, was like a frontier town in the American West. Frequently saloon altercations led to fights, and the rowdies of the town preferred knife and gun to fists. All too frequently those losers who were not killed outright developed peritonitis, and little could be done to save them. Dr. Reynolds remembers one glaring exception. A gnarled old drunk who'd had nothing to eat or drink but tequila for several days got into a row at a local saloon. When he was brought to the hospital examination showed that his intestines had been punctured fourteen times. Yet he recovered and was soon as good as ever.

"The moral of that seems to be," Dr. Reynolds said, "that if you're going to get yourself stabbed, don't eat anything and sterilize your intestines well with alcohol."

At that time in Mexico telegraph lines existed even where there were no roads. Dr. Reynolds frequently got requests for medication by telegraph; one message said simply, *"Lengua roja, manda medicina"* (red tongue, send medicine). Dr. Reynolds made the proper diagnosis immediately. What causes a man's tongue to get so red that the patient notices it, and makes him sick enough to want to do something about it? The answer is pernicious anemia. Dr.

Reynolds sent off a bottle of liver extract and that was all there was to it.

After building up his hospital and practice, Dr. Reynolds was one day informed of a new regulation requiring all doctors to be licensed by the national government. Dr. Reynolds was glad, in one sense, to hear of the new regulation, for it would enable the central government to check up on all quacks. But he also feared that the regulation would be used to harass the American doctors in Mexico, in keeping with the anti-American feeling prevalent at that time. His fears were realized; he sent in his application for a license to Mexico City, and it came right back with a demand for additional information. This included a copy of his certificate, his diploma, and transcripts of his undergraduate, premedical school and medical school grades. All transcripts must be signed by the registrar of the school in question. The registrar's signature must be witnessed by a notary public; the notary public's signature must be witnessed by the county clerk; the county clerk's signature must be witnessed by the secretary of state of the state in which the county was located; the state secretary of state's signature must be witnesssed by the American Secretary of State, and the American Secretary of State's signature must be witnessed by the Mexican consul in Washington.

Dr. Reynolds secured all these signatures, each in its proper place, and again forwarded his application with them attached to Mexico City. Hardly had they arrived in the national capital when a revolution upset the government and all of his papers were lost. He would have to obtain the same set of signatures all over again. This he did. Now he was informed that he must go to Mexico City to take an examination. However, he was reliably informed on the quiet by a national official, there would really be no point in it, for even if he turned in a perfect paper he would not pass the exam.

During all this time Dr. Reynolds was without a license to practice medicine. He got around it in various ways. At first he simply arranged for a Mexican doctor to be with him at all times. Dr. Reynolds would interview and examine the patient, then inform the Mexican doctor of his diagnosis and prescribed treatment, which the Mexican doctor would carry out under his supervision. The Mexican doctors selected didn't mind in the slightest; word got back to Dr. Reynolds that they all considered it an excellent postgraduate medical course. Dr. Reynolds' competition, another sanatorium which the local people referred to grimly as the *Matatorium*—which translates nicely into "slaughterhouse"—objected strenuously even to this procedure; Dr. Reynolds was prohibited from seeing patients under any circumstances and his hospital closed down. Still he maintained a semblance of a practice; top officials and influential citizens could secure special permission from the governor of Sonora to enable Dr. Reynolds to treat them.

The governor, tired of receiving long-distance calls day and night, suggested to Dr. Reynolds that he might find a solution to his problem at the University of Guadalajara; the governor of the state of Guadalajara happened to be a personal friend of his. Dr. Reynolds hired a young lawyer, who went to Guadalajara and spent a month playing golf with university officials. Through these contacts the lawyer learned of an almost-forgotten regulation permitting any qualified person to take the university's medical examinations; if he passed, he would be automatically licensed to practice.

Dr. Reynolds took elaborate precautions in going to the university. Guadalajara is south of Sonora; Dr. Reynolds went to the airport in broad daylight and took a plane to the north. He got off at the first stop, went to the railway station, and there boarded a train south, traveling back through Obregón with shades drawn on the way to Guadalajara.

His first day in Guadalajara was uneventful; he took the first series of exams with no difficulty. But during the night someone must have exerted powerful pressure, for when he reported on the second day not one member of the medical school faculty was available. Inquiring around the campus, he found that the professors had all fled to a town 130 miles back in the mountains. Dr. Reynolds calmly hired a taxi for the trip, found the professors, and brought them back to the university with him. They agreed to give him the examinations the next day.

When Dr. Reynolds appeared at the university the following morning he found a student strike in progress. Word had been spread that he was a quack and that giving him the examinations would reflect adversely on the university. Dr. Reynolds arranged a meeting with the ringleaders of the students and talked them into calling the governor of Guadalajara. The governor called the governor of Sonora, who in turn called the governor of Arizona, who consulted the state licensing board and called the governor of Sonora back. Then the governor of Sonora called the governor of Guadalajara, and he was finally able to assure the students that Reynolds was indeed entitled to take the examinations. He did take them, passed with flying colors, and was officially licensed to practice medicine in Mexico. It had taken just nine and a half years.

And then, of all times, Dr. Reynolds became seriously ill, and had to return to California. After a long convalescence, he joined the faculty of the College of Medical Evangelists. After fighting red tape for nine and a half years to obtain his license to practice in Mexico, he has never used it.

The strange situation of Dr. Reynolds, who had medical knowledge but was not permitted to use it, was exactly reversed in the case of a young Adventist missionary named Richard C. Hall. With his wife and three children, young Hall established the first mission of any denomination in northern Laos, shortly after the formation of the new Republic. Just getting into his new area was headache enough; the Halls could either take a small dilapidated bush plane or walk or ride horseback over the narrow jungle trails. They chose the plane. On their arrival, the Halls found themselves true pioneers in every sense of the word—there was not even a house for them. With native help Hall went into the forest, felled timber, cut, planed and sized it, and built his own house, a church, and a house for his native assistant.

As he was hewing timber, people from all over the countryside would come up to him and ask for medical aid. "But I'm no doctor," he'd protest.

"But you're an American, aren't you?" people would ask. "Americans can do anything, can't they?" And then they would wait for him to begin treatment.

Fortunately, not long after Hall had been on the scene, Dr. C. E. Randolph of the General Conference Medical Department flew in for a visit. Doctor and missionary sat down together and made a list of the most common ailments of the area, complete with symptoms and treatment. Under Dr. Randolph's direction the supplies department of the big Bangkok sanitarium made up a large supply of medicines, each one labeled according to the illness for which it was designed, and the whole shipment was flown in to the new "doctor." He has been in business ever since. By now, incidentally, he's also an accomplished dentist, entirely self-taught.

Pioneering in countries under Communist domination or near the Soviet Union has drawbacks of a different nature. Melvin Jacobson, a young missionary in Meshed, Iran, near the Afghanistan border, having no church building, held Sabbath services in the garden behind his house. Each Sabbath Jacobson had the strange feeling of being watched. Carefully peering around, he noted furtive movements behind the windows of a second-story apartment overlooking his garden from a neighboring house. One day he caught the reflection of the sun off a shiny object in one of the windows—he was being watched with field glasses! Casual inquiry in the neighborhood revealed that two Russian women had moved into that apartment under mysterious circumstances. They were obviously secret agents detailed to watch the activities of a young Seventh-day Adventist missionary and his small flock.

Although flattered by the attention, Jacobson thought it rather pointless of the secret agents to hide behind curtains; the very purpose of his being in Meshed was to get people to come to the services. He accordingly issued a cordial invitation to the two women to drop in any time. It was pointedly ignored. From time to time Jacobson would meet the women on the street; although they had never been formally introduced, they were certainly far more than mere acquaintances, and, being a polite young man, he always smiled and nodded to them. It greatly flustered the secret agents; this crazy young missionary obviously didn't know how to play the game.

One time Jacobson, with a group of teachers driving a surplus ambulance, drove up to Bandar Shah, almost on the border of the Turkmen Soviet Socialist Republic. The roads were heavily patrolled by Russian soldiers and Jacobson and his party were stopped and held for questioning. This was obviously a case for the Russian general himself, and messengers were sent out to find him. It turned out that the general had chosen that momentous day to go fishing, and he didn't get back until 11 P.M. He immediately began questioning Jacobson. Starting out with the cost of shoes and bread in America, he worked back through Jacobson's education, the grades he had received, and the names of his teachers from college back to kindergarten. Jacobson saw no reason to withhold the names of his teachers, not even the ones who had given him D's, and he obligingly gave the Russian general a complete picture of his personal education. The general seemed satisfied, and the first session ended. Next day, however, it began all over again; now the general wanted to know about Jacobson's wife. Where had she gone to school, what grades had she gotten, and who were her teachers, all the way back to kindergarten?

Jacobson had to laugh at some of the questions. "Really," he assured the general, "I was interested in my wife's pedigree when I married her, but not quite to that extent."

The Russian general looked at his subordinates and all shook their heads in wonder. Imagine a man not knowing the name of his wife's fourth-grade teacher! Jacobson was, of course, released after questioning. It was readily apparent even to the Russians that he, like all church workers, was keeping himself completely out of affairs of state.

Many eager young Seventh-day Adventists have found that it is by no means necessary to go to far-off places, to brush with secret agents in Iran, or to build log houses in Laos to be pioneers in the service of Christ. It is not even necessary, as a matter of fact, to go to the red-sand desert of Monument Valley in the Southwest. Mrs. Marjorie Campbell, for example, has found all the challenge, all the opportunity for serving mankind, that anyone could possibly want right in the hills of Kentucky, settled since pre-Revolutionary days. As a jeep nurse in the Kentucky mountains, Marjorie Campbell has her fill of adventure, every day. She had been on the new job less than a month when, driving along a muddy, back country road during a pouring rain, she felt the entire shoulder of the road give way beneath her. The jeep rolled down an eight-foot bank, turning over, and, according to Marjorie's report, "causing minor bruises to the driver and major impairment to the jeep."

There are some places, particularly during the winter rains, where even the jeep cannot go. Here in the heart of Eastern America Marjorie has had to walk as much as twenty miles across country, wade through swift, muddy streams and climb high bluffs—always carrying her nurse's satchel and frequently a basket of food—to reach the mountain people. Sometimes, sloughing along through the mud, she meets the postman, delivering his mail from muleback. They usually stop and pass the time of day.

Some days Marjorie feels that she could use a mule herself. One morning she heard that twin baby girls had been delivered by a midwife in a mountain cabin, and she paid a visit to see how they they were getting along. They were not doing well at all, and no wonder. Their parents shared a two-room shack with two other families. In the same room where the children were born, two elderly people were confined to their beds as permanent invalids. The mother could not be spared from her other children and the household duties, and it was deemed best to bring the two baby girls to the little hospital at Oneida, Marjorie's headquarters, for care. After two months they were doing nicely. Marjorie sent word to the parents that the babies would be coming home and to prepare for them, and then, several days later, set out to make the delivery. This was not exactly a routine trip, for in the meantime the parents, with the mother's parents, had moved to a cabin of their own. The only way to reach it was by foot, across a swinging bridge high over a mountain stream, then along a narrow path up the mountainside for a mile and a half to the cabin.

Marjorie got another nurse from the hospital to help her. They put the babies in a big bamboo basket, filled another basket with evaporated milk and Karo syrup. Then, taking turns, they carried the basketful of babies across the swinging bridge and up the mountainside.

Over the years—she began her work in October, 1956—Marjorie Campbell has learned to love the mountain people. She has found them to be friendly and warm after the initial barrier of suspicion has been broken down. She learned early not to play the role of Lady Bountiful, or tell the people what to do. Rather, she gains their confidence by getting them to show her something or tell her something. A banjo hanging on the wall is a wonderful means of establishing friendship. Marjorie sees it, asks to look at it, and before long the little cabin is ringing with a mountain ballad sung to the accompaniment of the plink-plunk of the banjo. Only after she and the family are friends does she attempt to better their life, and then slowly, with the most rudimentary knowledge.

One of her first visits was to a family of six children ranging from a child of ten to a babe in arms, abandoned by the mother. The father was doing his best to earn money to support them as well as care for them at home. One of the younger children, a little girl, had been badly burned when her dress caught fire. The father had treated the burns by the old mountain method of smearing a mixture of lard and bark over them. Rather than wading in and removing the filthy mixture, Marjorie first gained the confidence of the father. Then it was easy to convince him that the best treatment was to keep the burned area clean and protect it by fresh clean cloth. She made repeated visits to the cabin, showing the oldest children how to take care of the youngest while their father worked.

Though Marjorie is trained in home economics, and considers it a part of her duty to show the mountain women how to prepare healthful meals, her course of instruction is a far cry from those given in well-equipped school kitchens. For one thing, how do you demonstrate the preparation of a balanced meal when there is only one cooking utensil in the whole house—and it doubles as a water bucket and wash basin?

As she goes from cabin to cabin, Marjorie gives a complete course in living. Tactfully and gently, she explains to mothers such rudimentary hygienic facts as what to feed the baby, how and when, the importance of bathing it, and of fresh air and sunshine. She teaches the older children how to perform domestic work at home to take the load off their mother, and teaches the whole family such things generally taken for granted elsewhere as cleanliness of person and in handling and preparing food, and even how to burn or bury waste materials. She shows them how to plant gardens and can their produce, how to buy beneficial foods such as whole wheat flour and how to make bread from it, how to budget, and how to improvise.

Though frequently she finds the living conditions of the people appalling, and in too many cases she finds invalids too far gone for her to be able to do anything but make their last days more comfortable, she finds rewards aplenty too. One day she was asked by a friend with a leaky roof to stop by a handyman's house as she made her rounds and ask him to come fix it. At the handyman's home she found him deeply troubled. He had several other jobs to do, had even bought materials for them, but was too sick and sore to work. Meantime, his money was running out.

What was his trouble? Well, he had a bad cold which had lingered on, and pains in his lower back. "Would you mind," Marjorie asked, "if your wife and I give you a treatment? I think it will do you some good."

"I'll try anything," he assured her. Marjorie set to work preparing the good old hydrotherapy treatments which Dr. Kellogg had made famous back in Battle Creek days. Linens were gotten out, water was put on to heat. Working together Marjorie and the man's wife gave him hot applications to chest and spine, a hot foot bath and cold compresses to his head and throat, and a sedative massage. Next day she returned and repeated the same procedure.

About a month later, in town, she heard her name called, and the man came running up to her. He looked hale and hearty and years younger.

"I just want to tell you how much better I feel," he said "I've worked every day and I haven't felt better in years." He thanked her over and over again for the simple treatment which had been so easy to give.

Marjorie frequently pays brief visits to people along the way, just to be friendly, and perhaps stop trouble before it starts. One day she dropped in on a young woman whose husband had been killed in an automobile accident. She and her four-year-old daughter were obviously in distress. For one thing, it turned out that all her and her husband's relatives, thinking she was lonely, had taken to dropping in constantly, frequently at mealtime, sometimes even to spend the night. These visits of well-meaning relatives had become a burden to her physically as well as financially. Her husband had taken care of all money matters, and on top of everything else she was worried sick about this new duty. Marjorie's casual visit had not come a day too soon. The young woman's nerves were near the breaking point. She had not slept for three nights, and hadn't been able to hold anything on her stomach for that time.

Marjorie quickly ran out and got some buttermilk which, with a slice of dried toast, would be the easiest food for the distraught young widow to digest. She gagged, but she retained it. As for the relatives, from a few tactful remarks it developed that they were perfectly willing to go home and get a little rest themselves. Marjorie promised to stay until the patient was better. When they were alone in the house, Marjorie called on her old standby, hydrotherapy. She gave the young woman a hot application to enable her to sweat some of the poisons out of her system, then a sedative one to enable her to sleep. While she was sleeping Marjorie ran home, got some fresh vegetables out of her own garden, brought them back and started preparing them. She fed mother and daughter a wholesome, tasty meal and both cleaned their plates. Marjorie stayed on until the woman was completely rested and refreshed, and ready to take up life's duties once more. As they lived together, particularly when Marjorie was giving hydrotherapy treatments, they talked about nursing. One day Marjorie took the mother and little girl with her to one of the most remote areas.

When they returned the young woman was silent a minute, then burst out with, "This is what I want to do!"

Marjorie helped her find a nurse's school where she could earn her way through. With her daughter she has since moved there and started the courses which will enable her eventually to do for others what Marjorie Campbell, the pioneer jeep nurse of the Kentucky mountains, had done for her.

All the young men and women who go out to medical and mission work, whether beyond the seas or here at home, are, at least within the confines of their own experience, pioneering. No one is sent by the church into a strange area without receiving some indoctrination in what to expect when they get there, yet no place turns out to be exactly like one's mental picture of it.

Essie Petherbridge was certainly informed, before she left her native Sydney for the Mount Hagen Mission Hospital in New Guinea, that she was going to a country where many primitive customs still persisted. As she busied herself in the little operating room of the station one morning shortly after she arrived, however, she thought she might as well be in any hospital back home. There was the rustle of her own and the doctors' surgical garments, the soft sound of instruments being laid out on sterile towels, the deep breathing of the little native girl being prepared for surgery. Just another routine operation of which she had seen so many—and then, with a crash, the door of the operating room burst open. A giant of a native, hideously painted, leaped through the doorway, brandishing a sharp-edged native axe. His dark skin was covered with ashes and ochre. His face was violently twisted into a horrible expression.

The painted warrior, uttering strange, guttural sounds, advanced to the operating table behind which Essie stood, mouth open to scream, paralyzed with horror. Suddenly he reached out to the table, raised his axe high over his head. The axe fell; Essie looked down. On the table before her rested the warrior's own hand, one finger neatly severed, and the stump already spurting blood.

What is this madman going to do now? Essie thought in panic. *Is he going to kill us all?*

The doctor's voice broke into the silence. "Please take care of his finger, Miss Petherbridge," he said calmly, going on with his pre-operative procedure. Essie numbly reached behind her, got a roll of bandages, started around the table to the painted native. The doctor's voice followed her.

"I had forgotten you weren't used to native customs," the doctor was saying. "That's this little girl's father. This is his way of showing his grief. He intends us no harm. As soon as you staunch the flow of blood and clean up a little, we'll get on with the operation. Actually I do believe he wasted a finger—his little girl is going to be all right."

Essie, now equally calm—well, *almost* equally calm—quietly dressed the warrior's self-inflicted wound, then helped the doctor with the operation. Everything proceeded well, and it turned out that the savage parent had indeed wasted a finger. But, Essie thought, as she cleaned up after the operation, this was one experience she certainly had never been briefed about back home in Sydney!

Not every young nurse sent to the mission fields can expect to be scared to death by a painted warrior, but life in many mission stations can nevertheless be uncomfortable, rigorous, even dangerous. Despite this, there are many more young men and women ready, willing and able to go than there is money to send them, even though a new worker is dispatched to the mission fields each day of the year, on the average. The total number of church workers is over 46,000, including 11,500 doctors, nurses, and hospital employees.

By no means are all the applicants for service abroad acceptable. The church has found out, through bitter experience, that some of the most eager applicants prove unfit for the job. Although crack-ups have not been numerous, when they do occur the whole church suffers; not only does it create a bad impression among the very people the church is trying to win, but it means substantial financial loss to the foreign missions budget. Each new missionary family represents an investment by the church of some $10,000. To return a young man from missionary service costs the church not only the $10,000 he represents, but another $10,000 for his replacement.

For this reason, each applicant for foreign service, whether evangelical or construction and maintenance worker, doctor, nurse or medical technician, is carefully examined. The perfect prospect is a rare combination. He must be so filled with love of God and love of his fellow man that he is willing to undergo severe discomfort to serve them. At the same time he must be tough enough, mentally and physically, to face the adversities he is bound to encounter. The foreign mission service does not want sissies, nor the pompously pious, nor the fastidious. Any mission worker must have a thorough theological knowledge, a sound constitution and good health, and a wife; bachelors just don't work out. It also helps to have a sense of humor.

Once he leaves, it will be four to seven years before he sees home again, unless he is sent to Nigeria or Ghana, where the term is two and a half years. The reason for the distinction is a simple one; every other equatorial area is close enough to the hill country to enable the missionary to spend his annual leave in a temperate climate, wearing sweaters and sitting before a fire at night, recharging his heat-drained body. Nigeria and Ghana are so far away from the mountains that the church worker there may just as well save up his annual leave and take it all at home.

In return for his services, which are hardly limited to eight hours a day, the young missionary draws a salary of $65 to $70 a week. (The salary figures given here do not include the 5 per cent increase that went into effect in 1960.) If his rent is more than 10 per cent of his salary, the church pays the difference. If a jeep or other means of conveyance is necessary, the missionary buys it himself; the church gives him an allowance for its upkeep and he may sell it for a profit when he leaves. Nor does he have great riches to look forward to when his children reach college age and he decides to return home. If he becomes the pastor of a large church, his salary will be $78 a week, plus a rental allowance of $80 a month, auto depreciation of $35 a month and some allowance for his medical expenses. If he becomes the president of a conference, responsible for perhaps 200 employees and a budget of a million and a half dollars a year, his salary will be $82.25 a week, with the same allowances. The president of a union, supervising over a thousand employees and with a budget of over $5 million, draws a salary of $85.50 a week. The salary of the highest officer in the church, the president of the General Conference, is $89.50 a week. All other salaries, whether for hospital administrator, college dean, parochial school teacher, or administrative or clerical personnel, are commensurate. Salaries for medical personnel run slightly higher. If a college graduate goes on to attend the College of Medical Evangelists, at a cost of well over $2000 a year, puts in his years of internship and residency and over the years acquires such experience and administrative capability that he finally is rewarded with the post of chief of staff of a large overseas hospital, he will be entitled to draw the munificent salary of $104 a week. People do not work for the Adventist church for monetary reward.

As a rule, each division is responsible for its own personnel, as well as that of its assigned mission field. The Northern European Division, composed of Great Britain, Norway, Sweden, the Netherlands, Denmark and Finland, assigns mission workers to the Ethiopian Union Mission and the West African Union Mission. The Australasian Division handles the South Sea Islands, and the Southern European Division the French and Portuguese colonies of Africa. Frequently, however, when individual divisions have difficulty filling specific posts, chiefly those requiring special training or administrative skill, they refer the vacancy to the General Conference. Here is a partial list of some vacancies which existed one day recently:

General surgeon, Seoul
Pediatrician, Manila
Radiologist, Bangkok
Director of Nursing Service, Bandung
Evangelistic worker, Haadyai
College dean, Philippines
Elementary teacher, Bangkok
Surgeon, Port of Spain
X-ray technician, Puerto Rico
College dean, French- and Spanish-speaking, Haiti
Division and Union treasurer, Beirut
Pastor-evangelist, Alexandria
Lady laboratory technician, Addis Ababa
Lady home economics teacher, Konola
Secretary-accountant, Accra
Hospital business manager, Rio de Janeiro
Home missionary, Sabbath school and radio secretary, Manaos
Mission station supervisor, Lake Titicaca
Matron, Kendu (Kenya)

Mission director, Majita, Tanganyika
Science and math teacher, Ikizu, Tanganyika
Girls worker, Kamagambo
General surgeon, Karachi
Laboratory technician (single lady), Rangoon
College business manager, Poona
Colporteur supervisor, Pakistan

9 *The Lord Working with Them*

It is a strange paradox that in the world of today, wherein one man can drop a bomb which will eliminate the better part of a country, few persons admittedly believe in present-day miracles. Even devoutly religious persons who accept with complete faith the miracles of the Holy Scriptures apparently feel that the same God who performed these miracles 2000 years ago has for some strange reason lost either the power or the desire to produce similar manifestations in the modern world.

Not so the Seventh-day Adventists. Members of a church whose very cornerstone was laid in supernatural occurrences, the scientifically proven visions of Ellen G. White, and firm believers in an all-powerful but personal God, they wholeheartedly accept the verified reports from devout church workers of happenings which could have no other explanation than divine intervention. The literature of the church and the accounts of its workers are filled with examples of miraculous rescues, of dying persons saved by prayer.

One particular type of rescue occurs over and over again in the history of the church. Its first occurrence was in the days of Millerism, when James White dared to address a congregation near Augusta, Maine, in spite of the threats of a group of rough men who called themselves Universalists. White was only twenty-two at the time, slender but eager to spread the word of the Advent. The preceding evening a mob had thrown stones, even spikes, at him. When he was warned that the Universalists planned even more violent action to prevent the second meeting, he hesitated, but only to seek guidance in prayer. Then he headed for the schoolhouse in which the meeting was to be held.

When he arrived the little building was filled with people, and an overflow crowd clustered about outside. Though it was winter, windows were opened to enable those outside to hear. Most of the people in attendance were good Christians, many of them women and children, but interspersed throughout the crowd were many ruffians. As White appeared he was greeted with catcalls, and snowballs and other missiles were thrown at him. He ignored them, faced the crowd, and began speaking in his normal tones, but the noise of the mob drowned out his voice. He closed his Bible, and his quiet voice changed into a roar, cutting through the babel. Then he took an object from his pocket and held it up for all to see. It was a big iron spike.

"Some poor sinner cast this spike at me last evening," he said. "God pity him! The worst wish I have for him is that he is at this moment as happy as I am. Why should I resent this insult when"—holding aloft the spike—"my Master had them driven through His hands?" He stepped back against the wall, arms outstretched, in the position of crucifixion.

Someone cried, "Hark, hark!" And then all was still. For several minutes the young man preached his heart out, calling on sinners to turn from their evil ways, speaking of the love of God. When he asked all those who desired prayer to rise, over a hundred stood up, and he prayed for them. And then he made his way through the hushed audience out the schoolhouse door.

But on the outside the main part of the mob was waiting for him. Grim, menacing, they pressed forward. It was James White's most dangerous moment. Suddenly a man of noble countenance, with a strangely familiar face, stepped up to young White and locked arms with him. The two walked steadily toward the oncoming crowd, and the ruffians gave way and let them pass. Not a finger was laid on either of them. When they had passed through the crowd, White turned to thank the man who had walked with him.

There was no one there.

You remember how Leo Halliwell, cruising up the Amazon River in the *Luzeiro,* had been warned of the rocks ahead by two strangers, who then disappeared mysteriously. Halfway across the world, during World War II, one of God's strongest disciples, Kata Ragoso, a native chief of the Solomon Islands born of cannibal parents who became one of the church's staunchest workers, had a somewhat similar experience. When the war broke out, all white persons except the military were evacuated from the Solomons. Kata Ragoso, as both temporal and spiritual leader, was left in charge of his people. He organized things so well that hundreds of Allied military personnel were led to safety from Japanese-held territory. But that is another story. During the early days of the war in the Pacific, Kata Ragoso was ordered by the British officer in charge of the district to perform tasks which his religion and conscience would not permit him to do, and he refused. The officer, under the strain of those perilous days, ordered Kata Ragoso to be flogged. The churchman-chief was laid face down over a gasoline drum and was beaten with a cane until the blood flowed. Again the officer insisted Kata Ragoso obey, and again he refused.

"Sir, I am sorry," he said, "but my religion does not allow me to obey you. My answer is no."

The officer drew his revolver and struck Kata Ragoso full in the face with it, smashing his nose. Then he beat him on the head until he fell to the ground unconscious. When he regained consciousness, the officer selected a firing squad and stood Kata Ragoso up against a tree.

"When I say three, you fire," he told the squad. Then he started counting. "One, two . . ." the word "three" would not come. Three times the officer started counting, three times he could not get the fatal word out. He turned on his heel and stalked off. He was, incidentally, later dismissed from the service for his actions.

Kata Ragoso was taken to the prison compound, and, with one of his most faithful assistants, a man named Ludi, was locked up. The native Adventists, concerned over the imprisonment of their spiritual leader, called a prayer meeting to begin just as the moon came over one of the high mountains on the island. It was a strange meeting, with the faithful being called by the beating of drums which had once played for heathen dances. It was strange in another way, too. Not too many years before, these erstwhile savages, who outnumbered the British detachment on the island, might well have murdered them all. But now their weapon was prayer.

The moon rose just before ten that night. The prayer meeting began. At about the same time a tall man holding a bunch of keys walked to the prison gate, selected the proper key, opened the padlock, and then the prison gate. He called Kata Ragoso and Ludi to him, took each by the arm and led them outside and along a path toward the sea. Overlooking the beach, he pointed, "You will find a canoe there. Take it and go home."

The two men walked to the water's edge, and there they found a canoe with two paddles. They turned to thank their rescuer, but no one was there.

Subsequent investigation proved that the original bunch of keys had hung on its peg in plain sight of a sentry all that night.

And then there was Faole, a native of Papua. Certainly, of all the blood-thirsty natives of New Guinea, Faole would be the last anyone would expect to become a Christian, let alone a Christian leader respected by hundreds of Seventh-day Adventist natives. Faole killed his first man at the age of fifteen, then went on to kill three more, two women and a child, simply for the heathen joy of killing. Later the law caught up with him and he spent some time in jail. After he was released Faole appeared at a little Seventh-day Adventist mission and requested permission to go to school. The missionary tried to put him off, for his unsavory reputation had preceded him, but Faole insisted. In his insistence the missionary saw the possibility that this man could be brought to Christ.

The missionary was right. From the most feared man in the district, he became the most respected. When a new mission was opened, and the missionary was authorized to take with him an assistant, he chose Faole. Finally Faole became a teacher in his own right, and was assigned, with his wife, to the village of Maibikee. The bush people learned to love him. He built a new village, clean and neat. A fine church was erected, attendance at the school grew, and the village prospered.

But at the nearest village, a few miles over the mountain, there was no Faole. There the natives continued their evil ways. They were suspicious of what was happening at Maibikee, and when one day their chief suddenly died, the medicine man announced that a spell had been put upon him by the people of Maibikee. It would be necessary to destroy Maibikee, burn it to the ground and kill all its people. That night fifty warriors in full war paint, with tipped arrows and sharpened spears, set out to accomplish the mission.

One person in the village opposed the venture. At the risk of his own neck, he ran across country to the mission station on the coast to tell the missionary what was happening. Although it was a two-day trip, and by the time he arrived at the mission whatever was to happen would have happened, the missionary set out immediately for Maibikee. There, two days later, the perspiring missionary was pleased and surprised to find the village in perfect order and Faole himself fit as a fiddle. Questioning brought forth the fact that Faole had sensed something in the air that night, and had gathered his family around him for prayers. He had picked up the Bible and opened it haphazardly, and his eyes had fallen upon the Thirty-fourth Psalm, in which was written: "The angel of the Lord encampeth roundabout them that fear Him, and delivereth them."

Faole had promptly stopped worrying, and had gone to bed and slept soundly.

But what had happened to the warriors? The missionary set out for the village over the hill. There he found things in a most unsettled condition. The men seemed sullen, the women mocking. The missionary asked the headman where he had been four nights before. The headman at first refused to answer, finally admitted that he and his warriors had started out for Maibikee to kill Faole.

Why hadn't he? The headman was furious. "You know all right!" he said. "Because when we got there you and a whole group of white men, all dressed in white, stood in a ring around Faole's house, and remained there all night!"

The other warriors backed up the chief's account. When they reached Maibikee they had seen those men guarding Faole's house. All night long the raiders hid in the bush, and all night long they saw the white-clad guards standing there. When dawn came the painted warriors gave up and slunk away home.

Another type of miracle has repeated itself over and over through the years. One of its first manifestations occurred in the South American Andes, where Ellis P. Howard, an American missionary in a small village among the Aymara Indians, received a message from a nearby town that the people would like to establish a school for their children. The call happened to coincide with the visit of another American missionary named J. M. Howell, and the two men, with a native convert named Daniel Sosa, rode over to the town on horseback. They found it deserted.

There was bitter opposition to the new church in this area and they knew something was wrong. They decided it would be wise to leave immediately, and started out, but two boys suddenly appeared and offered to show them a quicker way out of the town. The boys led them up a narrow street with a solid wall of houses on either side to a dead end. Too late they realized they had been led into a trap, for now up the narrow street came a mob, armed with sticks and clubs. The three men rode down the street toward the mob, hoping the people would give way before the horses, but they continued their menacing advance. It was obvious that the Adventists had been lured there to be killed. Just as the leaders were reaching out for the horses' bridles, Howard noticed, for the first time, a break in the high wall on one side of the street. He called to the others, and they all rode through it. Strangely, none of the hostile villagers followed them, and they rode home without mishap.

Later the bitterness in that village cooled toward the Seventh-day Adventists, and Howard was asked to pay a bona fide visit. He did, and, as a matter of curiosity, went to the street where he and his companions had been bottled up. He found no break in the wall on either side, nor any sign of repairs. Nor, the townspeople said, had there ever been any.

To the northeast of the Aymaras lives the Quechua tribe. To them came a young teacher named Pedro Kalbermatter, son of one of the first converts in Argentina. At the village of Laro the Indians had donated land and begun helping Kalbermatter build a schoolhouse when an intense opposition on the part of the few white people, priests and wealthy landowners, developed. The new teacher was threatened with death if he stayed. Fortunately for the gospel, however, young Kalbermatter was not the type of man to flee. He had already undergone persecution in his native land, when he had been conscripted into the Argentine Army. Refusing duty on the Sabbath, he was made to stand at attention until his feet were so swollen he could not walk. On the next Sabbath he was whipped on the bare back with a heavy leather strap until he passed out with the pain. Each week the punishment grew even more severe and finally he was sentenced to a year at hard labor. There the chaplain, a Catholic priest, talked with the young man, believed his faith and sincerity, and interceded for him with the high command. Eventually not only Kalbermatter, but all Seventh-day Adventist conscripts in Argentina, were given complete liberty on the Sabbath.

This, then, was the man the white reactionaries tried to drive from the country. When he stayed, fighting broke out. On one occasion a band of mounted white men ambushed a group of Indians returning from Sabbath services and killed twelve of them. Still Kalbermatter stayed on. One morning, working with some Quechuas on the half-completed schoolhouse, he saw several horsemen galloping toward him. Kalbermatter told the innocent Indians to hide behind the rocks, but he himself determined to fight. He got together the rifles which the mission had on hand as protection against wild beasts and took cover behind the schoolhouse walls. But as he waited, prepared to kill, the thought struck him: *Is this what Jesus would do?* The answer, he was forced to admit, was *No*. He threw aside his small arsenal, committed himself to God, and then, unarmed, stepped forth to face the riders.

"Ride him down!" cried the leader of the horsemen, and they charged him.

But as the leading horseman approached the unarmed man, the horse suddenly shied away. So did the second horse, and the third and the fourth. The men whipped their steeds, raked their sides with spurs, but not one single horse would touch the young man of God. Finally the men rode away in confusion. And today the mission at Laro is still doing excellent work among the Quechua Indians.

Although Seventh-day Adventists have been persecuted for their faith in many lands, the tortures inflicted upon native converts in Kenya during the dread Mau-Mau rebellion were unsurpassed in cruelty and bestiality. The greatest atrocities of the Mau-Mau were committed on their own people who had adopted the white man's ways and religion. They knew that torture and death might result, but still many Seventh-day Adventists in Kenya defied the Mau-Mau. One of these was a teen-aged girl named Gakui. She had been to the mission school only one year, but her faith was as strong and determined as though she had been born into the church. Perhaps it was even stronger, for Gakui, born of heathen parents, had experienced within her own soul the joy of finding Christ. When the Mau-Mau leaders demanded that Gakui take their oath, and even her parents pleaded with her to submit, the native girl remained adamant. She had heard whispers of the obscene acts initiates were required to perform, and she knew that the oath included the promise to worship Jomo, the Mau-Mau leader, even over God and His Son, Jesus Christ. And Gakui could not possibly denounce her faith in Jesus, nor could she disobey that commandment which says, "Thou shalt put no other gods before Me."

Time and again Gakui slipped into the bushes and hid when the Mau-Mau came by. One day, however, a neighbor woman came by Gakui's home and asked the girl to mind her child. As evening came on, and the mother still had not come to pick up the baby, Gakui thought that she had better return the child to its home. She tied the baby on her back, and set out through the jungle paths. Near the baby's home three men stepped stealthily out from the vines beside the path and seized Gakui. It had been a trap, after all. The mother appeared and took the baby, and the men led Gakui to the Mau-Mau ceremonial hut. They demanded that she take the oath. She refused and they began to slap her face.

"Do you want to die?" they asked.

"No, I don't want to die," Gakui cried, "but I will not die. Jesus will save me. I know He will."

The men picked up clubs and beat her until she was unconscious, beat her even while she was lying senseless on the floor. She was still lying there unconscious when other members of the Mau-Mau brought in a group of young natives to take the oath. They picked Gakui up and threw her limp body over against the wall, then proceeded with the ceremony. She regained consciousness, only to lie helpless and watch her friends in the village, young people her own age, perform the filthy acts and swear the terrible oath the Mau-Mau required.

One of the men saw that she was conscious, and taunted her. "So your Jesus is taking care of you, eh?" he said. "Well, we'll see about that. But don't worry, we're not going to kill you yet. There's no need to. There's only one door and it's well guarded. You can't escape from us, Gakui."

And he returned to the ceremony, as Gakui lay in horror, weak and helpless from loss of blood. She could only pray.

As she prayed, Gakui felt strong hands grip her feet. She felt herself being pulled, slowly but steadily, through a hole in the wall of the hut out into the freedom of the night. Finally she was completely outside the hut, and rose unsteadily to her feet. She looked around to see whose strong hands had pulled her to freedom, but saw no one. She managed to make her way to the home of an Adventist native family, where her wounds were cleansed and she lay hidden while she recovered from her beating. Some months later, government officials rounding up the Mau-Mau came to ask her to identify her tormentors. Gakui refused. The men who had beaten her did not realize what they were doing, she said; there was still hope for them.

One of the government men asked her to tell about her escape. When she finished, they shook their heads incredulously.

"Gakui," one of the officials said, "we have been in that hut. We have examined it minutely. There is no hole in any of the walls, nor is there any sign whatsoever that there ever was such a hole. This is the most mysterious thing I've ever heard of."

But it was not mysterious to Gakui. She had known all along that her God would not let her die.

At this point, to cleanse the mind, in a sense, from the atrocities of the Mau-Mau, it might be appropriate to recount the charming, happy little story told by Alva R. Appel, who, like his father before him, has served many years in the Far East. "It was in Colombo, in Ceylon," young Appel said. "One of our most devout members, a darling little girl about twelve years old, had a terrible problem. Bright as a new penny, she had a good chance of getting the highest grade in her class in the public school. And then her dream crashed about her, for the final exam in her best subject was set for Saturday, and of course she could not take it on the Sabbath. She appealed to the principal of the school, but he was adamant; she must take it on the Sabbath, or not at all. The child was in tears."

Appel smiled. "And then what do you think happened? The exam papers had been made up and sealed, but on the very day they were to be given the teacher found that there had been a leak. Someone had stolen one of the papers and may well have shown it to the other pupils. And so an entirely new exam was drawn up, and scheduled for the next week. The little girl took it, and made an almost perfect score.

"Don't you think," Appel said, "that God worked out the answer to her dilemma in a marvelous way?"

As Seventh-day Adventist workers penetrate into the most remote areas of the world, they hear tales of sorcery and witchcraft, devil doctors and evil spirits. Naturally, as this is, after all, the twentieth century, they discount much of what they hear. But two Americans, both with masters degrees, cannot discount what they themselves saw and heard in a tiny mission deep in Tanganyika one Sabbath in the year 1957. They are Karl C. Fischer and Ruth M. White, both members of the faculty of the College of Medical Evangelists. They were on a special mission studying the health problems of the Ha tribe, one of the most primitive in Africa. On this Sabbath they went out for services to the small mud-brick church at the Heri Mission. The man conducting the services that Sabbath was himself a member of the Ha tribe, a man whose name they recall only as Paulo. He was a short, intense young man, conducting services with great dignity despite the fact that his only clothes were a pair of pants ripped off above the knee, and a suit coat over his naked chest.

Following the services, Paulo asked Miss White and Fischer to come to the front of the church and participate in special prayers with some of the natives. One of the women was obviously not a church member. She was dirty, her arms and legs were greased to a high shine, and she wore great metal bangles around her arms and legs. Just as Seventh-day Adventist women in civilized countries forego lipstick and rouge in what they consider a needless embellishment of God's image, so do the women of Africa cease wearing their bangles and pig grease when they become converted.

Paulo began praying. Suddenly, from the heathen woman came a piercing scream, and she fell back in a trance. The native pastor went to her and spoke. Then, from the woman's throat, both Miss White and Carl Fischer, two people of scientific training, heard come the voice of a man. It was a beautiful, well-modulated voice, speaking in the Ha language. A shiver ran down their backbones. Paulo, however, stepped bravely before the woman and replied to the strange voice. For several moments he carried on a conversation, obviously a debate, with the strange man's voice coming from the unconscious woman. Finally Paulo seemed to become angry. In a thundering voice, speaking in English, he commanded: "In the name of Jesus Christ and Almighty God I command you to get out of this woman's body."

A piercing scream came from the woman's mouth. She sat up, shook her head and looked about her dazedly. Then, suddenly, a smile of relief came to her face. "It's gone," she breathed. "I'm whole again." And then Paulo, the minister in tattered clothes, the woman in a coat of grease, and the two Americans all gave thanks to God together for the delivered woman. She happily agreed to cast off forever her bangles and grease, and become a devout subject of the Lord.

"I had no feeling of cynicism or disbelief," Fischer recalled later, "rather, I felt privileged and humble to have seen the power of God over witchcraft."

Frequently doctors admit that they have seen strange phenomena for which they have no scientific explanation take place in their patients. Many Seventh-day Adventist doctors make the same report but with one exception: They believe that these phenomena have an explanation, and that the explanation is the unseen Hand of God. Dr. Herschel C. Lamp, a full-faced young man with mild eyes behind big glasses, is one of these men. After completing his residency, Dr. Lamp, with his wife Trudie and their three children, was sent to a small hospital in a village known as Jengre, in Nigeria. He was the only doctor in an area the size of Montana.

In Nigeria, a British protectorate, outlying missions are known as being "out in bush," and the far stations are known as "proper bush"; Jengre could be described only as being in proper bush. The

Lamps could hear baboons crying around the town, frequently the hyenas would come into the village and drag off a dog, and occasionally a leopard would come loping unafraid down the main street of the village. Though the natives are principally members of the Amo tribe, six different languages are spoken within an area of forty miles around Jengre. The Amo are primitive people; the women wear only a garment of leaves about their hips, the men a leather girdle. When children, their cheeks are slashed with the marks of the tribe. At puberty, the young men undergo a strange initiation ceremony. Dr. Lamp witnessed one of these rites. The youth who was undergoing the ceremony stepped forward into a circle of his tribesmen. A muscular young man with a long staff joined him in the circle. As the boy stood motionless, the man feinted at him with the staff, pretended to strike. The boy did not wince. Finally, with a full roundhouse swing, with all his weight behind it, the man struck the boy in the chest with the staff. Blood spurted from the welt. The man repeated the performance several times, pretending, teasing, then swinging with all his force. When the boy was covered with blood, another man came forward and placed a penny on his forehead. The penny stuck, and immediately the onlookers began hissing and laughing at the boy; the few drops of perspiration which held the penny were considered a sign of weakness. Later Dr. Lamp examined the boy and found that several ribs were broken.

Dr. Lamp and his family had been at Jengre only a few days when their male nurse, a tall native named Wallaby, driving the hospital truck-ambulance, struck an old woman who stepped full into the path of the oncoming vehicle. She was taken to the hospital, where Dr. Lamp did all he could for her, but she died. Word reached the doctor that some of the natives, resentful, had vowed to take vengeance. He ignored the threats until that night, when, as the children were asleep, he and his wife heard the drums begin to beat an ominous rhythm off in the jungle. As Dr. Lamp and his wife stood by the tiny window in the little mud hut close to the dirt road just outside the village, they heard the drums getting closer, closer,

closer. Far up the road they saw a faint glow, which grew brighter and brighter, then became several bobbing individual lights of flaming torches. Urged on by the drums, the procession came closer, closer.

Just before the leading torchbearers came to the little driveway leading up to their hut, Dr. Lamp turned to his wife and said quietly. "I think we had better pray." Holding hands, they bowed their heads and asked God to spare, not them, but their children sleeping innocently behind them. They looked up to see the procession pass on by. Next morning they learned the whole thing had been just another native celebration.

As the work went on, the doctor no longer had time or energy to be frightened. Never, even on the worst night in the accident ward back home, had he ever dreamed that such terrible conditions could exist. Malaria was everywhere; so was leprosy. He treated an average of 300 lepers a week, men and women whose toes and fingers had already dropped off. The parasitic worms were terrible. One variety ate into the eyes, causing a disease known as river blindness. Another ate into the brain, causing sleeping sickness. People would simply drop to the ground and lie sleeping in the dirt. But it was to the children that the kind doctor's heart went out in pity. They were so innocent, so helpless, and they had so little chance of survival.

One day an Amo mother from a community several miles away brought her baby boy to the hospital. She had carried him all the way in a goatskin pouch tied to her back with matted grasses. The baby's head was lolling weakly; the child was dying of pneumonia. The disease had made too much headway for even the most effective of the wonder drugs to do any good. Dr. Lamp knew that the child had only minutes more to live. He could not possibly survive. And yet. . . .

"Let us pray," Dr. Lamp told the native interpreter, and knelt. The interpreter fell on his knees, and so did the nurse. The woman, not knowing what else to do, also got down on her bare knees, holding the dying baby in her arms. Dr. Lamp uttered a simple little prayer: "Oh God, we fear that this baby is dying, and I can do no more to help him. But you, O Lord, You who love this child, can do much more than I. And I ask it, in the name of Jesus, through Your love and mercy for Your people."

Even as he was finishing the little prayer, Dr. Lamp heard a sudden change in the baby's breathing. The mother noticed it too; so did the interpreter, and so did the nurse. Still on their knees, they looked at one another in wonder and awe. "Why," the doctor said, standing up, "that baby is going to be all right!"

He took the baby boy from the mother, and gave him medication. But he knew the medication was only secondary. The child had been saved through prayer. In a few days the baby's mother took him home, well and strong.

"Both as a doctor and as a Christian," Dr. Lamp said later, "I believe in prayer. I have seen God perform miracles before my very eyes, and I know them to be miracles because my scientific knowledge offers no other explanation."

A poet once wrote that God works in wondrous ways his miracles to perform, and perhaps one of the most wondrous yet homely little miracles of modern times occurred in Montemorelos Hospital in Mexico, in June, 1957. This is no story for the squeamish—indeed it might be called the Miracle of the Bedpan—but it does prove an important point: God looks after His people no matter how messy the plight in which they find themselves.

A twenty-six-year-old woman of Galeana, mother of four children, suffered a strangulated hernia of the small intestine. With the elimination tract blocked, the young woman's abdomen swelled up with the accumulation of waste material and gases until it was distended far more than in pregnancy. After three or four days, a patient suffering from a strangulated hernia has little chance for survival in the finest of hospitals. This woman, in her isolated village, lived on for four days, six days, eight days, even nine days. She had a great will to live but her family knew that she had no chance. They ordered a coffin made and had it ready outside the door. But a native missionary in the area heard of the case, came to the village, and insisted that she be taken to the hospital in Montemorelos. Weather was bad and flying was impracticable, so the suffering woman was literally thrown up on top of a produce truck and jounced over the most impossible of mountain roads for hours—the road made eighty-three crossings over the rocky beds of mountain streams—until finally she arrived at the hospital. The pain was so intense that she had lapsed into a coma early in the trip.

Dr. Donald B. Miller looked at the unconscious woman as soon as she arrived. She was barely breathing, and from what he could see, plus what the people who brought her in told him, he knew that there was no medical possibility whatsoever of her surviving. "The only question," Dr. Miller said later, "was whether she would die while I was trying to save her, or whether she would just die. I knew that if I cut into that swollen abdomen there'd be a frightful mess. And yet, well, I decided to let her die while I was at least trying."

He ordered the woman taken into the clean little operating room, had the young nurses in their fresh starched uniforms get her ready. He went outside, cut off a length of the new plastic garden hose he had just bought, and brought it in with him. He placed a large bucket by the operating table. Then he made the incision and thrust the hose into it. After cleaning out the abdominal cavity as best he could, he cut off the strangulated portion of the intestine, then took the smaller of the two ends, thrust it into the larger, and sewed it carefully, all around. He noticed that above the hernia the intestines were so distended that there was no elasticity left in them at all; they were like stretched-out rubber bands. Without this elasticity the woman, even if she lived after the operation, would be unable to eliminate afterward. She was doubly doomed.

Dr. Miller sewed the patient up, looked at her sadly and shook his head, then left the operating room. At the door he issued orders to start digging the grave. And then one of the nurses, María Inez Medina, stopped him.

"Couldn't we," she asked, "call the chaplain?"

"Of course," Dr. Miller said. It was a busy day, with many other patients waiting, but he and the nurses nevertheless remained in the operating room while the chaplain, Andrés Pérez, led them in prayers. Then he left, to see about his other patients.

Twenty minutes later, on his rounds, he saw María Inez running toward him. "Doctor, Doctor," she cried breathless. "The patient asked for a bedpan!"

"That's impossible," he said automatically. In the first place the woman, even if still hanging on to life, would be incapable of thought or speech. In the second place, it would be impossible for her to eliminate; those stretched intestines were simply incapable of creating peristaltic motion.

"Really, Doctor, please come!" the nurse pleaded, and he ran after her to the patient. She was lying on her bed, fully conscious, a smile of life and gratitude on her lips. And she was in the very process of filling the bedpan.

Dr. Miller looked around him, at the smiling faces of the chaplain, the student nurses, María Inez, and for a moment he was speechless. Then the impact hit—he had witnessed a miracle, here in this very hospital. The words burst out of his mouth:

"The Lord has answered our prayer! He is paying attention to our little hospital! Let us thank Him!"

And so, standing in a circle around the smiling woman, doctor, chaplain and nurses all bowed their heads and gave thanks to God for the miracle. The patient recovered rapidly, and soon Dr. Miller was able to fly her back to her children and family. But not before she had accepted Christ herself, and had been baptized by the chaplain who had prayed for her.

10 *Go, Ye Swift Messengers*

Though most of the men and women who first brought the new faith to distant lands were ordained missionaries and medical workers, they were also, in more than one sense of the word, traveling salesmen. Their line consisted of tracts and books published by the Seventh-day Adventist publishing houses. The church word for them was, and is, *colporteur,* pronounced "call porter" and meaning, in French, to carry from the neck. In many of the countries where the first emissaries of the church were the colporteurs, they not only carried their books from their necks, but the whole church on their backs. In the Philippines, in Russia, in many other areas of the world, the church sent missionaries only after the colporteurs had paved the way, spreading the gospel at no cost to the churchgoers back home, and making a living for themselves and a profit for the publishing houses.

From the very beginnings of the colporteur system right up to the present, some of these self-supporting emissaries in out-of-the-way places have faced scorn, vituperation, and physical danger. In the 1890s a pioneer colporteur in Brazil named A. B. Stauffer was walking through the square of a village when a local man, urged on by the authorities, stepped up and felled him with one blow from a heavy club. As Stauffer lay helpless on the ground, the club rose and fell, administering crippling blows. When the brutal beating was done, police appeared on the scene, and arrested, not the assailant, but the broken man, lying in his own blood. But though Stauffer was broken in body, he was not broken in spirit. As soon as he could get on his feet once more, he hobbled into the courtroom to defend himself against the trumped-up charges. And in the courtroom the balance of power shifted, for while his assailant was not permitted to bring his club into court, Stauffer proudly carried his weapon under his arm. It was his Bible.

The prosecution had summoned the assailant himself, and other witnesses, to court to testify that Stauffer had made an unprovoked assault on the innocent townsman. When the first witness stood up to give his false testimony, Stauffer confronted him with his Bible. The witness could not say a word. His tongue was paralyzed, and he left the stand. Then the assailant himself stood up. Stauffer, his Bible in his hand, confronted the man; the prosecuting attorney was amazed to hear him confess that he himself was the guilty one, then turn to the colporteur and ask his forgiveness. He even agreed to buy a book. The case collapsed, and the assailant himself became the first Seventh-day Adventist baptized in the village.

Not all colporteurs escaped with a beating in the early days. Rafael López, a Puerto Rican working in Venezuela, sat down and wrote a letter home one night. "I am leaving for another fanatical town," he wrote. "But I cannot leave the country to Satan, for he would laugh at his pleasure. Pray that I may have the courage and strength until the last moment." The next morning he started out over the rocky mountain road to the village. He never reached his destination; assassins attacked him on the mountain and murdered him. But his very death brought dividends to the Lord. For his bravery, dedication and faith were the factors which proved to many people of the area that the way of Rafael was the right way, and they were baptized in the Seventh-day Adventist faith.

The tradition of the colporteurs is a long and proud one in the history of the church. We have seen how, far back in 1845, Captain Joseph Bates sat down to write a book, saying, "I cannot go everywhere, but a book can." As the church became organized, groups of Sabbath-keepers formed tract societies which mailed out literature all over the world. Over the years they became in effect branch offices of the Seventh-day Adventist publishing houses, and grew officially into what are now known as Book and Bible Houses.

Still earlier, years before the church was officially organized, preachers at tent meetings had found it easier to sell their small variety of tracts and pamphlets, at prices ranging from two cents to thirty-five cents, than it was to give them away; the people were more eager to get, read and heed literature on which a value had been placed.

The first real impetus to the colporteur system came, as might be expected, from the mind and pen of Ellen G. White. She worked out the entire system. "Hundreds of men should be engaged in carrying the light all through our cities, villages and towns . . . ," she wrote in 1879. "In all parts of the field canvassers should be selected, not from the floating element in society, not from among men and women who are good for nothing else and have made a success of nothing, but from among those who have good address, tact, keen foresight and ability. Such are needed to make a success as colporteurs. . . . The efficient colporteur, as well as the minister, should have a sufficient remuneration for his services if his work is faithfully done."

At the time there were no colporteurs, no one to select and train them, and precious little for them to sell. But, as was the case in nearly everything Mrs. White said or wrote, it was purely a matter of time before it came to pass. Her instrument was a tongue-tied young Canadian named George King who had come to Battle Creek seeking to be a preacher. James White, feeling pretty certain that the young man would never be able to hold an audience, but not wishing to send him back home, prevailed upon one of the church's most stalwart supporters, Richard Godsmark, to give him a job on the Godsmark farm.

Young King insisted that he wanted to preach, and "Uncle Richard," as the old farmer was affectionately known to all Sabbath-keepers in southern Michigan, called a special meeting of the church just to give the boy a chance. Before the assemblage, however, the young man's impediment of speech became even more pronounced, and he could not hold the congregation's attention.

The young man was so crestfallen that Uncle Richard gave him another chance. "Here," he said on the spur of the moment, "I'll give you some of my supply of literature, and you take it out and see what you can do with it. Maybe you'll do better just talking to one or two people at a time."

King trudged off down the country road with his bundle of tracts; he was back within a week, with empty hands, full pocket, and a radiant face. Maybe he couldn't preach, but he could sure sell tracts!

George added the *Health Reformer* magazine, just about the only health literature then available, to his stock, and that went well too. But the entire lot of Adventist literature, magazines, pamphlets and all, could be purchased for three dollars. Like good salesmen in all lines, he wished that he had something really imposing and profitable to sell. He attended the General Conference in 1880 and buttonholed the church officials with his proposal: Take the two small tracts of Uriah Smith, *Thoughts on Daniel* and *Thoughts on Revelation,* then the most popular publications of the church, and bind them into one handsome, illustrated bound volume. The technicians of the publishing company, with Conference approval, gave him what he wanted, a large book, complete with full-page illustrations, and bound not only in cloth but in more expensive editions of sheepskin and morocco. Prices ranged from $1.50 to $5—expensive indeed for the year 1881. Few believed that even George King could sell a book at those prices, but he took the first copy off the press and sold it to the first person he encountered, without even leaving the building. His commission, incidentally, was 50 per cent; now, as Mrs. White had predicted, George King and his fellow colporteurs could bring the Adventist story to the people and earn a comfortable living besides.

Mrs. White's *The Great Controversy between Christ and Satan,* a book still selling well today, was soon added to the colporteur's stock, and then others, one by one. Under the leadership and training of George King more and more young men and women took up this way of life. Never, from the very beginning to the present, has just anyone been accepted as a colporteur. Devotion, sincerity and character come before salesmanship. As a result, thousands on thousands of people the world over have been converted to the Seventh-day Adventist church without ever seeing any church member save a colporteur.

Under King and his successors a small army of colporteurs went out into the world. In Australia, a profitable printing press was in operation long before the first church was organized on the continent. A colporteur named R. A. Caldwell was the first Seventh-day Adventist in the Philippines. His work went slowly at first; in 1912, seven years after he had first landed in the islands, there were 100 Sabbath-keepers. Another colporteur who came to join him was killed by bandits. But at the end of the next seven-year period there were 6000 baptized members of the Seventh-day Adventist church in the Philippines, and today there are 70,000, all descendants, you might say, of one colporteur.

In Czarist Russia, a German farmer in the Crimea received a stack of literature from a relative in Minnesota. He read it, but, afraid that it would be deemed subversive by the state and its official church, kept it hidden away. Finally, he showed one tract, *The Third Angel's Message,* to a trusted friend, Gerhardt Perk, after swearing him to secrecy. Perk hid the tract under his shirt, went to his barn, climbed up into the haymow and, safe from spying eyes, read it through three times then and there. Then he sent to America for more. Eventually, entirely through the printed word, he became the first Seventh-day Adventist in Russia. Later, an American, L. R. Conradi, became the first Seventh-day Adventist minister to visit that huge, sprawling country. He and Perk set out to sell their literature, and were almost immediately jailed for teaching "Jewish" heresy. For weeks they lived in a little cell with a dirt floor, eating black bread and borscht, before they were released. They immediately went right back to work, selling and preaching, though perhaps a bit more cautiously. Today the thousands of Seventh-day Adventists in Russia can thank Gerhardt Perk as the instrument through which they found their faith.

The stories of colporteurs are legion and worldwide. In the American South a colporteur, wandering down a hot, dusty road, stopped at a cool spring for a refreshing drink of water. As he bent over, a copperhead struck him in the wrist. Seeking help, he stopped at the first house down the road, but the occupants had nothing to give him but turpentine, which is certainly no antidote for snakebite. Strangely, however, the young man seemed to be suffering no ill effects. From all over the county people came to see the young man who was impervious to snakebite. He sold many books that way, too, but he did not recommend that other colporteurs adopt the same sales gimmick.

Probably nowhere in the world have the colporteurs more dramatic success than in Brazil. In some countries colporteurs travel by automobile, in some they travel by muleback or afoot, but in the Amazon valley their mode of transportation is a canoe. These canoes are about fifteen feet long, with high sides so that alligators can't crawl on and overturn them, with a roof made of palm and banana leaves to shed the rain. Under this roof the colporteurs both store their supply of books, and stretch their little cot. Most canoes carry a kerosene can lined with fire clay which serves as a stove. The colporteurs carry a supply of dried beans and rice, get what vegetables and fruits they can along the way. And, of course, there are always fish. These canoes date back to thirty years ago, when the lightbearer of the Amazon, Leo Halliwell, staged a great campaign with the slogan "Fifty Canoes with Fifty Colporteurs." In these fifty canoes the fifty colporteurs have ranged through the Amazon valley, frequently going far out ahead even of the Halliwells.

Because the colporteurs are interested in spreading the word of God as well as making a profit, they sometimes spend time on dubious prospects. One colporteur in Brazil had been warned that one of the cabins along the river was occupied only by an old blind man, so poor that he could not have bought a book even had he been able to read one. Nevertheless the colporteur paid a call; if he couldn't sell the word of God, maybe he could give it away. The colporteur spent some time with the old man, telling him of the future world that lay before him, where there would be no blindness, and all could see the glorious works of God. When he got up to go, the blind man said that he had certainly enjoyed the visit—but why had he come there in the first place? The colporteur admitted he was a salesman, and that his product was books that told in writing and pictures the faith he had just described.

"May I feel one?" the old man asked, and sighed as he passed his hands over the cover. He got up, took some money out of a secret hoard, and purchased the book. Then he wrapped it in a cloth and stored it carefully in the bottom of a trunk.

"My little grandson is almost old enough now to go to school," he explained to the colporteur. "Soon he will be able to read to me. This book will be waiting."

In spite of such departures from sound business practices in selling, the colporteurs do get their work done. Just recently in Brazil, Selemias Lima set a new record. He put together three large books to make one set, and personally took 274 orders, for a total of 832 books, in twelve days. Hilda Mascimento, tired of trudging around with her books, thought of a way to get her customers to come to her. She marched into the Rio de Janeiro bus station, set up a little stand, and now happily sells some 5000 copies of church magazines a month.

Sometimes their success amazes even the colporteurs. A member of another church in a town in the state of São Paulo asked a colporteur if he had a book on that church. The colporteur was sorry, he didn't, but he did happen to have a copy of *The Great Controversy* with him at the time. The man read the book, passed it around, then invited the colporteur to his church to discuss the tenets of the

Seventh-day Adventist faith. Within a month half the congregation, including the pastor, were holding services on the Sabbath.

Colporteurs sometimes run into fascinating experiences, for which there can be no explanation except that God is taking a hand in their work. On one occasion a colporteur named Sergio Cabalieri was trudging along from door to door when two Brazilian Army sergeants stopped him. One asked him what he was doing, and he explained that he was selling books. The sergeant asked what church published the books, and while the other sergeant heckled and made abusive remarks, Cabalieri explained what the Seventh-day Adventist church was, and its beliefs.

"Then this is the church for me," the sergeant said, as his buddy laughed loud in scorn. "Last night I dreamed that I was standing outside a great open church. Several people stood at the door, inviting the passers-by to enter. I know that I never saw you before in my life, but one of the people I saw in that dream was you. And you told me, 'Come in, but come in awake.' "

Within a week the sergeant and his wife were attending Bible study at the church. But that wasn't the end of the story. Many months later Cabalieri saw the sergeant who had been heckling them in a Seventh-day Adventist church. He, too, had been impressed with the message of God, and he and his wife had both become baptized church members.

And so it goes all over the world. Just recently in Texas, a colporteur named Herbert Morgan set out to make a record selling *Drama of the Ages* by W. H. Branson, and subscriptions to *Life and Health*.

He planned to devote four minutes to introducing himself and his wares, five minutes to showing them, five minutes to listing the order, and one minute for prayer—a total of fifteen minutes for each customer. Between each house he would also offer up a silent prayer. In ninety-one hours he sold $2500.75 worth of books.

In Indonesia colporteurs also do well. There are more Moslems,

75 million, in Indonesia than in any other country in the world. Moslems are health fanatics, and they love the Seventh-day Adventist health books. One such book has sold 60,000 copies in Indonesia. (A high official of a Moslem country once announced publicly: "The Adventists are a very good people, much like Moslems. They don't drink liquor, smoke, attend evil cinemas, nor do they have any other evil habits.")

The large Seventh-day Adventist publishing house in Singapore prints books in Chinese, Vietnamese, Malay, Siamese, Tamil, Dusin, Telegu and French. Its president, Henry W. Peterson, decided a year or so ago to stimulate sales in Laos by making a foray into Vientiane with a large supply of books. Getting the books into Vientiane was the first problem. He had them shipped to Bangkok, where he picked them up and personally started out with them to Laos. He rode all night in the baggage car of a slow, little train to the Mekong River, the boundary line between Thailand and Laos. There he had them transferred to a boat over the river, and to another train on the Laos side, haggling with the customs officials of each country to get his books through.

Once in Vientiane Peterson started his sales campaign with the Chinese merchants. He knew one word of Chinese, *towkay,* meaning "boss," and he made that word go far. He would walk into a store, pick out the most important-looking person, go up to him, point a finger, and ask, *"Towkay?"* Whether he was right or not, the person so addressed was flattered, and, by means of signs and a few words of pidgin English, Peterson would attempt to sell his books. After the first sale it was easy. He got the purchaser to put his "chop," or personal identification mark, in the order book. From then on all he had to do was find the towkay, and point to the chop. Naturally no Chinese merchant wanted any other Chinese to have what he himself did not have, and so he would purchase the book and proudly add his chop. After he ran out of Chinese, Peterson began on the other merchants of Vientiane, who naturally did not want the Chinese to have anything they did not have. And so he sold a thousand sets a week.

Seventh-day Adventist publishing houses around the world are both big business and interesting business. The church has 42 publishing houses in all, four in North America, publishing in 214 languages. This does not include houses which have been lost to the Communists. In Shanghai a big publishing house and a printing school have fallen into their hands and have been written off. The houses in Budapest and Warsaw have also been taken over. No word has been heard from the small printing shop near the Tibetan border. In both the Philippines and Indo-China the plants were blown up during the fighting, but have been replaced by new ones. (In Indo-China, colporteurs went right up to the front lines; six lost their lives.) In Korea, the Japanese took over the plant early in World War II, and simply wore it out. When the Seventh-day Adventists went back into Korea after the war, they were able to get their material out only through the friendly cooperation of several different groups. Their type was set by a Methodist printing house, and the cuts were made by Catholics. The paper was hauled in by the Army from Pusan, and when everything was ready to go, the Communist prisoners in the Seoul federal prison ran the press and folded the papers.

In Germany and Japan during World War II, the publishing houses continued as long as they could. In Germany the manager was called repeatedly before the Gestapo, and as a result he lost his health. But as soon as the war was ended, the presses started rolling again and the colporteurs got right back on the job. In Japan, too, the presses are rolling again; one of the best printers happens to be an ex-Kamikaze pilot.

Perhaps typifying the work of the 6000 colporteurs over the world —their sales total $25,000,000 a year—is André Gedrath, one of the veteran colporteurs of Brazil. Leo Halliwell tells how Brother André preceded him into the state of Maranhão by three years. He was received kindly there, and sold a great number of books. The church received so many letters telling of people observing the Sabbath in the far-off reaches of Maranhão that Elder Halliwell and Elder Roger Wilcox, the mission director, set out on a special inspection trip. They traveled for five days up a small river by launch, then hired mules and journeyed three more days by muleback. Finally they reached the town of Jeju, consisting of one dirt street three miles long. On the front of one of the buildings they found a big sign saying "Seventh-day Adventist School." And there indeed was a large, efficient school in a town that had never been visited by any Seventh-day Adventist except André Gedrath, the colporteur.

The two elders visited the home of the teacher, and were much impressed by the cleanliness of the interior, so different from the squalor of many houses that far inland. As Halliwell glanced around the parlor, he noticed a huge picture frame hung on the wall. In one corner was the picture of the president of Brazil, in another the governor of the State. Two other government officials were in the other corners, but in the center, mounted on gold paper, was a picture of André Gedrath. In that town, and with good reason, the most important man in the nation was their colporteur.

11 *Labor of Love*

Little Myrtle McClary began working for the Seventh-day Adventist church when she was barely big enough to pull out basting threads at Dorcas Society meetings. It was a labor of love, for the church was in her blood. She was a fourth-generation Seventh-day Adventist on her father's side, third-generation on her mother's; she had been born two doors from the church. But her greatest work began when she was in her thirties, married to Chester A. Meyer of Worcester, Massachusetts, and the mother of two children. One of the church elders suggested that she start a welfare center in the church, and to Myrtle Meyer the suggestion was enough. From then on she lived for her welfare society; to many of her fellow church workers she was a prime nuisance, to others she was, well, just a bit gone on the subject. She insisted that the center stock inordinate supplies of clothing, bedding, bandages and medical supplies. She had attractive green uniforms made, to be worn by members on duty. She had special forms printed up, with spaces for vital information and case histories of people who might need aid in the event of some dread disaster. She insisted that church members not only take first-aid training courses, but that they repeat them periodically to avoid getting rusty.

"But why are we doing all this, Myrtle?" her exhausted co-workers would ask. "What in the world can happen to us here in Worcester to make all these supplies necessary?"

"Anything can happen," Myrtle would reply grimly. "An enemy attack, a flood, even a—a tornado! It pays to be prepared!"

The friends would laugh—imagine a tornado in Massachusetts!—but they nevertheless kept working. It was easier to do the job than to face Myrtle Meyer. For years the women of the welfare center had to go out and find needy people to take some of the supplies that were pouring in. But gradually Tuesdays at the center became full, busy days, with often as many as thirty families coming to seek help. One of those Tuesdays, June 9, 1953, was a particularly hot and busy day. Nineteen families had been cared for, the center cleaned and clothing put away, the floor swept and the door locked, when Myrtle Meyer was finally able to leave. She got home just as a terrible thunderstorm broke, and lay down to rest for a few moments before getting supper for her family. As the wind roared outside, she thought of the tornado which had struck Flint, Michigan, just a few days before and which she'd been reading about in the papers. What would she do if a tornado struck Worcester and she was spared, she wondered. Probably hustle back to the welfare center, she thought wryly.

Just then her husband rushed in. "Myrtle!" he cried. "It's a tornado!" They dashed to the radio and cut it on. An excited voice was pouring out the news. Destruction was everywhere. Whole areas in Worcester had been completely leveled, with hundreds of people killed and wounded, thousands homeless. Everything was needed—blood, medical supplies, bandages, food, clothing, bedding, housing and comfort for the stricken. The terrible catastrophe that Myrtle Meyer had been preparing for was now full upon the city. And she did what she had thought she would do: She hustled to the welfare center.

After a night of agony, confusion and misery, the clear dawn broke on a terrible scene of anguish and suffering. War veterans who had seen the bombed cities of Europe said that there was even more destruction in the leveled sections of Worcester. A housing development where nearly 800 families resided had been completely destroyed, with men, women and children killed and injured. Fiberglass insulation had been used in the construction, and the flying stuff had become imbedded in the skin and eyes of many people, including children and babies. The lungs of some people had exploded. There were bodies without heads, without arms, without legs. A slide from a venetian blind had been driven through the body of one man, but still he lived; rescue workers, fearing to remove the slat themselves, had simply bent the ends flat and taken the man to the hospital. A man who had seen the tornado coming had fallen flat on his face; some flying object had ripped his back open, and he was taken to the hospital with one kidney hanging out of his body. A woman who had prayed for a child for nearly ten years of her marriage, and who had been blessed with a lovely baby just a few days before the tornado, had gathered the child in her arms and rushed out in the street. The wind had torn the baby from her grasp, and blown the little body several hundred yards away.

Hospitals were full. Thousands were homeless; many of them had no funds, clothes, food. All was confusion and chaos, except in one building. For by eight o'clock in the morning, Mrs. Meyer had secured the telephone priority and had rounded up a staff of assistants, all uniformed. A big sign RELIEF CLOTHING DEPOT OPEN was up in front of the church, and eggs were cooking in the kitchen. Victims and clothes began arriving at the same time. People in the undamaged area around the church took sheets and blankets off their own beds, emptied their closets for the welfare center. Most of the damage had been done to houses in the nice new section of town where people were used to good things, and the Dorcas Welfare Society did not let them down. Mrs. Meyer was passing out brand new sheets and pillowcases wrapped in cellophane while other organizations were still running around looking for ragged ones to give out. Other agencies sent people to the welfare center for items they themselves did not have, such as size 52 women's clothes and trousers with 46-inch waistlines. The center even passed out numerous layettes, complete, for the babies born during that period. From the first day on, Mrs. Meyer and her girls fed from 500 to 700 people a day.

At noon, the center started running canteens out to all the disaster areas, and continued until 3 A.M., day after day. They fed victims, guards, police and workmen. Bakeries provided hundreds of loaves of bread, one dairy donated sufficient milk for all needs, and other food industries came forward with hundreds of cases of goods. The center even had an abundance of paper cups. Although soldiers with bayoneted rifles guarded the police lines, the women in the green uniforms had no difficulty at all getting anywhere they wanted to go; those uniforms became the best pass in Worcester. The head of the local office of Civilian Defense, in an army jeep with two soldiers, preceded the canteens into each post and called out the wares over the loudspeaker system. Whenever a canteen would show up people would come down from roofs and up from cellars, crowd around, calling the green-clad girls angels.

The canteen girls even became rescue workers. Two days and nights after the tornado hit, girls from one canteen found a whole family, unhurt but dazed and unfed, sitting blankly in the debris of their home. The girls gave them food, and they turned out to be ravenous. After eating they were taken to the hospital.

All welfare agencies worked together, and all denominational lines were erased—Catholics, Jews and Protestants combined forces. In many surrounding towns all places of worship joined together to collect food, clothing and bedding, bundled it up in one lot, and brought it to the Seventh-day Adventist center. Although the primary mission of the welfare center was to serve the unfortunate people in need of so many things, one by-product was certainly evident: Everybody in Worcester today knows who the Seventh-day Adventists are.

The center dispensed money for necessary prescriptions, as well as dispensing thousands of dollars' worth of medicines donated by pharmaceutical houses. One store gave a hundred pairs of slippers, which people in hospitals appreciated. Others gave shoes and all types of clothing. Two baby furniture manufacturers even came up with truckloads of new baby carriages, cribs and high chairs.

Mrs. Meyer sent letters to all the patients in the hospitals, assuring them that there would be plenty of clothes, bedding and other supplies waiting for them when they left. Many of these patients said that this was the most thoughtful thing that had happened during the entire period; they had been lying helpless in their beds wondering and fretting about what they would do when they got out to find all the supplies already given out.

After a few days many of the women who had previously scoffed at her for her insistence on uniforms were now coming up and pleading not for a uniform, but just for the pattern. Other organizations, seeing how the green-clad ladies were waved through police lines, wished that they, too, had some such identification. But it was not just the uniform, nor even the desire and willingness to serve; what really counted in those first few days was the preparation Myrtle Meyer had carried on over a period of years in the face of apathy and even ridicule. Her one-woman campaign was repaid a millionfold in tearful smiles of gratitude.

All over America, and over much of the world, the Seventh-day Adventists have faced up to the true yet alarming fact that with the advantages of civilization have come potential dangers, too, which can strike where they are the least expected. Who would ever dream, for example, that catastrophe could strike the quiet, little town of Roseburg, Oregon? Yet when Elder Walter R. Riston moved to Roseburg as new pastor of the Seventh-day Adventist church, he saw to it that the welfare society was ready for whatever might come. The warehouse was well-stocked with clothing, bedding, bandages and other vital supplies. The women maintained a tight welfare organization, and the men repeated their first-aid training regularly, keeping themselves sharp and abreast of the latest information. Pastor Riston's flock was ready to serve the people of Roseburg, but there were some who did not appreciate his efforts, among them, some members of the ministerial association. He was denied membership in the local ministerial council.

One night the driver of a truck loaded with six tons of explosives, some of which were to be delivered to a local store, pulled into Roseburg. It was too late to make delivery so the driver parked his truck outside the store and went to a nearby hotel and to bed. Later that night a fire broke out in a building near the parked truck. The sirens awakened the driver and he ran to move the truck, but he was too late. The six tons of explosives went off in one mighty blast. Thirteen persons were killed; one was a policeman of whom nothing was found but his belt buckle. Over 125 people were injured and houses all around were leveled. The truck simply disintegrated; an axle was found several blocks away. The Seventh-day Adventist school, a full mile away, was damaged. The explosion left a crater fifteen feet deep, forty feet in diameter; the pilot of a plane passing over Roseburg at the time saw the explosion, and reported later that he had thought the Russians had dropped a bomb.

Pastor Riston, who lived some distance away from the explosion, was notified by telephone at 1:40 A.M.; he was at the welfare center, getting things organized before 2:00. The women of the church went directly to the hospital to serve as nurses' aides, while men went to the area to give first aid. They found hundreds of persons seriously injured, many in advanced stages of shock. One man was busy directing traffic, seemingly unaware that his arm had been blown off.

By five o'clock the welfare center was open, ready with food, clothing and bedding. The Red Cross turned over the problem of blankets and bedding to the center, and everyone who needed any necessary item was supplied. Troops of the National Guard, called out to prevent looting, were fed by the church ladies. The welfare society secured a truck, and collected more material. Strangely, the center was busy for weeks, as homeless people who had left town immediately began drifting back; actually, the center was busier a month after the accident than it was the next day.

From the experiences in Roseburg, the quiet little town where nothing ever happened, the welfare society was able to pass on several items that others had learned. To be fully effective in disaster work, Pastor Riston advised, the welfare society needs a mobile unit, with identifying decals, and identifying uniforms for its members. And though the men of the church did excellent first-aid work, they would have been even more effective had they had training in light rescue work.

As a final sequel to the tragedy, the townspeople honored Walter Riston and his flock for their work. He was also invited to join the ministerial council.

On a national level and in Seventh-day Adventist communities all over America, the church cooperates fully with the Office of Civilian Defense. OCD authorities point with pride to the excellent cooperation of the church, and use it as a model and inspiration for other groups and communities. Church officials see nothing unusual in being prepared for any eventuality. When asked why they are so strong on Civilian Defense, they reply, in effect, why not? They are adjured by the Bible to be loyal to their government, and part of this loyalty is to be ready in the event of war. Further, a good civilian defense set-up can be transformed immediately into disaster relief. The members of the church get a great satisfaction out of helping their fellow man in time of travail; also, their superlative welfare work helps them spread the gospel not only to the people they comfort, but to the millions more who hear about their activities. For remember that a primary mission of the church is to spread the gospel—and who will give a more attentive ear than a homeless family which has been fed, clothed, and helped to find new housing?

In their connection with Civilian Defense work, some individual congregations have carried on worthwhile experiments in evacuation work and large-scale emergency feeding. A group of students of Washington Missionary College, for example, carried out a complete evacuation exercise en masse, even including small children. Equipped only with twelve-pound survival kits containing a high-calorie, high-protein diet sufficient for three days, plus water, medicine, bandages and plastic table cloths for tenting, they proceeded to a wooded area twelve miles away and spent three days in near-freezing weather completely apart from civilization. They returned none the worse off for their experience and with many worthwhile suggestions to make to the Office of Civilian Defense.

The Seventh-day Adventist churches of Atlanta, Georgia, chose one subfreezing Sunday in the winter of 1960 for their wholesale evacuation from the city. Not only was the temperature twenty-two degrees, mighty cold for Atlanta, but an hour or so before the scheduled time for the evacuation a freezing rain began to fall. In spite of the lack of cooperation from the weather, in less than one hour, 554 people were evacuated from the church to an area some twenty miles from the city. Ninety-eight cars, one truck and one pickup truck participated in the movement. Once on the chosen scene, every one of the members was fed well, all in the space of fifty-five minutes, from ovens built in the area from the ground up. The whole operation was covered by local television stations and it received glowing congratulations from authorities of Civil Defense.

Nowhere is the Seventh-day Adventist–Civil Defense organization in better shape than in the state of Texas. M. H. Jensen, State Welfare Director, and the Texas organization have had the dubious benefit of much experience in working out their program; the welfare societies have been active in a dozen disasters in the state. One of their first lessons came in 1953, when a tornado hit the town of Waco. The welfare society in Waco was on the job immediately, feeding 200 people a day and dispensing clothing. Within ten minutes after being called, Jensen was on the road from headquarters at Fort Worth with the conference truck, delivering more supplies. When they didn't last Jensen got in touch with other local societies and had more rushed to Waco. Other organizations turned over what they had to the Adventists for processing and delivery.

All in all, they handed out about 25,000 pounds of clothing and tons of food. They built a new home for one of the particularly hard-hit families—and built it in one day. At 7 A.M. one morning a labor force of sixty volunteers bowed their heads in a short devotional service in a vacant lot, then went to work. That night the house was built, lights, gas and water were on, and the family moved in. The head of the family, a man who had lost both legs in a previous accident, was almost speechless with amazement and gratitude. What seemed to impress him most was that he was not even a member of the church. "The Seventh-day Adventists building a home for a Baptist!" he kept repeating.

No question about it, the Seventh-day Adventist program in Waco was a success. Everyone in the area knew who they were, and what they had done. "This is Christianity in action," many people said. "This is practical religion," said others. A colored minister, after watching a house built in a day, said, "I call this religion on wheels."

But Jensen knew that the church could have done a better job in Waco. He set to work immediately on the part of welfare work that does not make the headlines, the preparation and organization. Before Waco, the central office had been chiefly for administration. Organization on local levels had been eager and enthusiastic, but haphazard. Under Jensen's direction the program is constantly being improved, but the basic pattern is set.

Central headquarters is located in a newly erected building in Keene, between the major cities of Dallas and Fort Worth. It contains classrooms, facilities for mass feeding, and a warehouse area. Tons of food and clothing, plus supplies and equipment of a complete 200-bed hospital, are stockpiled in this building. Clothing is stored in standard size boxes, plainly marked with labels of a separate color for each category, so that at a glance you can tell whether a box contains bedding, medical supplies, or men's, women's or children's clothing. The clothes are clean, mended, pressed and mothballed, and the boxes are sealed.

Before Waco the welfare societies had thought they could get along with local transportation. But when trucks were needed immediately, many were found to be loaded, out of town, or in the garage for repairs. So now central headquarters has its own truck, a huge army surplus tractor-trailer with ten gears and a ten-wheel drive. It can go anywhere. Each local welfare chairman keeps an up-to-date list of all equipment that may be necessary, including trucks, cranes, hydraulic jacks—everything. The local chairman keeps in constant touch with Civilian Defense, Red Cross, and other such organizations, city leaders, police, highway patrol, and the National Guard. Each chairman has a list of buildings which can be used in an emergency—churches, warehouses, school buildings—and has on hand written permission to use them in a disaster. He also has an up-to-date list of all trained personnel available—all men and women with training in first aid, mass feeding and rescue work, doctors and nurses, as well as electricians, plumbers, shortwave radio operators and anyone else who can do a specific job in an emergency.

Seventy communities in Texas have this kind of efficient set-up. Each one, of course, rests upon the shoulders of dedicated members of the local community, people like Mrs. Sermon of Athens. Mrs. Sermon was visiting in California when she suffered a severe heart attack. Doctors told her that her only hope was to go to bed immediately for a long period of recuperation. But Mrs. Sermon refused. "I've got to get back to Athens," she explained. "We don't have a church there yet, just a few isolated members, and they need me to help start the welfare center."

"You'll never do welfare work and you'll never see Texas if you start out now," the doctor told her grimly. "You'll be buried in Arizona or New Mexico."

But Mrs. Sermon got back to Athens. There her family doctor examined her, and, expressing amazement that she had made the trip at all, told her she had to go to bed and stay there for a long, long time.

Mrs. Sermon had no intention of going to bed. First she went out to find a location for the welfare center. Jensen went to Athens to inspect the place she had selected, and told her that as a welfare center it would never do. But she proved him wrong; it is now an excellent center, and the rent is one dollar for five years. She supervised the stocking and inventory of every item in it. A year later she appeared at the state meeting bubbling over with enthusiasm, reporting that the center had helped 126 people. She seemed in perfect health.

"My doctor says for me to do all the welfare work I want to," she said, proudly, "it must be good for my heart."

With such an organization and such people helping, the Adventists were ready when the terrible Dallas tornado struck. Shortly after he heard the news on the radio, Jensen had help on the way. The trained team found welfare work in a terrible mess. Of the thousands of persons needing equipment of all kinds, the boldest had pushed to the front and gotten what they needed, while the timid, and often those in most need, were left out. The first thing the Adventist team did was close and lock the doors, and get things in order. They handled the whole production on an efficient, businesslike basis. With a van load of supplies to work with, and with the Red Cross doing the case work to determine the neediest, the Adventist team was able to give every qualified person two complete work outfits from tip to toe and from inside out, and one outfit for Sunday best, all in the correct size. Every qualified family was given food for a balanced diet for five days. In the meantime clothing and food was pouring in from businesses, institutions, and people from all over the state and country. As one group of Seventh-day workers were dispensing equipment, another was receiving, inspecting, sorting and packing every item which came in. When it was all over, each item of clothing left over was apportioned to the local centers to be mended, cleaned, packed and sent back to the depot, ready to go out again.

It all came in just in time, too, for a flood wiped out a good part of the city of Lampasas. Again the Red Cross and other organizations simply turned over the distribution of clothing to the Seventh-day Adventist team, and again, they did a good job.

Though the welfare societies carry out their work in an efficient manner, this does not mean that they are impersonal. In Waco a woman came to the welfare center and asked for help. She was asked if she was a disaster victim and, almost sadly, she replied that she was not. Because of that, she had been turned away from several other organizations. But, she explained, her husband had left her several weeks ago, taking all the money there was except twenty-five dollars. She had six children to feed, and she was not in the best of health. Her family was out of money, out of food, out of clothing.

One of the volunteer workers put together a box of supplies for her, loaded it into a pickup truck, and took it to her home himself. He quickly saw that the situation was truly one of desperate need. One of the little girls, in ragged clothing and with the pinched face of hunger, ran up and asked, "Mother, did you get us anything to eat?"

"Yes, darling, I did," the mother replied, then fell on her knees by the child, enfolded her in her arms, and burst into tears.

When the volunteer worker returned to the welfare center and reported to Jensen, the director asked him if he had said anything. "No," the man replied sheepishly, "I didn't say a word. If I'd opened my mouth I would have burst out crying myself."

After the Dallas tornado Jensen and his crew took over the disaster area on the Texas-Mexico border near Brownsville, where the flooding Rio Grande rendered 14,000 people homeless. A cold rain was falling, the whole area buzzed with mosquitoes, but thousands upon thousands of homeless slept night after night on the built-up highways; everywhere else was under water. The clothing the Seventh-day Adventists handed out was probably far better than that most of the people had ever had.

At one o'clock one morning in the fall of 1959, Jensen received a long-distance telephone call from the Mexican Red Cross. A hurricane had struck the west coast of Mexico. Villages were wiped out completely; the proud seaport of Manzanillo was simply a pile of ruins. Flooded streams buried the populations of whole villages alive in up to thirty feet of mud. Survivors were in great danger from disease and snake bites. Particularly dangerous were the millions of *alacranes,* poisonous scorpions which lived in the thatched roofs of the houses; scores of people were dying from their bites daily.

Jensen loaded up tons of clothes, food and medical supplies, particularly antibiotics, vaccines and antivenom. The wife of the president of Mexico, Señora Eva de López Mateos, was supervising the relief operations herself; Jensen thoughtfully consigned everything to her care. As a result the convoy breezed down the 700 miles from the border to the stricken area with a police escort. When customs officials opened the boxes of clothing before Señora Mateos, and they all saw the beautifully packed, plastic-wrapped garments, their eyes opened wide with wonder and gratitude.

But the Texas Adventists were not the only ones to go to the aid of the stricken area. G. Herbert Fleenor, administrator of the Montemorelos hospital, flew a team of doctors and nurses from the hospital over the mountains in his plane. Fleenor landed in places which seemed impossible—"You're either a great pilot or a big fool!" a Mexican Air Force general told him—but they brought help to thousands of miserable sufferers. "I have seen the destruction of war in the islands of the Pacific," Fleenor said, "but never have I seen such complete destruction as this."

Altogether the Seventh-day Adventists spent a full two weeks in the stricken area. Their work was never pleasant; in one community alone 800 bodies were pulled from the flooded river. The atmosphere over the entire area was sickening. They vaccinated thousands, distributed food and clothing to thousands more, and prayed with thousands of local people who wished to seek solace from God. Even out of this nightmarish catastrophe some good was derived;

when it was brought home to the local authorities in such striking fashion that there was not one graduate nurse in the state of Colima, a spontaneous movement to organize a nursing school, with help from the Montemorelos school, got started immediately. Eventually the people of Colima will have their own nurses, and, surely, many of them will be Seventh-day Adventists.

The church maintains its welfare societies in many parts of the world, and they are always ready to help. Just recently, one Sabbath morning in Millicent, Australia, as the congregation was going into church, word came that a home was on fire just a couple of blocks away. The men of the congregation ran to help put out the fire, but they were too late; the house burned to the ground. Members of the family, newly arrived from Latvia, were not at home at the time and returned to find that they had lost everything. But on hand to soften the blow were the ladies of the Dorcas Society. They took the little family over, and did not permit them to miss one meal. They provided furniture, clothing, bedding, utensils, and a Bible, and then went on to organize a community drive to outfit the family completely.

To choose one more area at random, let's take the Dorcas Federation for the São Paulo area in Brazil, composed of thirty-four local societies. The federation carries on a constant work of providing food and clothing for the poor in the rural areas of the state of São Paulo. The local societies make much of the clothing themselves, mend and clean what they collect from their friends and neighbors, and pack and store it, along with food supplies.

And so the welfare work goes on all over the world, for in the Seventh-day Adventist church, there are many Myrtle Meyers.

12 *With Strength to Battle*

To many a young man, the arrival of a letter from his draft board is hardly a welcome surprise. To Desmond T. Doss, a young Seventh-day Adventist from Lynchburg, Virginia, the draft notice which arrived during the early days of World War II was both. It was welcome for many reasons. As a deeply religious young man, Doss knew that he was urged by the Holy Bible to give worldly allegiance to his country, and he gave it wholeheartedly. Like all Seventh-day Adventists, he was no conscientious objector but a non-combatant, a man who would serve but would not kill. While working as a carpenter in a shipyard he had taken courses in first aid to prepare himself for service as a medic if the call would come. Yet, when the summons did arrive, Doss was pleasantly surprised; there had been talk that the shipyard was seeking to have him exempted from military service.

During Desmond's first few months in the army his anticipated pleasure was not forthcoming, neither for him nor for the officers and men of his unit. He got into trouble his first day in the army. Ordered to scrub down the barracks, Doss refused; it was the Sabbath. Then, instead of being shipped to a training camp for medics, he found himself in the infantry. He refused to serve on the Sabbath, refused to carry a gun. He even refused to get out of the army, when his commanding officer tried to have him discharged as a neurotic. He was transferred out of the infantry, but it was from the frying pan to the fire, as his next unit was a tough engineering outfit. There he again refused even to touch a weapon, and as a result served so much kitchen police that the skin peeled off his hands from overexposure to lye.

Finally, through the efforts of the church's liaison bureau with the Armed Forces, Doss was put in the medics where he belonged. (So powerful was this influence that the orders came not only from General Marshall, Chief of Staff of the United States Army, but from the Commander-in-Chief himself, President Roosevelt.) To many GIs the transfer would hardly be anything to be thankful for, for now Doss was a company aid man attached to an infantry platoon of the 77th Division, bound for combat in the Pacific. A company aid man's chances of survival in battle are even less than that of the front-line soldier. The aid man not only goes with his unit into battle, but must move about to care for the wounded, while the infantry soldiers can seek cover.

Although his duties might call for him to risk his life to save theirs, the officers and men of his new unit still resented him. He had an altercation with his platoon leader, Lieutenant Cecil Gornto, when Gornto delayed in getting water to the troops in a stateside desert maneuver. Doss reported the incident to higher-ups, and Gornto hardly appreciated it. As for the company commander, Captain Frank Vernon, he thought all medics were goldbricks. His fellow soldiers were resentful of his getting Saturday off to go to church. It made little difference to them that Doss had made arrangements with a Catholic aid man by which each pulled double duty on the other's day of worship. They called him a sissy, and when he knelt to say his prayers both epithets and shoes came flying through the air at him.

But then came combat. The 77th was in the forefront of the invasion of Leyte in the Philippines, and Doss, a stretcher bearer with the first wave, was one of the first men on the beach. For a solid week of fighting he worked with compassionate fury. He dragged wounded men to safety over dead bodies as bullets whistled around him. He was caught in a counterattack and Japanese soldiers with bayoneted rifles ran right over him as he played dead. Another time he was cut off behind the enemy lines. Once again he crawled so close to an enemy machine-gun nest to rescue a wounded man that the Japanese machine gunner could have hit him with a rock. But for some reason the gunner did not fire.

With the Leyte fighting under its belt, the division moved on to Okinawa, the biggest and bloodiest of all the Pacific battles. By now Doss was popular with the men, but the officers still resented him. One day, learning that a platoon had gone out on patrol without an aid man, Captain Vernon ordered Doss to catch up with them. The platoon, composed mostly of green replacements, confused Doss with the enemy and shot at him; he didn't want to get shot by his own men, and returned to the company command post. The captain ordered him court-martialed. When the colonel of the regiment heard the full story he chewed out the captain instead of the aid man.

The regimental medical officer commented, "Vernon's got the best medic in the army and he doesn't appreciate him. Well, he doesn't have him any more." And he transferred Doss back to the base hospital.

Not long after that Captain Vernon came down with the dread jungle rot, a fungus disease which attacks the feet. Doss volunteered to go back and treat the captain, and got him on his feet again. "You were right and I was wrong," Vernon told him. "If there's anything I can do for you, tell me and I'll do it."

"Well," Doss said, "I'd like to stay up here with you."

Doss rejoined the company just in time to participate in the company's bloodiest battle. It was the battle for the escarpment, a big hill, heavily fortified, that lay in the path of the American advance on Shuri. Lieutenant Gornto's platoon had the murderous job of scaling a low, steep cliff and taking a plateau swept by machine-gun and mortar fire. The men would get up the cliff by means of a cargo net fastened to a tree on top of the cliff. Everything was in readiness for the attack, but there was no medic. Captain Vernon did not command Doss to go, for this day happened to be the Sabbath.

But Doss volunteered, without hesitation. Jesus Christ had healed people on the Sabbath; could mortal man ask a better precedent?

Before jumping off on the attack, Doss led the men in prayer. That first day, although units on either side suffered a terrible toll in casualties, and although they wiped out eight machine-gun nests, the platoon didn't suffer one casualty. The second day the platoon advanced up the slope toward the crest of the mountain. The Japanese poured out of their dugouts on the back side of the mountain and with superior numbers, position, and fire power, drove the Americans back, across the plateau, back down the cliff. But of 155 men who had scaled the cargo nets, only 55 went back down again. The rest were killed or wounded, and Doss stayed with them. One by one, under fire, he helped, dragged, and carried, a dozen men back to the cargo net. They tried to get down by themselves, but couldn't. Doss pulled up the rope, took a couple of turns around the tree, then tied one end of the rope around one of the wounded men, using the double bowline he had learned back in the Adventist Youth program. Though exposed to enemy fire, he calmly lowered one man at a time. Then he went back out on the fire-swept plateau, dragged more men to the top of the cliff, and lowered them, one by one, to the stretcher bearers waiting below.

"Come on down, Doss!" Captain Vernon yelled. "You'll just get yourself killed!"

Doss paid no attention to the company commander. He knew his danger, but he thought of the men whose lives he was saving, men who might have wives and children back home. He went back again and again and again, pulling and dragging and carrying the wounded men scores of yards across the open field. One severely wounded man was on the far side of a deep gully. Doss found a rickety wooden ladder stretched over the gully, pulled the soldier across on it. He kept going back until every last man had been evacuated, and only then did he himself shinny down the rope.

His uniform was completely soaked with blood. Captain Vernon looked at him and shook his head in speechless admiration.

Next day, in a new uniform especially brought up for him, Doss went back to work. He crawled across the battlefield to treat four wounded men, then, again under fire, he brought them each back separately. Several days later Doss dived into a shellhole with three other men as the Japanese counterattacked. Doss saw something hurtling across the sky above him, heard it land in the shellhole. It was a grenade. He jammed his foot down on it, hoping to protect himself and the other men even at the cost of a foot. The explosion blew him into a back somersault and embedded sixteen separate pieces of shrapnel into his legs and thighs, but Doss kept his foot. They all got out of the shellhole lest another grenade come in. Doss, left alone, tried to crawl away, but lost consciousness from shock and loss of blood. Eventually he was picked up by stretcher bearers. On the way back to the rear, in an evacuation train of stretcher cases and walking wounded, through sniper fire, he figured some of the walking wounded were worse off than he, and rolled off the litter to give his place to someone else. A few yards farther on he was hit by a sniper's bullet. It went in and out of both his forearm and upper arm, one bullet leaving four wounds.

Finally, in the hospital, Doss realized with a shock that he had lost his Bible, the leather-covered Bible that his wife, Dorothy, had given him on their wedding day. The loss hurt more than the wounds. Back at the company command post, officers and men dropped the war to find that Bible. A patrol braved a hail of bullets and mortar fire to locate the shellhole which Doss had shared with the grenade. They found the Bible, and delivered it with humility and gratitude to the man they had once cursed and reviled.

That was not all that was delivered to Desmond Doss. Sometime later President Harry S. Truman personally presented him with the Congressional Medal of Honor, the highest award a grateful nation can bestow on a hero.

Corporal Desmond T. Doss is no forgotten hero. His name, which the War Department declared a "synonym for outstanding gallantry" lives on in a rare combination of the Seventh-day Adventist church and the United States Army, Camp Desmond T. Doss. To this camp, which is located at Grand Ledge, Michigan, in odd years, near Portland, Oregon, in even, come, each summer, an average of 225 young men of the church who pay their own way to take what amounts to an army basic training course, in order to be better company aid men when called upon to serve their country.

Many a military man just simply can't believe it when he first hears of Camp Doss and the work it is doing. "It would be incredible enough if this were a camp for young men itching to fight," a hard-bitten infantry general once remarked, "but when members of a church pledged to nonviolence pay good money to attend an installation of this size with such rigorous training—all I can say is—*wow!*"

The camp opens immediately after the close of the school year, so that it will not interrupt summer jobs. The cadets—many more apply than can be accepted—pay a total of $31.50, which includes registration fee, board and room, use of uniform, equipment, and books, accident insurance, and a half unit of college credit on completing the course. An additional four or five dollars is necessary for laundry, incidentals, and Sabbath school and church offering. Cadets bring their own blankets, sheets and pillows, toilet articles, Bible, recreational items such as softball gloves or tennis rackets, and class A uniform—suntan shirt and trousers and black shoes.

Cadets can come back repeatedly, for Camp Doss offers both a basic and an advanced training course, including drill, military courtesy and instruction in the techniques of the medical soldier, and an officer training course.

The church also sponsors a medical cadet corps in its colleges and academies. The corps, whose motto is "God First Always," has units in some sixty institutions in the United States and other countries including Japan, Korea, Indonesia, Philippines, Brazil and the British colonies. The corps was founded in 1933 at Union College in Lincoln, Nebraska, by Everett N. Dick, who commanded the corps for twenty-five years. Dick, a Marine in World War I, was shocked to learn after the war that there had been 162 court-martials held during the war growing out of Sabbath-keeping. On Armistice Day, 1918, he learned, there were thirty-eight young men in the military prison at Fort Leavenworth, serving sentences from five to twenty years for Sabbath-keeping. How terrible it must have been for those young men, Dick thought, to be thrown into the harsh life of a military prison, along with offenders of the worst military crimes, for no other reason than obeying God's Fourth Commandment to His people. As a former member of the Armed Services and a patriotic American, Dick also realized that the nation had been deprived of many fine young men eager and willing to serve their country.

For Seventh-day Adventists are loyal citizens. They have no moral reservations whatsoever about paying taxes, saluting the flag, singing the national anthem, repeating the pledge of allegiance—rather, they are proud to do so. They believe sacredly that they owe allegiance to their government, for they believe that the principles of government were established by God. But they also believe that their duty to God comes first, and God himself, in the Fourth and Sixth Commandments, specifically directed all men to remember the Sabbath and not to kill.

Young men of the Seventh-day Adventist faith would make excellent soldiers in noncombatant capacities, especially in the medical department, Dick thought. Surely the advantages of having such men in the armed services would outweigh the small administrative matter of giving them permission to observe the Sabbath day. Today the church and the government have a firm understanding relative to the participation of Seventh-day Adventists in the services. When young church members reach their eighteenth birthday and register for the draft they are classified, all other things being equal, 1-AO, which means that they will not bear arms. (Conscientious objectors are classified as 1-O.) Government and church work well together; Clark Smith, who directs this work for the church, gives a concrete example of this relationship.

"Occasionally," Smith explained with a little smile, "one of our boys suffers a reverse of some kind—usually girl trouble—and he runs off and joins the army. When this happens, he has to serve where the army puts him, and it isn't too long before he realizes what a great mistake he has made. Well, the government makes special provision for these cases—we have a wonderful government —and the boy is permitted to leave the Armed Forces without stigma and come back in in the normal course of events as a 1-AO."

Many Seventh-day Adventist recruits already have a better background in military training than many medical soldiers who have completed basic training. For, thanks to Smith's sincerity and eagerness, he has ready access to the War Department, and is able to get the newest training methods for the Medical Cadet Corps, sometimes even before they are put into effect in army training.

Sometimes, students being students, the boys in the Medical Cadet Corps ask themselves if it is really necessary to learn their first-aid training with such painstaking thoroughness. After all, they figure, it will be a long time, if ever, before they have occasion to put this knowledge into use. The boys of the Medical Cadet Corps of the West Indian Training College in Jamaica had their answer to this question in the dark hours just past midnight on the morning of September 2, 1957. They were sleeping soundly in the men's dormitory when a knock came on the door of Neville Gallimore, the chief officer of the corps. A train wreck had occurred near the college. Preliminary reports said that there were hundreds of dead and injured. The Medical Corps was needed, and needed desperately. So were the girls of the Home Nursing Class across the campus in the girls' dormitory. Boys and girls piled into the college pick-up and all the available cars. There were so many that several trips had to be made to get them all to the scene.

And what a scene it was! A bomb could not have caused more

damage, death and suffering. An excursion train, taking some 2,000 people back to Kingston from an outing at Montego Bay in old wooden cars packed and jammed with people, had overturned on a steep grade. Cars were smashed and disintegrated. Bodies were everywhere. Some were pinned in the wreckage, some were thrown clear only to suffer crushing injuries of impact, some were screaming with pain, some moaning, and some were permanently still. Cadets, student nurses, instructors and the doctor from the school went hastily but efficiently to work. They tied tourniquets on bleeding stumps of limbs, administered injections—marking with lipstick on the patients' foreheads the type of drug, made rough splints for broken bones, and, when nothing else could be done, at least uttered comforting words.

One student found a man lying in agony with a broken back and obvious internal injuries. The student leaned over him and said, "Don't be afraid; you are still alive; perhaps God wants you to have another chance."

But the man looked up and said, with no light of hope in his eyes, "You sound like a Christian, but I'm not. I've put it off. And now I'm dying without God." The student could do nothing but pray for him as he died.

But there were miracles, too. It seemed inconceivable that anyone could be alive in one badly smashed-up car, as the students dragged out body after body. One of them saw a tiny leg extending from under a pile of rubble, dug gently, and managed to extricate the body of a two- or three-year-old little girl. Although she could not be alive, although there were others calling for aid, the student nevertheless laid the body gently down beside the row of dead. The cadet thought he saw a flicker of motion in her face, and bent over just as she opened her eyes wide, looked at him, smiled, and said, "Papa." Of all the people in that car, she alone survived.

The sun came up over the lovely green mountains, its yellow rays shining down on that acre of blood, and still the cadets and the other volunteer workers toiled on. They sorted out the dead—over 200—from the living, and prepared the injured for a trip to the makeshift aid station in the depot, thence to the hospital in the nearest town. They worked all that day on the scene, on into the night. And then, when all the 700 injured had been taken to hospitals, cadets and nurses worked on shifts day and night for the following week, assisting doctors, serving as best they could. There can be no way of estimating the number of lives the Cadet Corps of the West Indian Training College saved.

In addition to the Medical Cadet Corps, the 324 Seventh-day Adventist colleges and academies also provide work opportunities for their total enrollment of some 50,000 students. Many educational institutions throughout the world are self-supporting, through farms and industries drawing labor supply from the students themselves. This has been the tradition from the earliest days of education in the church.

One of the first Seventh-day Adventist schools of this type, and the very first in the South, was a school for colored students near Huntsville, Alabama. The church bought an old plantation, with both worked-out land and run-down buildings, and S. M. Jacobs and his family were sent from Iowa to put it into shape. Two students arrived on the first day, and there on hand to greet them were the president of the General Conference, Ole A. Olsen, and the superintendent of the district. Both of these church officials put on their overalls and worked along with Jacobs and the students to get the old place in shape. One of the first jobs was to clear the mud and débris out of the old well. Local rumor had it that a Yankee cavalryman had been buried in the well during the Civil War. When, after digging down through seventeen feet of mud, they found a spur, the two students quit the job cold.

Gradually the old house was rebuilt and the lands restored to fertility. At first the local people were decidedly hostile to the venture. The Adventist movement had begun in New England, with many members who were also Abolitionists, and the church was finding much prejudice in the South. One local farmer was particularly harsh in his criticism of the school. After one of his most bitter tirades, his barn caught on fire and burned to the ground, with all his work animals and tools. When word of his misfortune reached the school, Jacobs and the boys promptly hitched up a half a dozen cultivators and drove them over to their neighbor's place.

"What do you want?" the farmer asked them, hostility in his voice.

"Why, we've come to plant your corn," Jacobs answered.

The farmer was silent for a long moment, looking piercingly at the superintendent and the colored students whom he had so bitterly criticized.

"Is that the kind of man you are?" he asked.

"Yes," Jacobs answered. "That's the kind of man I am."

The farmer again looked over the small group who had come to help him, and cleared his throat. "Well, I've got something to do before you begin," he said. "I've said some mighty hard things against you for starting that school. Now I ask you to forgive me for all I've said."

"If I hadn't forgiven you a long time ago I wouldn't be here," Jacobs said, "and neither would the boys. Now let's get to work."

Jacobs led his task force out into the field, and they all, with the farmer, put in a good morning's work. When noon came Jacobs called a halt to the work and led the boys to the wagon to get their lunches.

"Oh no you don't," the farmer said. "My wife has been getting dinner. We'll all eat together, in the house."

Making friends in such fashion, the school grew steadily both in the respect of the community and in size and academic stature. Today Oakwood College is a leading educational institution.

One of the finest examples of Seventh-day Adventist colleges is the Southern Missionary College near Chattanooga, Tennessee, which is not only a school, but an industry. Through its corporation, College Industries, Inc., the college produces $2 million worth of goods annually, with a payroll of $400,000 going to its student workers. The major operation is a furniture plant, manufacturing chairs and desks, which employs 150 students and grosses $600,000 a year. The broom factory employs up to 100 students, and grosses $400,000. The printing plant and foundry do about $100,000 a year apiece. In addition there is a dairy and creamery, a cabinet shop which furnishes equipment for both the college and other schools, a department store, an auto service center, and a few smaller businesses. Students can make up to $3.80 an hour, and work up to twenty hours a week. Though not all the students work, 80 per cent of the student body earns at least one-fourth of their college expenses, and 25 per cent earn all their expenses. Some students have, by working summers, attended the college for four years and left with money in their pockets without spending a cent of their own. Further, over the years, records show that the students who work are at the top of their classes.

Thanks both to the opportunity offered by this system, and to the desire for knowledge evidenced by most young Seventh-day Adventists, in America three times as many Seventh-day Adventists are college graduates as the general public, and twice as many have completed high school. The church also offers a graduate school and theological seminary, offering advanced degrees in education, history and theology. The College of Medical Evangelists, with campuses in Loma Linda and Los Angeles, has major schools in dentistry, medicine and nursing, and related schools in dietetics, medical technology, physical therapy, X-ray technology, tropical and preventive medicine, and graduate studies. The College of Medical Evangelists alone represents an investment of over $15 million, with an annual operating budget of over $12 million. The church also cooperates with medical schools at Velore, India, and Monterrey, Mexico, and maintains nursing schools in many countries.

On the lower level, the church maintains over 5000 elementary and secondary schools, with an enrollment of a quarter of a million. Adventist parents pay tuition for their children to attend these schools. "We support public schools through taxes, our own schools through tuition," a Seventh-day Adventist spokesman explained. "We believe in both, and we have no complaints."

The Seventh-day Adventist schools in America look just like any other schools. In Switzerland they are typical of Swiss schools—with latticed windows and frames decorated by carvings or paintings. In the Philippines the schools are usually on stilts, with walls of bamboo, floors of split bamboo, and roofs of fronds from the nipa palm.

Teaching varies, too, from region to region, but only superficially. Around the Equator, when the children sing the song about souls being whiter than snow, they usually substitute coconut meat or lamb's wool, for they have never seen snow. One of the most popular primers contains a story of a pair of shoes. But in Korea and Japan, where the children don't wear shoes, the story is omitted; it was found that the children simply couldn't make the transfer.

Even more esoteric is the word "skyscraper." How do you describe a skyscraper to a child in the Belgian Congo? One brave teacher thought she had the answer. A skyscraper, she told her big-eyed pupils, is twenty houses one on top of each other. But, the children asked, how do the people who live in the top house get up there? The teacher started to say that they take an elevator—but how do you describe an elevator to children completely unfamiliar with electricity and electric motors? Should she say that someone pulled the elevator up with a rope? Finally she gave up, but not before she gathered that the children think that anyone who'd pile twenty houses on top of one another is pretty silly.

Teachers are constantly learning from their pupils. A home economics expert was making the rounds of the schools in a region in Africa, teaching the older girls improvements in cooking. It would seem to be a worthwhile endeavor, but the teacher failed miserably. In that area, cooking in the home is impossible; there are no windows, and the smoke would drive everyone out of the house. Consequently, outside each native hut is a fireplace made of three stones on which the woman of the family prepares all the meals. When the teacher began her cooking lesson, she first had trouble building a fire. The pupils had to help. After the fire was going and the teacher was beginning to prepare the demonstration, a sudden shower came up and put the fire out. The girls took a dim view of higher education. Here was a woman with a master of science degree in home economics, but she didn't have sense enough either to make a fire or build a roof over it to keep the rain off.

But despite the occasional failure of education on a higher level, learning goes on, elevating the children of the most primitive lands from savagery to civilization. G. M. Matthews, who is in charge of elementary education around the world, is one of the fortunate people who can see primitive peoples changing before his eyes. Recently he went on a safari deep into the heart of Sierra Leone. For hundreds of miles he traveled through regions ruled by native chiefs, untutored and heathen, and then came into an area in which the church has been active in the past decade. There the chief is a man of handsome bearing, clean, resplendent in a bright tunic, with a gold ring in his nose. He is the absolute monarch of over seventy villages, in which live hundreds of his children. The only education in this entire district is furnished by the Seventh-day Adventist church, and the chief, clean and tolerant, intensely desirous of better education for his people, cooperates with the church's educators to the fullest extent. His area is an oasis of cleanliness and increasing learning in a desert of sloth.

Matthews visited a girls' school in Africa and was greatly impressed by the neatness of the students' quarters. The dormitory was a one-story structure with floors of packed dirt, but shining clean. The girls themselves all came from poor native families; each one had a small box on a wall shelf in which she kept all of her personal belongings. They lived six to a room, with sleeping mats radiating out from the center. Mats, shelves and boxes comprised the sole furnishings, and yet no room seemed barren, for in each Matthews saw bunches of scarlet bougainvillea—who needs interior decorators and lavish appointments when flowers are there for the cutting?

Matthews knew from personal, itching experience that this region abounded in chiggers; he asked why the girls weren't bothered with the little bugs, since their mats were on the floor. The girls smiled and giggled and refused to answer. A day or two later the mystery deepened when he was politely asked not to visit the dormitories that day, as the girls were treating the floors. Curious as to what they did to make the floors so shiny and at the same time impervious to chiggers he insisted, and found the girls spreading a mixture of cow dung and water. This simple treatment served as both polish and insecticide.

"I couldn't help but marvel at the bounty of God," Matthews said on his return to Washington, "that He would give His people this common thing and the wisdom to use it."

In spite of the worldwide educational and medical program, many Seventh-day Adventists feel that neither the church nor they themselves are doing enough to benefit the people in remote areas. A group in California has organized the Pan-American Mexican League—known to its members as the *Liga*—to carry on additional work. The *Liga* has some 500 members, most of them Adventists who contribute their time and money. The fine sanitarium and nursing school in Montemorelos, for example, was started by the *Liga;* it is now self-supporting. A grateful former patient at Montemorelos bought a large tract of land at Navajoa and turned it over to the *Liga*. Currently a large farm and school are being operated on this land, and it, too, will someday be self-supporting. A former missionary named Frank Chaney, retired at the age of seventy-five, found after a period of inactivity that he was much too young to stay idle, and started a school at Yecora. Aided only by sporadic native labor, he built an airplane hangar and school building. The school was so successful—it now has 100 pupils—that it became the nucleus of ten small schools scattered out in the mountains around Yecora. The first schoolteacher, a man named Teneo, became the superintendent in effect of the little complex of schools, and makes continual rounds inspecting the little mountain schools, encouraging the children and teachers. The trips can be made only by burro, and each round takes two months.

The church also operates homes for orphaned and underprivileged children. Perhaps nowhere is the benefit of this work more strikingly apparent than in Korea, where, years after the cessation of hostilities, there are still many homeless children. One of the Seventh-day Adventist orphanages, Sam Yook Wan, is for disabled children only; of the more than 300 orphanages of all denominations in Korea, it is the only one operated exclusively for the disabled. Here, among their own kind, the children have found a happiness they cannot have at the other institutions.

Take little Yung Sook Kim, for instance, six years old and totally blind. Nobody knows where she comes from, who her parents were, or what happened to them. They know only that her first few years of life were spent in another institution where the other children, with the unthinking cruelty of the young, had made her life even more miserable, teasing her and hitting her. Somehow an American soldier heard about her and about Sam Yook Wan, and brought her there. She quickly found that here the children were not cruel, but sympathetic. One of the children is always with her, perhaps hobbling ahead on crutches, serving as her eyes. At every meal, in company with the hundred other maimed, scarred and disfigured boys and girls, she sits on the floor with her legs tucked under her and hands folded and sings a blessing of gratitude over her little bowl of cooked rice.

Or take little Lim Daik Koo, who was brought south from the fighting front years before by his parents. Something happened to the parents, nobody knows what, and little Lim Daik Koo was found crouching along the side of the road, clothed only in rags, in the dead of the Korean winter. His legs were frozen, and had to be amputated. But at Sam Yook Wan the boy is no longer legless, for he has friends who will take him with them wherever they go, carrying him in their arms. Here Lim Daik Koo has many, many legs.

Kids the world over, disabled or healthy, love to belong to organizations like the Boy Scouts and Girl Scouts. Unfortunately, because of their strict observance of the Sabbath, it is difficult for Seventh-day Adventist boys and girls to be Scouts, and the church consequently has its own Scoutlike organization. Boys up to ten years old join the Adventurers, whose activities closely parallel those of the Cub Scouts. From ten to fifteen they belong to the Pathfinder clubs, complete with uniforms. They progress from Friends to Companions to Explorers to Guides, just as Scouts advance from Tenderfeet to Eagles. For a boy under sixteen to work his way up to the top rung of the ladder is no snap. To be a Wilderness Guide, for example, he must pass the following tests:

1. Be able to build a fire on a rainy day or in the snow. Know where to get the dry material to keep it going.
2. With lashings, build a wilderness object.
3. Demonstrate ability to properly tighten and replace ax or hatchet handle.
4. Complete Orienteering Honor.
5. Know on sight, prepare and eat ten varieties of wild plant foods.
6. Know proper formations and movements of a color guard.
7. Citizenship: prove yourself a good citizen at school and at home.
8. Go on one overnight hike which totals fourteen miles. List the proper equipment for back-packing. Pack a pack correctly and demonstrate a horseshoe pack.
9. Go on two overnight camping trips. Demonstrate the proper care and storage of camp foods and how to build various caches to protect food from animals.
10. Keep a month-long log on the earning of the Missionary Endeavor Certificate.
11. Be up-to-date in club dues.

12. Collect, preserve and label one of the following categories: 25 wild flowers; 25 tree leaves; 25 butterflies; 25 moths; 25 shells; 25 rocks and minerals.
13. Be able to send and receive 35 letters a minute by semaphore code or be able to send and receive 15 letters a minute by wigwag using the International Morse Code or be able to send and receive Matthew 24 in one-hand sign language for the deaf.
14. Stalking and concealment.

From sixteen to twenty the youths belong to teen-age clubs, which go in for hiking, nature studies and similar activities. Seventh-day Adventists participate in competitive sports like baseball, but many specialize in outdoor sports. "Frankly," one strapping youngster explained, "we like things a little more rugged than playing ball. We like mountain-climbing. We go snow-camping—spend nights out right in the snow. We have a wilderness survival program—we go out with no food of any kind, even in winter, even in the desert. When you know the only way you can get something to eat is to find it yourself, it's a lot more fun to look for it. There's always something new in nature. We play a game in which each of us takes an area just exactly ten feet square and sees what he can find of interest in that area. You'd be amazed at some of the fascinating things we come up with. Then we play a game called Capture the Flag, which is a regular small-scale military engagement. Compared to some of the things we do and enjoy, playing ball is pretty tame." But ball playing has its followers too.

As if the Seventh-day Adventist kids didn't have enough to do, they also participate heavily in the church's famous investment program, in which kids and adults alike undertake a year-round project to bring in money for missions. Some kids invest in seeds, and sell the flowers and vegetables they grow. Others bake and sell cakes and cookies. Others make small handicraft objects, baby sit, collect pop bottles for return to stores for deposit or wire coat hangers for sale to laundries. Many unique little projects come up. In Lockhall, Maryland, three little boys named Dick, Wayne and Robin Gatling suggested to their parents, proprietors of a family bakery, that they sell the doughnut holes. Now, every Sunday, the tasty little pieces of doughnuts cut out to make the holes are placed on sale. They last only a few minutes. The Gatlings' Catholic friends are their best customers; one doctor stops by the bakery on his way back from Mass and buys five dozen holes each Sunday.

Sometimes the kids of a particular church have an extra-special reason to raise money. In Caldwell, Idaho, for example, where Wes and Joanne Schultz were youth leaders before they went to Pakistan as missionaries, the forty kids in Sabbath school set the nearly impossible goal of $500 for the year. They earned money in several different ways. They went out to the sheep camps, found motherless lambs, and raised them to healthy, plump maturity. Two boys trapped gophers and sold the tails for twenty-five cents apiece. One boy raised chickens, a girl sold greeting cards, and a whole class made candy together and sold it from door to door. At the end of the year the total profit came to not just $500, but $600.

This work goes on all over the world. In Guinobatan, the Philippines, the finest papaya tree in town was the one that was planted for Seventh-day Adventist investment. It continuously yields big, sturdy fruit for foreign missions. In Brazil a boy came across a skinny, sorry-looking, almost-featherless young rooster which had been chased away from home by a dog. The boy made an honest effort to find the owners of the rooster, and, failing in that, made the rooster his investment project of the year. He took such good care of the rooster that some months later the handsome creature was sold for a good price.

Adults, too, of course, participate in the investment program. In Hawaii a man goes fishing on his day off, and through sales of his catch contributes a hundred dollars or more each year—truly a wonderful inducement to go fishing!

For many students who go into active church work, the church's over-all youth program is excellent training. A young couple named Wellesley and Evelyn Muir have particular reason to be thankful for their outdoor activities as youths and youth leaders. After two years at the Lake Titicaca mission in Bolivia, the two had visited every mission station except one. There was a good reason for this omission; the Tambopata Mission station is more than fifty miles beyond the end of the last road, over a twisting trail that winds through jungles and over steep mountains. But the young couple felt that the isolated church members and Indian workers living in the remote area needed the encouragement of a visit. Wellesley, who had received a serious leg injury sometime before, also wanted to see if his leg could take the hike. And Evelyn wanted to be the first woman missionary ever to visit all the stations.

They started out by truck for Sandia, the jumping-off place. For two hours they drove along at the 12,500-foot level of the lake, then started to climb up the rocky, bumpy road. There were many rivers to ford, and some of them were deep, but the mission truck crossed each without coughing. They stopped for lunch under a glacier that glistened like a giant diamond in the noonday sun. Now they were up to 17,000 feet. Crossing the continental divide, they started down the eastern slopes of the Andes, the lowest gear whining. That night they reached Sandia, and their lunch amidst the glaciers was followed by supper amidst orchids and other tropical plants of the jungle.

After two days with the church members of Sandia, they engaged two Indian *cargadores* named José and Raul to help with the sleeping bags, Sabbath clothing to wear when they reached their destination, and food for the three-day, fifty-mile hike. They started at dawn, and for the first several hours kept up a good pace along the trail by the Sandia River. The bodies of pack animals which had died along the way, and crude mounds signifying the graves of people who had met the same fate, were not good omens. After the noonday lunch stop the trail began getting difficult. Now the river ran through a deep, rocky gorge, and the trail skirted the edge of a cliff, high above the water. One misstep would be certain death. Just a day or two before, José and Raul told them, a teen-aged boy had fallen off the cliff and had not been seen again.

The river gradually became a mere trickle, and the trail left it to wind up the steep, rocky side of a high mountain. The afternoon sun beat down on them; the jungle helmets which had seemed silly in the Andes were now a great comfort. But it was no comfort when one of the *cargadores* slipped. Although the only damage was to get the outside of one of the sleeping bags muddy, neither Wellesley nor Evelyn could help asking themselves the pertinent question: "If *cargadores* can't keep their footing on this trail, how can we?"

They were glad when dusk came along, and they had an excuse to stop for the night.

As Evelyn sank down in exhaustion to a sitting position, she sighed, saying, seriously, "I just don't see how I can possibly finish the trip. My feet are killing me." Wellesley helped her off with her boots. Together they counted seven big blisters on her feet. Wellesley took his own boots off and together they sat by the side of the little river, soaking their aching feet in the cool mountain water.

"I think you'd be better off if we opened those blisters," Wellesley said, tentatively.

"I was afraid you'd say that," Evelyn said wryly. "But I'm afraid you're right."

With a sterile needle, and to the accompaniment of several cries of "Wow, that hurt!" plus a few tears, Wellesley performed his pedal surgery, dabbing burning merthiolate on each blister when he had finished. Then they feasted bountifully on dried fruit and oatmeal cookies washed down with fresh mountain water flavored with halazone. The guides ate the same thing they had for breakfast, lunch and dinner—hot soup made by adding dried ingredients to water heated over a small fire.

Rolling out their sleeping bags and blowing up their air mattresses sapped the last bit of their strength. They studied their Sabbath-school lessons with the aid of a flashlight, thanked the Lord for protecting them on the trail thus far, and dropped off to a sound sleep.

Next morning they hit the trail again. Evelyn's feet seemed much better, and they made good time. By the afternoon they were over the mountain and once more in jungle country, with birds of bright plumage, perching in lovely palms, watching their progress and being watched in return. The sun was blazing hot. At the infrequent rest stops they stretched out flat on their backs; watching the birds in the trees above them gave an excellent excuse. But in the late afternoon the trail wound up again and once more it was hard going. They made camp on a level spot of a high ridge where a cool wind swept down from the Andes. A small group of Indians driving a train of twenty mules loaded with coffee from the jungle made camp with them, but not even the sound of the mules moving around and the snoring of the drivers could keep them awake. A short heavy rainstorm just before dawn did manage to awaken them, but only long enough to pull the flaps of the sleeping bags up over their heads. The morning sun quickly dried out the equipment, and soon they were off on their third day on the trail.

Though the trail was winding and dangerous, it was the only thoroughfare between the mountains and the jungle and there was a steady traffic of people and animals carrying cargoes of coffee from the jungle, and general supplies back. The trail was so narrow that no one dared ride, and everyone, men, women and children, carried loads on their backs. Children under ten carried twenty-five pounds, José and Raul explained, women fifty pounds, and the men seventy-five, sometimes even one hundred. The Muirs, with their aching muscles and blistering feet, stared at the Indians in wonder as they went by, carrying their loads without complaint—and without shoes. They all, kids included, carried a small kettle, in which they made soup. At night the Indians would stop at *tambos,* built along the way, which were nothing more than thatched roofs held up by four poles. The third night the Muirs joined the crowd at a *tambo,* but they vowed never to do it again. The people were constantly moving around, singing, laughing, shouting at the children and one another, with the children adding to the uproar. Further, the place was infested with fleas.

Next day the trail started off level, but a level trail has its disadvantages too; the torrential rains had made it a quagmire in years past and the jungle road-builders had placed logs across it. The *cargadores* explained that when a burro or mule slipped off the corduroy roadway the drivers would simply go off and leave it there to die, as it was practically impossible to pull an animal out of the deep ooze. After several miles of walking over the slippery logs, Wellesley's leg, which had stood up well over the mountains, began to pain him severely, and he wondered how he could possibly finish the trip. But word had been sent to the believers at the Tambopata church that the Muirs were coming, and he did not want to disappoint them. Besides, now they were close to their destination. He limped on.

In midafternoon they arrived at a *tambo* to find the deacon of the church waiting. Although he didn't speak Spanish, and the Muirs could not speak his *patois,* he made them understand that he was the advance guard of the welcoming committee. After several hearty embraces he brought out a large bag of big, juicy oranges. Water had been scarce for the past several hours, and the oranges looked good. The deacon obviously liked them, too, for he went through nine big oranges in well under ten minutes. Wellesley managed to put away eight oranges, but in twice the time.

While they were eating the oranges, their strained muscles tightened up, and the ensuing few hours were by far the worst of the trip. The trail went down a steep ridge, and walking was agony. But in the little village of San Juan de Oro the second section of the welcoming committee was waiting, and the Muirs were nearly drowned in orange juice. Now it was only an hour's walk to the mission station and they made it easily. Fortunately, a little river was flowing right in front of the mission property, and off came the boots and into the cooling water went four aching feet. Evelyn now had a total of twelve blisters and Wellesley's right leg was badly swollen.

But it didn't matter. The director of the mission station was waiting with more tall glasses of orange juice, freshly squeezed, and, with cool glasses in hand, the Muirs could look around at the lovely mission station surrounded by banana and orange trees.

The next three days were fully occupied with mission business. The Muirs helped the brethren with plans for a new school building to take care of the 143 boys and girls crowding the current little building. Wellesley examined the baptismal candidates, and both made as many visits as they could to the members of the congregation. But although their days were crowded and they had little time to rest their feet and aching muscles, they had before them a constant inspiration to keep going. It was the little whitewashed church, with a galvanized metal roof, each length of which had been carried fifty miles on human back.

On the Sabbath morning members came from everywhere—over 300 of them. At the close of the service the crowd gathered at the edge of the beautiful little river and Wellesley baptized nineteen persons who were pledging their lives to the service of Christ.

Finally it was time to hike the fifty miles back to the road. They started at night in order to climb the steep ridge out of Tambopata without benefit of the scorching rays of the sun. They heard pumas rustling in the brush as they walked along. After only a few hours' sleep in the early morning they continued on all that day. José and Raul wanted to make Sandia by nightfall the next day, and suggested starting about four o'clock the next morning. The Muirs agreed, turned in, and, it seemed, almost immediately afterwards were awakened. They looked at their watches; it was 1 A.M. The *cargadores* had already had their breakfast and were ready to go, and there was nothing for the Muirs to do but roll out of the sleeping bags and start walking. Guided by the full moon and the occasional use of their flashlight, they found the dangerous trail not too bad at first, but they had made barely a mile or so when heavy clouds obscured the moon. They had to use the flashlight continually, and the batteries burned out. Heavy rain began to fall and the trail was soon as slick as glass. After slipping in holes and nearly falling several times, they found themselves on a ledge over the river listening to the sound of unseen rushing water beneath them. Continuing was out of the question.

For two hours they sat in the mud, leaning against the bank, in the drenching rain. The rain ended just as dawn broke, and they resumed the journey. After walking several miles, a new deterrent was added to Wellesley's aching leg and Evelyn's blistered feet: diarrhea. The last miles of the trip were miserable ones. The little truck had never looked so good. They reached home at two o'clock the next morning. For days the Muirs wore slippers.

"Throughout the high Andes," Evelyn wrote home to her friends, "the sandy coastal deserts and the steaming jungles that make up the territory of the Lake Titicaca mission, thousands are being reached with the gospel. As we had walked for days and seen trails leading off to other areas of large population where our workers have not yet gone, we were impressed with the urgency of reaching the millions in our mission territory who are still waiting to hear the story of Jesus, who died for their sins.

"When we remember that Wellesley arrived in Peru on crutches, it makes us appreciate even more all that God has done for us when we have been able to walk over a hundred miles together in His work."

13 *So Shall I Be Saved from Mine Enemies*

Desmond Doss, the American hero of Okinawa, didn't know it, but all the time he was in uniform he had thousands of allies, muscular black men with bushy hair, serving the same cause in the same way in the islands of the South Pacific. In New Guinea on the Owen Stanley Track, in the Solomons, on Bougainville, on Guadalcanal other Seventh-day Adventists, many of them sons of headhunters, were aiding the Allies in their own valuable way.

One of the great leaders of the war effort in the Pacific, a man whose name will live in both church and military history, was Kata Ragoso; we have met him before in the chapter on miracles. Jet-black and straight as an arrow, with a bristling mane of black crinkly hair, Kata Ragoso, when war broke out, was the native leader of the Solomon Islands Seventh-day Adventists. Just five years before he had attended the General Conference in San Francisco and had toured the United States. When the Japanese started their march through the islands of the Pacific, the Australasia Conference of the Seventh-day Adventist church, like other churches, felt it wise to evacuate the white missionaries from the islands. The responsibility of both the mission stations and the thousands of natives who had found the peace of God fell on the broad shoulders of Kata Ragoso. The big chieftain took on another responsibility. He knew that the Japanese would occupy his island, and he knew that the Allies—

Americans, Australians, New Zealanders—would some day return to drive them out. But he also knew that before they could reoccupy the Solomons they would send out planes; Kata Ragoso set out to ensure the safety of the pilots who might be shot down over the islands.

With his native pastors, he organized the islands into one big network of life savers. Over the entire archipelago, at five mile intervals, thousands of keen eyes scanned the heavens constantly in search of Allied planes. When the spotters did see a plane come down, they sent out word immediately by jungle drum or fleet-footed messenger to rescue squads. On several occasions when spotters saw an airman bail out of his plane, rescue squads were on the way to him before he landed.

Rescue work was all the more difficult because the Japanese were particularly suspicious of the natives who were Seventh-day Adventists. The Japanese destroyed the churches, even destroyed the natives' gardens. Among the Solomon Islanders who, with their families, were forced to flee their mission station were two men named Pana and Jimaru. They fled to the mountains, walking upstream so the Japanese scouting parties could not track them. They existed in the mountains for almost three years. They tried to plant gardens for food, but the Japanese always found them and destroyed them. And yet they survived; strangely, they frequently found small gardens with food ready to dig and eat tucked away in the hills, even though there seemed to be no habitation within miles. Pana and Jimaru were positive that angel hands had prepared these gardens.

Even in their mountain hideout, the two men kept abreast of the progress of the war by the mysterious jungle telegraph. On one occasion Jimaru learned that one of the big planes belonging to the Allies had been crippled in an air battle and had fallen somewhere nearby. Jimaru and the men in his group immediately set up a systematic search for the plane. They found it, but saw no signs of life. Some distance from the plane Jimaru came across a canteen lying on the ground. Looking up, he saw the pilot. His parachute had caught in the branch of a large tree and he was dangling helplessly forty feet from the ground. Jimaru called for help, and he and his fellows built a huge pile of leaves and ferns directly underneath the airman. When it was ready, he looked up and cried, "Mastah, you come down along tree."

The pilot had no idea whether the natives were friendly or not. Besides, it was a long drop, even to the pile of leaves built to soften the fall. He hesitated a long time, but finally unhooked his harness and fell. Despite the cushion of leaves, he lost consciousness when he landed. Jimaru examined him, saw that his body was terribly cut and bruised, and that one arm was broken. Jimaru and his men built a crude stretcher and carried the pilot to the cave in which they were hiding out. When he regained consciousness they tried to feed him, first with mashed banana, which he couldn't eat, then with birds' eggs beaten up in coconut milk. This the pilot drank, and then went to sleep again. Jimaru was concerned about the long, deep gash in the pilot's face; he knew that it had to be sewn up. Unfortunately, he had no surgical equipment of any kind, no anesthetics. Sadly he told the pilot what should be done, and the pilot agreed for him to do it. Jimaru took a large thorn and a small, tough vine, sterilized both in water boiled in a coconut shell, and then sewed up the wound as the airman gritted his teeth and held on.

After the pilot had gotten some strength back, Jimaru led him across the mountain to the other side of the island, where he secured a canoe. Traveling at night, he paddled his patient through the Japanese lines and delivered him to safety. After the war was over, Jimaru received a letter from the pilot. It said:

"I can never forget those days of sickness, for the scars are still on my face; the marks are there where you sewed. These marks remind me of what you did to keep me alive and I want to thank you."

The Allied airman was only one of over 200 men rescued by Kata Ragoso's people. Each rescue had its moments of fear for both rescued and rescuer; the airmen could not know whether or not the natives would turn out to be friendly, and the Solomon Islanders, to whom all men not black looked somewhat alike, were never sure whether the man they were rescuing was American or Japanese. One time, just as Kata Ragoso was finishing Sabbath services, two planes got into a dogfight overhead. One plane fell, but the pilot seemed to have it under control, and when last seen it was heading for the water. Kata Ragoso sent his men out to find him. An islander named Tiri rounded a small promontory in his canoe and came across the pilot paddling away in his rubber boat. The encounter nearly scared both of them to death, and each stopped paddling and sat warily eying the other.

Finally the airman forced a smile to his lips. Tiri, encouraged, asked, "You fella man belong American or Japanese?"

"Me no Jap," the airman answered. "Me American. Where you from?"

"Me from mission, me Christian," Tiri answered proudly.

But Tiri was still suspicious. He helped the pilot, who was injured, into his canoe, and took him to Kata Ragoso. The chief was upset. He thought that the man was Japanese, and began scolding Tiri for bringing him to the secret hiding place. The pilot now became apprehensive all over again. How was he going to convince these people that he was an American?

The big chief bent down and scrutinized the man's face carefully. "Are you really an American?" he asked, in good English.

"Yes, honest I am," the pilot said.

"What part of the United States do you come from?" Kata Ragoso asked him.

The pilot hesitated. How could this bare-chested black man possibly know one part of the United States from the other? Finally he said, "I'm from Hollywood, California."

Instantly Kata Ragoso's face broke into a big smile. "Good!" he said. "I've been there—I know Hollywood well!"

The islanders gave him oranges, pawpaws and coconuts, and cooked sweet potatoes for him. They gave him a shower, and one of the first-aid men looked after his injuries and bandaged his leg. They helped him into a big war canoe, and twenty-one men paddled him to the secret wireless station. The following day a seaplane dipped down out of the sky, landed on the water, and took the pilot back to safety.

While Kata Ragoso and his brethren were doing their best for mankind and the Allied cause, other native Seventh-day Adventists were busy to the north, in New Guinea and New Britain. When the Japanese started their push down through New Guinea, destination Australia, through the malaria-infested jungles and over the forbidding Owen Stanley Range, the Allies made a full-scale attempt to stop them. One of the big decisions was whether to ask the help of the natives. Some of the old-timers in the islands opposed the recruiting of natives bitterly and vehemently: "They'll steal everything that isn't nailed down; you can't trust them out of your sight, and they'll let you down in an emergency," they said. But others, having seen in Seventh-day Adventist villages and missions clean, intelligent, trustworthy men and women, insisted that they be given a chance. Thousands of natives were recruited as cargo carriers, litter bearers, and "doctor-boys."

From the beginning they proved a pleasant surprise, as when an Australian general attempted to interview one of the first recruits.

"You fella boy, spik English? You understand?"

The young man, not knowing what else to do, bowed humbly to indicate that he did understand. After all, the general had every right in the world to doubt; the young man himself, whose name was Lawrence, came from Goodenough Island where only a few years before his grandfather had been a headhunting chief. The general had no way of knowing that the Seventh-day Adventists had come to Goodenough Island, built schools and missions, and educated and imbued the young people of the island, of whom Lawrence was one, to live a Christian life of self-betterment.

But the respectful bow wasn't enough for the general. He persisted. "You talka English? Savvy words?"

That was too much. "I think, sir," Lawrence replied in perfect English, "that I shall be able to understand everything you say."

The people of Australia know full well the service Lawrence and his fellow natives performed in New Guinea. No one knows how many thousands of sick and wounded soldiers were given first aid treatment and helped back to the rear by the native doctor-boys and litter bearers. Always gentle and kind with the suffering, frequently irritable soldiers, the litter bearers often had to slice their way through the narrow jungle trails, ease the stretcher down rocky precipices, ford swollen rivers and wade through waist deep mud, and at the same time shield the patient's face from the frequent rains with broad leaves plucked from jungle bushes on the run. An Australian soldier wrote a long poem in tribute to the Fuzzy Wuzzy angels on the Owen Stanley Track, ending with:

"May the mothers of Australia, when they offer up a prayer,
Mention the impromptu angels with the fuzzy-wuzzy hair."

An Australian mother answered with a poem of her own:

"We, the mothers of Australia, as we kneel each night in prayer,
Will be sure to ask God's blessing on the men with fuzzy hair;
And may the great Creator, who made both black and white,
Help us ever to remember how they helped to win the fight!
For surely He has used these men with fuzzy-wuzzy hair
To guard and watch our wounded with loving, tender care;
And perhaps when they are tired, with blistered, aching back,
He'll take their yoke upon Himself and help them down the track.
And God will be the artist, and this picture He will paint,
Of a fuzzy-wuzzy angel with the halo of a saint;
And His presence shall go with them in tropic heat and rain,
And He'll help them tend the wounded in sickness and in pain.
So we thank you, Fuzzy Wuzzies, for all that you have done,
Not only for Australia but for every mother's son;

And we're glad to call you friends, though your faces may be black,
For we know that Christ walked with you on the Owen Stanley
Track."

Despite the valiant efforts of Australian and New Zealand soldiers, backed up by the natives, the Japanese hordes pouring down the island in the winter of 1941–1942 just couldn't be stopped. After the fall of Rabaul many of the soldiers were cut off and had to escape as best they could. One of them wrote this letter home to a friend in Australia who was a member of the Seventh-day Adventist church:

"We were endeavoring to reach the coast, which entailed our crossing a high and extremely rugged range of mountains. We had passed through several rather dirty, ill-kept villages, which contained very few gardens and scarcely any surplus native foods, and we were feeling particularly tired and hungry when one evening we arrived at a small village and were met with the welcome sight of extensive gardens surrounding the clean, well-laid-out native houses. It was Saturday, and we heard the sound of singing from the large house-lotu [church] in the center of the village. We waited until the service was over, and then approached the luluai [headman] and told him we would like some food and a house to sleep in. He immediately offered us his own house and insisted on our having it, while the women set about preparing a meal for us. The most striking thing about the villagers was their shining white teeth. It was the only village we passed through in which the natives did not chew betel nut, which so discolors the teeth and mouth of the average native and makes him constantly expectorate the red juice. The marys wore spotless print smocks, and all the boys were wearing clean lap-laps.

"That evening we enjoyed a sumptuous repast which included a whole variety of native vegetables, bananas, and papaws, and that was indicative of the hospitality we received for the next two days. On the second evening we were invited to the evensong conducted by the mission boy; and to listen to them sing with feeling familiar hymns, and to hear the mission boy read a short lesson from the Bible, brought us much nearer home.

"But the weary being rested, and the wounds and cuts healing, we had to push on. To help us over the last, and by far the worst, stretch, we asked the luluai to provide us with some carriers to relieve us of some of our loads and to take us as far as the beach. Although the village was small, young and old volunteered, and by taking the 'monkeys' [children, some of them no more than twelve years old] and giving them small loads, we got what we required. We stipulated that we would want the carriers for only two days, but alas! Rain, back-breaking tracks, and tropical sores greatly impeded our progress, and at the end of two days we had scarcely covered half the distance. Hourly we expected the carriers to drop their loads and go bush, as we had scarcely any food left and could give them very little to sustain them for their hard work. As we had said we wanted them for only two days and, moreover, could not feed them, we hardly expected them to stay. But for three more days they kept with us, until at last we dropped down onto the beach.

"We felt deeply grateful to those natives who gave us such help, and grateful to those who had taught them the principles of cleanliness and honesty, which they are now putting into practice. It was the only Seventh-day Adventist village we passed through, but I can honestly say it is the one of which I have the most pleasant recollections. It was a credit to your church."

Multiply this man's experience by hundreds and you have the work of the Seventh-day Adventist natives in New Guinea. One entire regiment, including many wounded, was rescued and led to safety by a group of Seventh-day Adventist native teachers. The heroic efforts of the natives did not go unrewarded; after the battle of Milne Bay, which marked the turning point of any enemy penetration southward, seven natives were decorated with the highest honors of the Australian Army for their heroism. One of these was Lawrence of Goodenough Island, and the other six were also all Seventh-day Adventists. On Bougainville, just off the coast of New

Guinea, a Seventh-day Adventist native named Okira was responsible for rescuing hundreds of soldiers and sailors, and was also decorated with the highest honors.

The natives in the villages overrun by the Japanese, particularly the Adventists, suffered particular cruelties and indignities. By the very appearance of their persons and their villages, the Japanese could tell which natives were Seventh-day Adventists, and quite rightly suspected them of allegiance to the white man who had brought them their knowledge. The Seventh-day Adventist natives were perhaps their own worst enemy, in that they were incapable of telling a lie. Other natives had no moral compunction about saying "I don't know" to the Japanese questioners. The Adventists were forced by their own consciences to answer, if they did know, "I won't tell you." And then the beating and torture began. One native schoolteacher, who knew where some Australian soldiers were hiding but refused to tell, was brutally clubbed, then forced to dig his own grave and stand in front of it while Japanese soldiers leveled their rifles at him. He was standing before the grave, awaiting death but still refusing to talk, when a shell landed behind the soldiers; in the confusion he managed to escape.

The story of the American lieutenant, Gordon Manuel, was told in the popular best-seller by Quentin Reynolds, *Seventy Thousand to One*. The title of the book was descriptive; when Lieutenant Manuel was shot down near Kambubu in New Britain, he was outnumbered by 70,000 Japanese, all of whom were searching for him. A Seventh-day Adventist native teacher, Dennie Mark, who was in charge of the rescue work in the area around Kambubu, found the seriously wounded lieutenant, built a hut for him in the jungle, and fed him and nursed him while his wounds were healing. Dennie Mark and his fellow natives kept Manuel hidden for six full months, then guided him through the jungle, through Japanese lines, to another section of the island where there was an Allied outpost. After Lieutenant Manuel had reached safety, Dennie Mark was picked up by the Japanese. His only answer to their questions was, "Dennie

Mark no talk." He died from the brutal treatment he received. He was buried near the spot where he had taken care of Lieutenant Manuel.

Remember Faole, the one-time murderer who had become a worker for Christ and who escaped from a stockade only through miraculous intervention? Faole's village was occupied by the Japanese after fierce fighting in which most of the houses were burned and many people killed. Faole, whose own family had now grown up, had taken several orphan children into his home, and when his home was destroyed by bombs he and the children hid in the jungle. Shortly after, the battered remains of an Australian company of soldiers, cut off behind the lines, came up to the neat, little grass hut Faole and his children had built in a small clearing. The soldiers could hear voices coming from the hut, and came to the conclusion there must be Japanese within. They lay on the grass at the edge of the clearing, fingers on the triggers of their rifles, waiting for the enemy to emerge. Suddenly from within the hut came the strains of "Anywhere with Jesus I Can Safely Go."

The officer in charge of the Australians jumped to his feet exultantly. "Come on, boys," he cried, "there are no Japs here."

Faole and the children found food for the hungry men, and tended the wounded. The best care was not enough for one of the men, shot through the pelvis, and he died. Faole dug his grave with a pointed stick, and conducted the funeral services over his grave, weeping as he sang, "There Is a Place of Quiet Rest."

Then Faole and the children undertook to guide the men back to their own lines. The Japanese were on the main track and controlled all the trails, which meant Faole would have to lead the men across the ravine-split, jagged country. It would be difficult not to get lost, and if he did get through, Faole knew that eventually the Japanese would hear of it and a price would be put on his head. Nevertheless they started off. Faole led, followed by the officer and his men, with the orphans walking behind, covering their footprints. Frequently they heard parties of soldiers coming through the jungle, and their only hope was to freeze in their tracks, standing motionless almost without breathing. For days they walked, and then it was Friday. In midafternoon Faole abruptly stopped; the party must prepare for the Sabbath before it began, at sunset. All the next day they rested in that one place in the hostile jungle.

The Australian officer, when Faole explained the delay, could only smile and shrug.

"You are the master," he said simply. "We will do as you wish."

On Sunday they resumed the journey. Several days later when the trail became too arduous for the children, Faole left them in what he hoped would be a safe hiding place, and went on with the soldiers. As they wound around through ravines and hills the inevitable happened. Faole became lost. He had to admit it, and the spirits of the hungry and exhausted men dropped like shot birds. Faole asked the soldiers to gather around and kneel down while he prayed. "Me ask 'im big Fella Marsta, 'im 'e stop long heaven 'im 'e tell pickaninny belong 'im which way 'e go."

The officer and his men silently knelt down as the old man prayed, and as they did so, listening to the old man talking with his God—who seemed to be his Friend—they felt something come over them. Suddenly Faole rose, and without hesitation, started back in the exact opposite direction. Within an hour they were safe behind their own lines.

Strange stories are told of the happenings in the jungle islands of the South Pacific during the war years, but perhaps the strangest of all is the story of the mission schooner *Portal,* the ship that would not burn. The *Portal,* with the *Dadavata* and the *G. F. Jones,* had been commandeered by His Majesty's Navy. They were anchored in the Marovo Lagoon in the Solomons when a panting native came running up to the commander of the little fleet at his headquarters on shore. The Jap man was coming in a plenty big fella ship.

The commandant of the little navy sighed. He had been dreading this moment. He gave orders for the three ships to get underway. The deck boys were able to start up the engines of the *Dadavata* and the *Jones* right away, but the *Portal's* tired old diesel refused to turn over, even though the deck crew followed the customary procedure of heating the cylinder heads with a blow torch. The officer reluctantly gave orders to destroy the *Portal,* to keep it from falling into enemy hands. As the Adventist natives watched in horror from the shore, two full drums of gasoline were poured over the deck, in the cabin and the engine room, and the officer himself threw an ignited bundle of waste into the cabin. A burst of flames shot out, and the officer, satisfied that the *Portal* would soon be at the bottom of the lagoon, hurriedly left with his little fleet.

The Solomon Islanders, watching as the little schooner which had brought them missionaries, their education and their hope, began to burn, silently prayed that somehow the schooner would be spared. Suddenly, despite the two full drums of gasoline which had been poured on her, the fire went out as though snuffed by a giant hand. A joyous shout went up from the islanders.

"*Portal* 'im 'e boat belong God. 'Im 'e no burn," they cried, and, swimming, paddling canoes, they hurried out to the schooner. Pushing, pulling, poling, they worked the boat into the mouth of a little creek, and pushed it up into the mangroves. In the meantime fourteen Japanese gunboats were pursuing the two other schooners. The natives didn't worry, for they knew the two boats were manned by crews who knew every reef and shoal of the twisting lagoon, and they were right. The boats escaped.

Now the islanders went to work on the *Portal.* They unshipped the masts and removed the awnings and rigging. They cut down whole palm trees and lugged them through the jungle on their backs to put them over the boat. When dawn broke you would never know, whether looking from the sea or from the air, that the *Portal* was there.

Weeks, months and years went by. The Japanese took possession of Marovo Lagoon, and day and night planes of both sides flew over. But during all that time the *Portal* remained undetected, nor, among all the bombs dropped in the lagoon, did one come close to it.

Finally the war was over. One day in May of 1945, Elder Norman Ferris, a missionary of some twenty years in the islands, was landed by the American forces on the shores of the lagoon. What a joyous reunion there was! After several minutes of celebration, with shouts and tears of joy and prayers of gratitude, a group of islanders whispered among themselves, then ran, like happy children, to the beach and launched a canoe.

"Where are you going?" Ferris called after them.

"We go catch 'im *Portal!"* they hollered back.

"But the *Portal* was burned and sunk!"

"Government 'e no savvy 'e all time 'e gammon, *Portal* 'im 'e boat belong God 'im 'e no burn. *Portal* 'e stop, we get," one of the men told him with a sly chuckle.

And they did get it. The loyal old boat looked like a wreck, but after she was cleaned up she proved to be staunch and seaworthy. She'd been lying in the mangrove creek for three years, but there was not a sign of a worm or bore. Ferris walked over her, nodding his head in wonder. But when he went down into the engine room his spirits fell. The engine was gone.

But once again the natives passed around their sly chuckles and winks. Word went out: "Masta, 'im 'e want engine belong *Portal* one time quick." And immediately bits and pieces of the engine began to arrive. Each family had been entrusted with a certain part. Some had been hung high in trees, others carefully wrapped and buried in the sand. One of the girls stood before the pastor, and grinning mischievously, took several shiny ornaments out of her hair and handed them to him. They were springs from the engine. A boy untied a belt he wore around his waist and, giggling, handed it over. It was composed of all the nuts from the engine, strung on a strong cord. When all the parts were together, not even one tiny screw was missing.

The men who had disassembled the engine stepped forward and, from memory undimmed by three years, put it back together again. The tank was filled with fuel, the cylinder heads heated with blow torches, a rope given two turns around the flywheel, and then, with a mighty heave on the rope, the men turned the engine over. With a happy cough the temperamental old engine came to life and roared contentedly. The *Portal* was scrubbed and painted all over except for one small patch of charred timber near the cabin door. That one blemish has remained to this day, for it is evidence that the *Portal,* 'im 'e boat belong God, 'im 'e no burn.

And the good old *Portal,* just as the islanders and the missionaries, returned to the rewarding work of bringing the light of the gospel, of education, of cleanliness, to the people of the islands of the Pacific, the Fuzzy-Wuzzy angels.

14 *But the End Is Not Yet*

To the critical eye and burning heart of youth, nothing is ever perfect. Young men and women do not accept things as they are. Persistently curious, they ask questions and seek answers to them; constantly restless, they are never satisfied with the answer. Young men believe that they can change the world, and the young men of the Seventh-day Adventist church are no exception.

One of these young men, through birth, background, education and training, was particularly well equipped not only to ask questions about the present and future direction of the church's work over the world, but to go out himself and find the answers. Saleem A. Farag was born in Egypt, an ancient land now driving fervently and furiously to catch up with younger nations. His father had been an official in the Coptic church in Alexandria, but a question bothered him: Why, when the Ten Commandments plainly stated that it was the seventh day mankind should keep holy, did his church deliberately pass over that day and worship on the first day of the week? He met and talked with members of the small Seventh-day Adventist congregation in Alexandria, and left the church of which he was an official to become just another member of the small congregation.

At the time of his father's conversion, little Saleem was just a few days old. He grew up in an atmosphere of enthusiasm for this newfound faith, and he determined to follow it. He attended the American University at Beirut and took his graduate work in America. Young Dr. Farag married an American girl and joined the faculty of the College of Medical Evangelists as a research biologist. He was certainly fully in accord with the principles of medical ministry, the right arm of the church. He believed completely, as a man dedicated to both science and God, in healing the sick. But, he wondered, is healing the sick enough? He had seen the impressive figures on numbers of people treated each year—over three million—but a nagging thought remained in his mind: How many of that number were treated, even cured, to go back to their own communities and be straightway reinfected all over again? How many moved constantly in a revolving door betwen sickness and health? In his native land and other countries of the Near East, he knew, 90 per cent of the people have schistosomyasis, a disease transmitted by a parasite carried by the snail. Treating persons suffering from this debilitating disease was all very fine, but why not get at the cause of the disease, at the parasite or the snail? Dr. Farag also knew that, in curing the sick, the medical ministry was creating an attitude favorable to reception of the gospel in the minds of its patients. But Dr. Farag believed that medicine could go further than curing the sick; it could help keep them from getting sick. Through preventive medicine, long practiced by the right arm of the Church, but now more efficacious than ever before, he believed that many of the world's ills can be eradicated.

"If we can bring the word of God to the sick," he asked himself, "can we not even more effectively bring the gospel to hale, healthy, hearty people?"

Other thoughts buzzed through Dr. Farag's mind. In his own native Africa, he knew, Communists were doing a highly effective and efficient job of propaganda and proselyting. Their aggressive bid for the manpower and natural resources of the Dark Continent was showing signs of success, much more so than the softer and unrealistic approach of the free world. The Communists understood the basic needs of Africa. They knew that in many parts of that huge continent, as in other parts of the world where men, women and children lie down at night hungry, the concepts of freedom and liberty mean far less to the people than freedom from hunger, freedom from poverty. But there is another freedom that they are seeking, too, a freedom that the church can help them attain: freedom from disease.

Dr. Farag was by no means the only Seventh-day Adventist who thought along the lines of prevention of disease; preventive medicine has prominent mention in the history of the Church's medical missions. Others helped him narrow his broad aspirations down to a definite program of medical assistance, with emphasis on health, education and preventive medicine, to the underdeveloped areas of the world. The important correlatives of this work, it was fully realized, would be the fostering of friendly international relationships and research in tropical medicine.

The program is divided into three phases. The first phase would entail a comprehensive survey of the area, not only in regard to the indigenous diseases and their causes, but in the very nature and patterns of culture of the people themselves. The second phase would be the execution of the program, helping the people to help themselves. Indigenous students would be carefully selected, and, by means of the most modern educational techniques blended with the specific characteristics of the people, given an eighteen-month course of instruction in the elements of personal hygiene, sanitation and nutrition. Finally, in the third phase, the trained students would return to their communities as health educators to work under the supervision of a physician or medical officer of the area. American personnel would withdraw to begin a similar project within another area.

The church itself put up some funds, and private and governmental agencies and individual philanthropists contributed to the project. The success the church has had in working with native peoples, a success to which explorers, travelers, scientists and military personnel have personally attested, was a great help in this important preliminary. The College of Medical Evangelists, as a center of health education, with close-knit ties connecting it to some 235 medical units scattered throughout many primitive areas of the world, would be a natural choice for a directing agency.

Dr. Farag, of course, was named to head the first pilot program. For his first area of study and assistance, he chose the area of the Ha tribe, in western Tanganyika. He had many reasons for his choice. The Ha tribe itself is one of many large groups of people throughout the world in general and Africa in particular who are largely generally unknown to civilization. The tribe numbers about 300,000 in an area of about 10,000 square miles. The people themselves are proud and intelligent, though largely illiterate and living in the most primitive conditions. In their language, incidentally, singular and plural are expressed by prefixes, and thus one member of the Ha tribe is called a Muha, whereas two or more members are referred to as Waha.

As Tanganyika is a mandate of the United Kingdom, with which America has excellent relations in general, it was comparatively easy to obtain permission to carry on the program. The church had some time before established a small mission hospital in the area, at the village of Heri, and, thanks to the excellent work the hospital had done, the members of the tribe were favorably disposed to Americans. The Ha tribe provided Dr. Farag's program with an excellent starting place.

At first the Waha themselves were astounded at the manner in which Saleem came among them. Following the classic pattern of some of the great Seventh-day Adventist pioneers, he did not live in the white frame houses of the mission, but moved right into one of the huts in a native village. Nor did he seem to be on the go from dawn until dark, the way other white men were; on the contrary, he blended in with the tribe, learning its language, sitting around by the hour, entering into conversations with his new friends when they felt like talking, saying nothing when they felt like remaining silent. In this manner, despite its seeming indolence, their young visitor was learning far more about their way of life, their values and ways of thinking than he could have learned in many, many hours of hurried, stark interviews.

Had Saleem lived in the mission house and conducted surveys, he would probably have remained just as unaware as were the rest of the white visitors to the area that, far from being trusted implicitly by the Waha, the white man was the object of positive, if secret, distrust, even fear. He would surely have never suspected the cause. Dr. and Mrs. William H. Taylor, the Adventist husband-and-wife team who ran the little mission hospital, had seen a hint of this distrust in the reluctance, frequently downright refusal, to permit the doctor and his wife to take samples of their blood. Busy with their practice, the Taylors had considered this reluctance to be based on native superstition and thought little of it except as a hindrance to their diagnostic work.

Only through living with the Waha, almost as one of them, did Saleem Farag discover the shocking import behind this attitude toward blood-sampling, and the reason for it. After he had been in the village for sometime a white woman, a sister of one of the missionaries of another denomination, came to the remote area for a visit of several days. Externally, except for a somewhat liberal use of lipstick and rouge, she did not seem greatly unlike Mrs. Taylor, whom the Waha knew; and Saleem could not at first understand the undercurrent of fear and revulsion he noted among the Waha when she passed by. It was a casual remark which revealed the reason for this.

"At least," one of the Waha observed after she had passed by one day, with lipstick freshly applied, "she could wipe the blood from her lips after drinking it."

Saleem's ears perked up, but he did not immediately ask the speaker what he meant by that remark. He bided his time, then, at the right moment, casually brought the subject up again. And finally he learned that the Waha believed that white men and women drank the blood of African natives! They were positive that the redness of the woman's rouged lips was caused by fresh blood. This, of course, was the reason why they so insistently resisted giving their own blood, even to the Taylors. They thought those samples of blood were transmitted to cities in America and Europe, there to be drunk by the white people. It was obvious that a full-scale educational campaign on blood tests would have to be instituted, not merely for the convenience of the doctors, but to dispel a misapprehension which caused far-reaching prejudice and distrust.

Another of Saleem's discoveries dealt with sanitation. Although the Seventh-day Adventist doctors and missionaries have had splendid results the world over in getting the native people to burn or bury human waste or garbage, there still remains room for improvement in this elementary hygienic necessity. The people of the Ha tribe, in particular, ignore waste disposal. The British government requires every native hut to have a pit latrine, constructed according to government specifications. Saleem was amazed to find that Ha families, even after they had constructed the latrine pit, refuse to use it.

Why? After the people of the village had become used to him, and, he felt, would speak frankly, he undertook to find out. First of all, he learned that the Waha simply did not believe that the flies, which bred in the little piles of waste scattered everywhere throughout the community and then crawled on the people and their food, had anything to do with disease. They flew, therefore they were birds. No one accused the other birds of carrying disease—why should the fly be set apart? Another reason for not using the latrine pits, the tribespeople told Saleem, was because they smelled bad. The odor emanating from the human waste on the ground was not nearly as unpleasant.

But even as the tribespeople were explaining these points to him, Saleem knew that they were holding something back. It was only after some months of his residence with them that he learned what they really thought about the white man's ideas of waste disposal. And when he did learn, the knowledge came with a shock. For generations the white man had been going forth into primitive areas, carrying with him the conviction that he was bringing the virtue of cleanliness to the unclean. But to the members of the Ha tribe, at least, the shoe was on the other foot. In their minds it was they who were clean, the white man who was dirty.

"All the white people seem to think about is relieving themselves," one of his Ha friends told Saleem. "They are constantly after us to be the same way—use only one place, think about it and plan for it and then sprinkle lime on it afterwards. When we have to relieve ourselves, we just want to do it, get it over with, and walk away from it and forget it."

Although the Waha live in an area blessed with fertile soil, more than adequate rainfall and a perfect climate for the growing of delicious fruits, their diet almost completely excludes them. A mango for which a resident of a North American city would happily pay sixty-five cents falls on the ground and rots in the land of the Ha tribe. What the Waha smack their lips over is casava. They dig the white, pulpy root, pound it into powder in a hollowed log with a long stick, mix it with water to the consistency—and taste—of glue, then eat it. When not pounding out the root, the people leave the stick used for that purpose lying around on the dirt floor of the hut. As they also keep their cattle in the hut at night, the stick is hardly sanitary.

Naturally this whole process raised many questions in Saleem's mind. Why would they not eat fruit? Why did they prefer this tasteless casava gunk? Why would they not take better care of the implement they used to prepare it? For that matter, why keep their cows with them in the house all night long?

Saleem is still looking for the answer to some of these questions. Apparently to wean the Waha away from their insufficient diet and get them to include foods which grow so prolifically in their area will take time and education. But he did learn, and in a striking manner, why the Waha keep their cows in their huts. Late one night he woke with a start. From the noise and caterwauling going on outside the hut he thought surely several leopards had attacked the village. He dashed outside. Everyone was running up and down and screaming. One old woman seemed to be making more noise than all the rest put together. Finally Saleem learned what had happened —her cow had been stolen!

"Is that all?" he asked. "I thought something terrible had happened."

The people looked at him in amazement. "Something terrible *has* happened!" they told him. "The woman's cow was stolen!"

And as the night wore on, and the excitement increased rather than abated, Saleem Farag realized why the Waha keep their cows in their huts. It's for the same reason that people in America rent safety deposit boxes for their valuables, insure their houses, and teach their children to look up and down before crossing the street. In short, a Muha's cow is his most valuable possession, and he wants it under the same roof with him at night.

And so, by living with the natives as one of them, Saleem acquired knowledge and understanding which will help the church improve its relationships and, consequently, its results. One of his little discoveries proved that the doctors of the church are on the right track. Learning from the very way the Waha talked about it that they much preferred the Seventh-day Adventist doctor to another physician who had once come through the area, Saleem questioned them further in an effort to find out just what the Seventh-day Adventist doctor had done to become so popular. It was a simple thing; other doctors had seemed reluctant to put their hands upon the Waha, but the Seventh-day Adventist doctor did little things like knuckling the kids' hair, patting a man's arm. The natives were perceptive enough to see this difference in the men who came to treat them, and responded to it.

Saleem's venture was no one-way street; he went prepared to learn native remedies for the ailments of civilized man as well as to find ways of helping the natives make better use of the white man's remedies. He returned to the United States with several samples of native herbs, including a plant which the natives use to increase lactation in mothers of newborn children, and another purported to be of value in the treatment of mental derangement. Finding this second plant was a project in itself. Saleem learned that a local native schoolteacher had become so mentally disturbed that it had been necessary to take him to the small mission hospital and keep him under observation. When he showed no improvement in the hospital his family took him away and called in the witch doctor. This was a decided affront to the mission, for the witch doctor had never cooperated in any way with the white doctors. He then proceeded to add insult to injury by curing the patient completely. He administered a native drug to the deranged man which put him into a three-month coma. When the schoolteacher awoke he seemed to be in perfect mental health, returned to the school, and at last reports was doing just as good a job as he ever had.

What was this plant? Saleem was unable to find out. He did learn, however, of another herb supposed to cure mental disorder, and, after a series of cloak-and-dagger arrangements, made a journey of several days to visit another witch doctor who had promised to be more amenable. After much palaver, the witch doctor took Saleem to the back of his hut where there were some banana trees. Although there was no human being in sight, the witch doctor suddenly stopped and, at the top of his voice, ordered all trespassers to leave. In an instant the area became alive with natives falling out of the trees and taking to their heels. The witch doctor then, with great secrecy, left Saleem alone and went to another part of the orchard, whence he returned bearing some plants subsequently identified as plain old jimson weed. Even so, Saleem took them, along with the plants supposed to increase lactation, back to the College of Medical Evangelists, there to perform lengthy tests on their efficacy and possible toxicity.

Young Dr. Farag's experiences with the Waha strengthen considerably his belief that the church should go even more heavily into the field of preventive medicine. "If only preventive medicine can be practiced in conjunction with the work of every Seventh-day Adventist hospital all over the world," he says, "the welfare of the world's peoples will be greatly enhanced. This is our hope of the future. Nor do we have much time. Americans don't realize the extent of the powerful Communist drive in Africa. Theirs is the positive approach, the approach of food for hungry bellies. Even in the remotest villages of Africa I found Communists, and people talking communism. This is a challenge we must face and we must face it now. In these times of action we must be men of action."

In every corner of the world the church and its emissaries are facing new problems, new challenges. As whole areas emerge suddenly from the Stone Age into the blinding light of the new dawn of self-determination, missionaries and doctors must proceed with a new caution, if, indeed, they are permitted to proceed at all. Many countries considered friendly have closed their doors to missionaries per se, although trained technicians, administrators and, of course, medical men are welcome.

Even for doctors, the way is no longer as easy as it once was; many a country today requires that national licensing examinations for physicians be given in the indigenous language. This has not stopped all Seventh-day Adventist medical missionaries. In 1953, Dr. Richard Nelson, just finishing his residency at the White Memorial Hospital in Los Angeles to crown years of training directed toward the practice of medicine in Japan, learned that all those years were for naught unless he could pass his exam in Japanese. Dr. Nelson continued with his plans. He went to Japan, and, along with his hospital duties, plunged into a study of the incredibly complicated Kanji characters which make up the written Japanese language. After three years he tackled the exams. They lasted two days, but Dr. Nelson became the first non-Japanese to complete the exams successfully.

Typical of a nation pulling itself up by its boot straps is Egypt. Not too many years ago missionaries could carry on their work in that ancient land without much fear of governmental supervision. Today, Egypt is a land of fierce nationalism; foreigners, even those who want only to bring salvation to the people, must watch their step. Recently a minister was walking along the streets of an Egyptian town when he saw an appealing child before him; he took out his camera and snapped a picture of her. Almost before he knew it, he was in jail. Because the child was wearing a humble and soiled dress, the thin-skinned authorities accused him of taking the picture for propaganda purposes.

But because of this very fervor and ambition, the nations which have recently embarked upon a program of new nationalism make fascinating fields of endeavor for those who would preach the gospel to all nations. "In these lands," L. Hugh Cowles, a young missionary who has spent several years in Egypt, said, "you can see eager and earnest people making a valiant and solid effort to leap across the centuries in one bound. We see persons, who, like their forefathers before them, have lived all their lives in mud huts, now moving into the new government villages, into new homes, into a new atmosphere of energy and progress. In the schools, no longer is reading, writing, and arithmetic enough. Now training in agriculture and industry is considered a vital part of a school's curriculum. Our Seventh-day Adventist schools have always featured these vocational pursuits, and so we are keeping abreast of the times. But we must be on our toes in order to stay abreast."

Under its God-given mandate to preach the gospel in all nations, the church has entered all of the 213 countries and political subdivisions listed by the United Nations except 24. Though these countries represent only 1 per cent of the population of the world, and although political developments in these countries have made once-difficult entry into them now virtually impossible, still the church has not given up. Before Tibet was taken over by the Communists and its ruler, the Dalai Lama, deposed and exiled, two missionaries whose names cannot be revealed were nearing completion of their plans to go into the forbidden land. They knew that if caught they would probably be sewed into the green skins of recently killed animals, then placed in the open sunlight to be crushed to death as the hides contracted. But still they planned to go ahead. When the iron curtain enveloped Tibet they were forced to call off their planned mission, but not forever. It may even be possible that the expulsion of the Dalai Lama will in the long run aid the Seventh-day Adventists in penetrating Tibet. For one of the first men of the Western world he encountered, when he reached sanctuary in Mussoorie, India, was Alva R. Appel, an Adventist missionary.

"The Dalai Lama is a man of marvelous insight," Appel reported later. "We spoke for several hours, talking in the Chinese language. I can't report the details of the conversation, but I can say this: If the Dalai Lama ever returns to Tibet as leader of that country, the Seventh-day Adventists will be permitted to enter. The Dalai Lama has promised it."

The world leaders have been particularly heartened by reports from representatives traveling in Russia and neighboring countries in recent years. The 1960 yearbook places church membership in Russia at 40,000, with 843 churches organized and operating. These figures in themselves are not impressive, but bear in mind the fact that in 1928, the last year in which there was any contact between the U.S.S.R. division and the General Conference, there were just 632 churches with 13,519 members. This tripling of membership has occurred despite laws specifically prohibiting all churches from evangelizing, and despite great difficulty on the part of individual members in finding work which permits keeping the Sabbath.

In 1959 Francis D. Nichol, editor of *The Review and Herald,* had the heart-warming experience of visiting fellow Adventists and attending Sabbath services in both Warsaw and Moscow. In Poland he found Seventh-day Adventists enjoying a real measure of freedom. In 1945 the conference had only 600 members; at the beginning of 1959 the membership was 3700.

The environment is hardly friendly to religion, however, and evangelical work is difficult; half of the 74 churches in Poland have to meet in private homes or in other Protestant churches. Under such conditions many other Protestant bodies find their ranks depleted.

"But we have," the editor wrote, "what other churches do not have, a valorous, ardent band of colporteurs. They sell their books and papers in a community. Then an evangelistic meeting is held. Those who have bought books are specially invited to attend. The result? A company of believers is raised up. God bless our colporteurs! They toil without stimulus of trumpets. They toil in the heat and the cold. They toil for the God of the harvest, as they do their exploits bold."

Nichol had "a most friendly forty minutes" with the government officer in charge of all religious bodies. He pointed out that the church believes in separation of church and state, hence its ministers do not become involved in politics.

"Render to Caesar the things that are Caesar's, and to God the things that are God's," the official surprised him by replying. "I know Adventists. They have a good name by their good lives. And we like your temperance work."

The Poland conference opened a new school for training workers in the fall of 1959, and saw in this an omen of greater growth and strength.

In Russia Nichol found that the church has positive rights. Even though the Soviet Union itself is antireligion, it grants freedom of worship. In Moscow the congregation is assigned a meeting place for Sabbath and Wednesday night services. Over-all guidance of the work is carried on by an elder of the church who serves as president of the conference. Though the church is not permitted to evangelize, though children attend public schools—parochial schools are not permitted—where there is definite hostility to religion, still when Nichol attended Sabbath services he found some 500 people in attendance. Sabbath school began at 10 A.M. with a song and a prayer. The minister discussed a chapter of the Bible for an hour, and the choir sang a number to conclude the Sabbath school. Then, without anyone's moving, the minister went directly into the regular preaching service. The congregation sang a hymn, the minister preached a sermon for about an hour, and then a second minister spoke on the significance of foot-washing, for this was the day of the Communion service. The congregation filled both the main floor and the balcony, but on this Sabbath only those on the main floor participated. The following Sabbath they would change places with those in the balcony, and Communion service would be repeated. After the final prayer, Nichol was introduced, and stood up, but was cautioned by the interpreter not to reply. Then Sabbath services were ended—and the hour was 2:20 P.M.

"Actually," Nichol wrote, "I had not much noticed the passage of time, or even that I had not yet eaten anything that day. I seemed to be transported into a new, strange world. At times I seemed so near to these dear people, especially when the minister, in his prayer, asked a blessing 'on God's people in all the world.' "

After the service he talked with some of the conference leaders. He reminded them that Adventists always seek to be the most loyal, upright citizens in every land. "We seek both to serve our God and our country with all our heart and sincerity. I called their attention to the fact that Adventist churches everywhere follow the Bible admonition to pray for rulers and dignitaries. Our talk closed with prayer. I asked God to guide His people in Russia, and to guide the officials of the Soviet Union that they might wisely lead that great land in paths of peace."

Because Adventists are never a threat to the state, but rather stable and dependable citizens whose very love for God gives them a love for their fellow man and for their country, the work of the church may be carried on in any country without causing suspicion on the part of the authorities. Adventists the world over have every hope that the work will continue in the Soviet Union.

It might also be pointed out that long ago the first church workers in every country newly pioneered started immediately on a program to train nationals for leadership in their own countries. Foreign missions will someday be a thing of the past in nearly all countries of the world as nationalism increases, and yet the work will be carried on, as in Russia, by trained nationals, loyal to their own country, who render to Caesar the things that are Caesar's, and to God the things that are God's. The church has always planned ahead, its leaders thinking of the future as they preached the gospel of two millenniums ago.

Constantly seeking new ways to spread that message, today's leaders make full use of the latest scientific achievements and techniques in education. Its weekly television program goes on, for one example, bigger and better than ever. Another example of greater things to come occurred in late 1959, when a medical missionary in Okinawa, Dr. George M. Tolhurst, Jr., carried on a medical consultation with other doctors 6000 miles away, through short wave radio. Some months before a cinder had gotten into one of the doctor's eyes, but as he was working night and day to aid victims of the series of typhoons which had struck the island, he was unable to take proper care of it. A virus ulcer formed. Calling in from his own set to radio station W6–EDL, owned and operated by the personnel of the College of Medical Evangelists and White Memorial Hospital, he gave a complete description of the ulcer and received back a diagnosis and prescribed treatment from eye specialists at the college. In this way he was able to arrest this rare type of ulcer himself. The station has been used on other occasions too, to impart specific medical information over thousands of miles of land and sea. Its operators plan to install an even more powerful transmitter which will enable them to reach other doctors throughout the world.

Thanks to the Seventh-day Adventist contacts in other lands, medical and dental students of the College of Medical Evangelists, many of them future members of the medical ministry, are now able to visit and treat, under faculty supervision, peoples of primitive rural areas while still undergraduates. In 1958, thirty-five students and faculty members of the college spent three weeks among the Chamula Indians of the high mountains of southern Mexico, treating the mountain people in thirteen clinics located in the remote north-central area of the state of Chiapas. This program is expected to grow larger over the years.

In Monument Valley, which the Seventh-day Adventists themselves pioneered only in recent years, a new program is underway. It enables nurses and public health workers to spend several weeks as part of their undergraduate training among primitive peoples of a strange culture and almost incomprehensible language, all without ever leaving the United States.

Not only is the Seventh-day Adventist church itself seeking new ways to meet the great challenge of a changing world, but some of its ideas are finding their way into other denominations, and even into the science of medicine. Since Dr. Jack Provonsha began conducting a class in theology in the College of Medical Evangelists, other medical schools and hospitals have begun similar programs. A chair in theology has been established in the Chicago Medical School, for example, and each year finds more doctors taking courses at the Theological School of Harvard University, the better to bring religion into hospital routine. More hospitals will doubtless follow the example of the Massachusetts General, which recently underwrote a full year of theological study for one of its doctors. The time may not be far off when the medical profession as a whole will accept what the Seventh-day Adventist doctors have known all along, that therapy for the body is far more effective if accompanied by therapy for the soul.

And the Seventh-day Adventists themselves, dedicated, tireless and resourceful, can be counted upon in the future as well as in the past and present to continue to preach the gospel, to heal the sick and, ever-increasingly, to maintain good health in the healthy, looking ever forward to that glorious day when Christ will come again, and they shall live in the house of the Lord forever.

15 *Minutes to Midnight*

Tilted back in the big leather chair in the office he has occupied for nearly a third of a century, beneath photographs of out-of-the-way places of the world to which his youthful energy and curiosity have taken him, Francis D. Nichol, the slender, silver-haired editor of the *Review and Herald* and the church's leading interpretive historian, was musing on the first century of the Advent people.

"From our very beginning in the 1840s we took the unpopular view, based directly on the scriptures, that we could look forward only to increasing wars and wickedness that would climax in the destruction of the world under the judgments of God," he said. "We were charged with being calamity-howlers, we were caricatured and ridiculed. I remember well, as a young minister forty years ago, being dismissed as an intellectual anachronism by other Protestant ministers in my community for preaching that cataclysmic times were coming, wars and increasing wickedness."

He paused, remembering those days. "They laughed at us then," he said. *"Well, they don't laugh at us now!"*

The one and a quarter million Seventh-day Adventists find themselves, in this atomic era, in two strange paradoxes. They are convinced that the time of the deliverance of righteous men from an evil world is near at hand, but they go calmly about feeding the hungry and healing the sick while they are still here. They find themselves vindicated in their direst predictions by the words and actions of the very groups which most bitterly criticized them, yet they find no satisfaction in their vindication. For it is, as Nichol says, an awesome thing to be right about.

When William Miller and his followers, in the early 1840s, looked deep into their Bibles and predicted that the world would become far worse before it suddenly got better, they were simply echoing the view long before set down in Christian creeds.

For example, the Apostles Creed of the fourth-century Christians (probably the oldest of all creeds), the Augsburg Confession of the Lutheran States, the Thirty-nine Articles of the Church of England, the Baptist Confession of A.D. 1688, the 1784 Methodist Articles of Religion, to cite representative creeds, all affirmed the solemn belief that Jesus Christ will return to earth to judge the quick and the dead. The Millerites, from the strict theological viewpoint, really added little to this classic Christian doctrine; they simply sought to revive it and to bring it into sharp focus by avowing that the time was near. The Millerites believed then, and the Adventists believe now, neither more nor less than what is written in the Bible: that on the final day the righteous will be taken up into the clouds to meet Christ, the wicked destroyed, the earth cleansed with fire. Then in heaven above the righteous will reign with Christ for a thousand years, a millennium. On this last point the Millerites were not all clear, but Adventists are.

But between the time of the Protestant Reformation in the fifteenth century and the rise of the Millerite, or Advent, movement four centuries later, a new view of the Advent had become popular in Protestant theology. By the opening of the nineteenth century churchmen were declaring that the millennium would not take place in a heaven physically apart from the earth, but would be a period of heaven on earth resulting from the ever-advancing triumph of the good in man over the evil. The coming of Christ would be spiritual, the coming of the divine spirit into men's hearts.

This new theology was given a boost by the pleasing philosophy that there was a law of progress in the universe which ensured betterment for the world. Charles Darwin was later to give this idea great impetus with his Theory of Evolution. Furthermore, churchmen came to look upon the performance of miracles as in conflict with the fixed laws of nature. The idea of a personal God who actively directs the world grew to be at variance with the scientific concept of an orderly world moving inexorably along under natural control. The Biblical prophecy of the sudden, cataclysmic end of the world was pushed aside by the theory of gradual progress and the idea, of course, that miracles are impossible. The belief that wickedness and wars would ravage the planet seemed defeatist and negative in comparison to the new dream of ever-improving man. The rapid strides of science gave positive indication of eventual health, happiness and peace for all the world.

Thus the Millerites, though preaching, basically, a biblical doctrine, found themselves out of step with the rest of Christendom. The Advent doctrine as set forth by William Miller was viewed by the learned as not only pessimistic, but irrationally unscriptural. In a long letter to William Miller in 1844, Professor George Bush of New York University argued that rather than the end of the world, the expiration of the prophetic periods of Daniel—and he, with others, believed they were about to end—would introduce, "by gradual steps, a new order of things, intellectual, political and moral." He added, italicizing his key phrases: "The great event before the world is not its *physical conflagration,* but its *moral regeneration....*"

In 1887, D. M. Canright, the bitter critic of Adventism, recalled an 1849 statement by the leading Adventist writer Ellen G. White: "The nations are now getting angry." Canright retorted:

"That was thirty-eight years ago. It takes a long time for them to get fighting mad! Pshaw!"

On through the years the savants spoke of a better world in the making. In 1913 Dr. David Starr Jordan, a great leader of the movement for world peace, declared of the great war of Europe which Adventists predicted: "We shall say that it will never come. It is humanly impossible." President Woodrow Wilson, in December of that year, spoke of "a growing cordiality and sense of community of interest among the nations, foreshadowing an age of settled peace and good will." Eight months later, when World War I began, Wilson cried, "Incredible!"

But the idea of a better, warless world persisted. Soon the first world war became "the war to end war." Ten years after it ended the nations of the world signed a treaty, the Pact of Paris, renouncing war. Charles Clayton Morrison, editor of the *Christian Century,* who witnessed the signing, said, "Today international war was banished from civilization."

Yet Adventists remained steadfast in their doleful but Bible-founded belief that wars and wickedness would increase over the earth. They rejected Darwinism, and held to the Creationistic origin of the earth as given in Genesis; they rested on "the seventh day," in obedience to the explicit words of the Ten Commandments and in witness to their belief in a transcendent, omnipotent God, who ere long will "create a new heaven and a new earth wherein dwelleth righteousness." They believed that the Ruler of the Universe was a personal God, perfectly capable of performing supernatural acts. They not only believed, but preached their beliefs in all the world. They deliberately went counter to the contemporary views of much of Christendom. They exposed themselves, completely and deliberately, to ridicule and scoffing.

And now more and more people—responsible people—are coming around to the views the Seventh-day Adventists have constantly held since the 1840s, modified only by their refusal to set a time for the Advent. The evidences of the validity of their preaching are on the pages of current history for all to see. Their vindication has been dramatic, as in the answer to the great challenge hurled at William Miller by Professor Bush. Speaking of the coming of Christ as a spiritual coming in terms of "moral regeneration," Bush had written: "Such is the dominant faith of all Christian communities at this day, and to the *tribunal of time,* as the only arbiter, they willingly refer its final decision."

Just a century and a year later a group of atomic scientists at Los Alamos, New Mexico, exploded the world's first atomic bomb. The tribunal of time, with two world wars and an atomic bomb in the scales, began clearly to render its verdict.

It is strangely ironic that those who scoffed the loudest in the early days of the Adventist movement, the scientists, today are the most pessimistic about the wan hopes for the world as we know it. For it is a military and scientific fact that there exists, in the thermonuclear stockpiles of the two greatest rival nations of the world today, enough explosive material to obliterate civilization.

On the front cover of the journal, the *Bulletin of the Atomic Scientists,* each month, is portrayed in stark simplicity the face of a clock, with its hands pointing just minutes to midnight—minutes to midnight. The *Bulletin* was founded in 1945 under the impetus of the nuclear scientists' Emergency Committee—Albert Einstein, chairman—in an effort to arouse the public to the need of international controls for the potentially world-destroying energy they themselves had released. Just five years later, in one of the most pitiful documents of all the ages, the editor of the *Bulletin* wrote of their failure to secure controls:

"What then have we to show for five years of effort, except the relief of having 'spoken and saved our souls'—and the doubtful satisfaction of having been right in our gloomy predictions?"

Said Thomas E. Murray, commissioner of the Atomic Energy Commission, in a speech at Manhattan College in New York: "For all we know it may be the incomprehensible and the inscrutable Will of God to make the twentieth century 'Closing Time' for the human race."

Or, in the words of Harold C. Urey, Nobel prize-winner and atomic scientist, "Future history, in fact, may not last very long."

"Once," Nichol has observed wryly, "the scientists considered the Advent people to be crackpot criers of doom. Now they themselves are crying 'doom' louder than we ever did. We can't hold a candle to them when it comes to sensationalism!"

Some learned Protestant theologians, who once considered the Seventh-day Adventists a group of calamity-crying oddballs, no longer scoff. Rather, they seem to have taken over the Adventist line. The official message of the Provisional Committee of the World Council of Churches, at the time of its creation, contained these words:

"The world stands today between life and death. Men's hopes of a better world have not been fulfilled.... We face this crisis as Christians whose own consciences are gravely disturbed.... But the time is short."

When the World Council held its notable meeting in Evanston, Illinois, in 1954, some of the key addresses by overseas theologians sounded almost as if a Seventh-day Adventist had written them.

Professor Winthrop S. Hudson of the Chicago Divinity School, writing in the *Christian Century,* the much-quoted, liberal voice of American Protestantism, declared:

"We must stop smiling complacently at the way in which the Millerites once played upon the fears of the credulous. This time the final explosion can too easily occur. This time it is not the credulous who believe but the incredulous, not the hysterical but the coldly scientific. The task of the church is to make their fear real to the great mass of the people."

Scientists and churchmen are not the only people whose words can be used to vindicate the once-ignored doctrine of the Adventists. Perhaps Joseph Alsop, the nationally known Washington columnist, was speaking for all when, on the subject of atomic-energy control, he wrote:

"If control is not achieved, wise and informed men must join the Seventh-day Adventists...in making ready for something not too unlike the end of the world."

In one respect, the Seventh-day Adventists are still at variance with all those fearful of the destruction of the earth by atomic power. They look upon this dreadful store of cataclysmic energy not as the means of earth's purging, but only as an indication that the tragedy and warfare of a sinful world are soon to end. For they are positive that it will not be man who will destroy the world, as we know it, but God. They do not believe that God has abdicated, leaving the destruction of earth to man by bombs or radiation. They do not believe that on the day of the Second Advent Jesus Christ will return to a scorched sphere of cinders covered with wretched, irradiated bodies. Rather, He will return in glory, visible to all, to an earth still filled with men, good and bad. Hence if man is making ready to destroy himself it is time for God to act.

It is not the Adventists who wail in terror as the hands of the celestial clock close together on the midnight hour. For over a century they have preached the end of the world as others have turned their backs. Now, as the savants and the scientists look to the future with increasing horror, the Advent people look to it with increasing joy. To them the final day is only the beginning. They are increasing their already prodigious efforts to spread the gospel. In answer to the mournful that since the coming of the thermonuclear bomb there is no place to hide, they reply: "Ah, but there is, within the mantle of God's promise that He will deliver, on that dread day, all who accept His proffered salvation."

To the preaching of the nearness of that day and the universality of God's offer of salvation, Adventists have dedicated their lives. Theirs is not the defeatist dirge of "Minutes to Midnight." Rather, they say, the time is now Minutes to *Morning*—the glorious morning of the Advent!

About the Author

Mr. Herndon was born and raised in Charlottesville, Virginia, and, being the true Virginian that he is, returned there eight years ago with his wife and children to pursue his career as a free-lance writer. After attending the University of Missouri and the University of Virginia, he worked for New Orleans newspapers for several years. With the U.S. Army during World War II, he participated in the Normandy invasion and four other major European campaigns. After his military duty, he went to New York to get started on a serious writing career. A well-known magazine writer, Mr. Herndon has written articles for many of the major magazines throughout the country and is also the author of *Bergdorf's on the Plaza* and *Young Men Can Change the World.*